Managing Bermudagrass Turf

Selection, Construction, Cultural Practices, and Pest Management Strategies

Managing Bermudagrass Turf

Selection, Construction, Cultural Practices, and Pest Management Strategies

L. B. (Bert) McCarty and Grady Miller
Clemson University and University of Florida

This book represents information obtained from authentic and highly regarded sources. Reprinted material is quoted with permission, and sources are indicated. A wide variety of references are listed. Every reasonable effort has been made to give reliable data and information, but the author and publisher cannot assume responsibility for the validity of all material or for the consequences of their use.

Ann Arbor Press
310 North Main Street
P.O. Box 20
Chelsea, MI 48118
www.sleepingbearpress.com
Ann Arbor Press is an imprint of Sleeping Bear Press

Printed and bound in the United States.
10 9 8 7 6 5 4 3 2 1

Library of Congress Cataloging-in-Publication Data

McCarty, L. B. (Lambert Blanchard), 1958–
  Managing bermudagrass turf : selection, construction, cultural practices and pest management strategies / L. B. (Bert) McCarty and Grady Miller.
    p. cm.
  ISBN 1-57504-163-4
  1. Bermuda grass. 2. Turf management. I. Miller, Grady L. II. Title.

  SB201.B35 M33 2002
  635.9′ 642—dc21
                                                                    2002006100

Dedication

To my children, Sara Emily and Max McCarty, and to my niece and nephews, Betsy, Brett and Will McCarty, and Mike Smith Jr.

In memory: my father, W. Tyrone McCarty and uncle, Woodrow W. Boozer Sr., two members of the greatest generation. Also, to my brother-in-law, Michael Lawrence Smith. Each is dearly missed.

Contents

Preface

Bermudagrass golf courses are continually increasing in number, sophistication in terms of design and management, and increased scrutiny from the general public and regulatory agencies. This book is intended as a reference guide for golf course superintendents, assistants, club managers, greens committee members, students, and regulatory agencies in their efforts to grow and maintain some of the most prestigious courses in the world. The information is as complete and up-to-date as possible. However, management and pesticide recommendations are constantly being updated. New products, grasses, and management techniques continue evolving, while older ones often disappear. Contact your State University Turf Specialist, County Cooperative Extension Service office, and attend the various Turfgrass Field Days and Turfgrass Association's Annual Conference and Trade Show for the latest recommendations.

The pesticide recommendations presented in this publication were current with state and federal regulations at the time of publication. The user is responsible for determining that the intended pesticide use is consistent with the directions on the label of the product being used. All chemicals mentioned are for reference only. Not all are available for turf use and may be restricted by some states, provinces, or federal agencies; thus, be sure to check the current status of the pesticide being considered for use. Always read and follow the manufacturer's label as registered under the Federal Insecticide, Fungicide, and Rodenticide Act. Mention of a proprietary product does not constitute a guarantee or warranty of the product by the authors or the publishers and does not imply approval to the exclusion of other products that also may be suitable.

About the Authors

Bert McCarty is a Professor of Horticulture specializing in turfgrass science and management at Clemson University in Clemson, South Carolina. A native of Batesburg, SC, he received a BS degree from Clemson University in agronomy and soils, MS from North Carolina State University in crop science, and PhD from Clemson University in plant physiology and plant pathology. Dr. McCarty spent almost nine years as a turfgrass specialist at the University of Florida in Gainesville. While at the University of Florida, he oversaw the design and construction of the state-of-the-art research and education turfgrass facility, "The Envirotron." He also was author or coauthor of the books, *Best Management Practices for Florida Golf Courses*, *Weeds of Southern Turfgrasses*, and *Florida Lawn Handbook*. In 1996 he moved to Clemson University and is involved in research, extension, and teaching activities. He has published over 200 articles dealing with all phases of turfgrass management and has given over 500 presentations. He is currently coordinating author of the books, *Best Golf Course Management Practices* and *Color Atlas of Turfgrass Weeds* and is active in a number of professional societies.

Grady Miller is an Associate Professor of Turfgrass Science at the University of Florida in Gainesville. He is a native of Louisiana with a BS from Louisiana Tech University in agriculture, an MS degree from Louisiana State University in agronomy and soils, and a PhD from Auburn University in turfgrass science. Dr. Miller's research program includes activities that address the environmental concerns of the commercial and urban turfgrass sectors. His research involves the investigation of nutritional and physiological influences on growth and development of turfgrass species. Current research activities include: turfgrass water relations as related to drought stress, inorganic soil amendments and plant nutrition for improved turfgrass establishment, and evaluation of athletic field performance characteristics. He teaches undergraduate and graduate courses in turfgrass culture, golf and sports turf management, and landscape management. He is a member of the International Turfgrass Society, American Society of Agronomy, Crop Science Society of America, United States Golf Association, Golf Course Superintendents Association of America, and the Sports Turf Managers Association.

Managing Bermudagrass Turf

Selection, Construction, Cultural Practices, and Pest Management Strategies

Section I

Introduction

1. Bermudagrass Characteristics

1 Bermudagrass Characteristics

Bermudagrass is a long-lived perennial grass originating under subhumid, open, closely grazed rangelands characterized by hot, dry summers around the Indian Ocean ranging from eastern Africa to the East Indies. It is believed to be introduced to the United States from Africa in 1751 or earlier and is now quite cosmopolitan (Figure 1.1).

The *Cynodon* genus is comprised of nine species with chromosomal numbers ranging from 18 to 54. Both common and hybrid types are used in turf (Figure 1.2). Common bermudagrass (*Cynodon dactylon* [L.] Pers. var. *dactylon*) has 36 chromosomes (Tifton 10 is an exception with 54) and produces pollen and seed. Triploid hybrids (*Cynodon* X *magennisii* Hurcombe [= *C. dactylon* X *C. transvaalensis*]) have 2n=3x=27 chromosomes and are male and female sterile. Vegetative propagation of hybrids makes a uniform turf possible. Only common bermudagrass types can be propagated by seed. However, a stand of common bermudagrass from seed can appear mosaic over time because each plant is genetically different.

Common bermudagrass such as Tifton 10, Quickstand, FloraTex, and Vamont have unique characteristics such as increased cold temperature tolerance and are vegetatively established, and thus produce a uniform turf. Although they produce pollen, these cultivars do not set much seed unless they receive pollen from an adjacent different bermudagrass type. Due to their upright growth habit, intolerance to low mowing heights, and coarse texture, common bermudagrasses are not used on golf greens but are sometimes used on roughs and less so on fairways.

ADVANTAGES

Bermudagrass produces a vigorous, deep-rooted, light to dark green, dense turf that is well adapted to most soils and climatic regions into the lower portion of U.S. Department of Agriculture (USDA) plant hardiness zone 6 (Plate 1.1). Bermudagrass has excellent wear, drought, and salt tolerance and is a good choice for oceanfront property (Table 1.1). It establishes rapidly, produces lateral stems, and is competitive against weeds and, depending on the variety, is available as seed, sod, or sprigs. Bermudagrass has inherently few pest problems, especially with diseases.

DISADVANTAGES

Bermudagrass has several cultural and pest problems which may restrict its use in certain situations. In most temperate areas when temperatures approach 50°F (10°C), bermudagrass becomes dormant (turns brown) (Table 1.2). Overseeding in fall with

Figure 1.1. Approximate bermudagrass use range for golf greens in the mainland United States (note: overlapping ranges often occur) (McCarty, 2001).

Figure 1.2. Hybrid bermudagrasses are characterized by desirable denser stands and thinner (or tighter) leaf textures than coarser, less dense common bermudagrass (center).

Table 1.1. Advantages and disadvantages of bermudagrass for golf courses.

Advantages	Disadvantages
Tolerates low height of cut	Turns brown (dormant) with temperatures below
Good soil salinity tolerance	~50°F (10°C)
Good traffic tolerance	Higher nitrogen requirements (1/2 to 2 lb N/1,000
Good drought tolerance	sq ft, 24 to 98 kg/ha) per growing month
Rapid recovery from damage	compared to cool-season grasses (1/4 to 1/2 lb
Has rhizomatous and stoloniferous growth habit	N/1,000 sq ft, 12 to 24 kg/ha)
Responsive to nitrogen fertility	Thatch/mat production potential
Uses approximately 68% less water than	Winter-kill potential
cool-season grasses	Very poor shade tolerance
Adapted to varied soil drainage conditions (sand,	Unstable genetics potential
clay, silt, or loam)	Encroachment into other grasses
Good tolerance to a range of soil pH (5.5 to 8.5)	Off-color (purpling) potential from cool
Good disease resistance	temperatures (chill injury)
Good pesticide and growth regulatory tolerance	
and compatibility	
Excellent utilization of effluent water	

Table 1.2. Parameters of hybrid bermudagrass used for golf greens.

Parameter	Bermudagrass Characteristic
Morphological Characteristics	
Leaf texture	fine (1–3 mm)
Lateral shoot type	stolons + rhizomes
Leaf vernation	folded
Ligule type (length)	hair (1–3 mm)
Auricles	absent
Leaf blade tip	pointed
Inflorescence	4 or 5 digitate spikelike racemes
Chromosome count	2n=3X=27
Seed viability	sterile
Growth Characteristics	
Carbon metabolism type	C_4 (warm-season)
Sunlight requirements for maximum photosynthesis	100% full sunlight (1,200 μmoles)
Photorespiration presence	absent
Optimum air temperature for shoot growth	85 to 100°F (29 to 38°C)
Optimum soil temperature for shoot growth	80 to 95°F (27 to 35°C)
Optimum soil temperature for root growth	75 to 95°F (24 to 35°C)
Growth limiting high soil temperature	100 to 110°F (38 to 43°C)
Lethal soil temperature	120°F (49°C)
Minimum air temperature for growth	55°F (13°C)
Air temperature which causes shoot dormancy (browning)	≈ 50°F (10°C)
50% Root loss soil temperatures	18 to 23°F (–8 to –5°C)
Food storage type	starch
Pesticide tolerance	very good
Disease susceptibility	low
Salinity tolerance	high (1,000 to 2,000 ppm)
Mean summer ET rates	0.15 to 0.28 in./day (0.4 to 0.7 cm)

Figure 1.3. Bermudagrass inherently has very poor shade tolerance, requiring six to eight hours of full sunlight daily when grown under short mowing conditions such as golf greens and tees.

ryegrass, bentgrass, and/or roughstalk bluegrass is a common practice to maintain year-round green color. Bermudagrasses are susceptible to several nematode, insect, and disease problems. Bermudagrasses also have very poor shade tolerance and should not be grown underneath tree canopies or building overhangs (Figure 1.3). Due to its rapid growth, thatch buildup can become a problem, particularly on golf greens. A reel mower should be used to produce the highest possible quality turf stand. Bermudagrass also periodically 'winter-kills' when grown in the upper transitional zone in the United States where temperatures periodically drop below 10°F (–12°C).

A major problem in recent years is finding and maintaining pure bermudagrass stands. Although sterile hybrids, off-type patches of different color and texture bermudagrasses in greens have plagued the industry (Plate 1.2). Typically, 7 to 10 years after planting, these patches begin to slowly develop and then rapidly spread, most often, by cup changing. Over time, greens become mosaic and difficult to play, drawing complaints from players and management.

BERMUDAGRASS CULTIVARS

Prior to the mid-1940s, golf courses used common bermudagrass (also called Arizona common) from tee to green. Common bermudagrass provided a coarse-textured, uneven, and thin putting surface. Common bermudagrass seed was not certified until 1963 in an attempt to rid seed from a tall, rapid growing giant bermudagrass *(Cynodon dactylon aridus)*. Due to the lack of water, desert-located golf courses often use sand greens where a roller smooths the ball line toward the cup and heavy oils or diesel fuel are applied to pack the sand.

In 1947 the first recorded release of an improved vegetatively established bermudagrass occurred when 'U-3' bermudagrass was provided by the U.S. Golf Association (USGA) in cooperation with the USDA. During the 1950s and 1960s, Dr. Glen W. Burton with the USDA in Tifton, Georgia released several interspecific hybrids, including 'Tiflawn,' 'Tifgreen,' 'Tifway,' and 'Tifdwarf,' which are still widely used. These are from various crosses of common bermudagrass (2n=36) with African bermudagrass (2n=18) to produce sterile triploid hybrid bermudagrass (2n=27). In recent years, a wave of ultra-growing bermudagrasses have become available. These tolerate routine mowing heights of 1/8 inch or closer, allowing courses to rival putting characteristics of bentgrass at much lower costs and stress to employees and medium.

Tifgreen (or Tifton 328)

This cultivar was released in 1956 and is a hybrid between a fine-textured *C. dactylon* and *C. transvaalensis*. It is a medium dark green bermudagrass with high shoot density, fine texture, soft leaves, and low growth habit. Tifgreen produces few seedheads at putting green height. It requires a high level of maintenance in terms of irrigation, fertilizing, dethatching, close mowing, and edging frequencies. Tifgreen is also popular for golf course tees, baseball and softball fields, tennis courts, and lawn bowling activities. It does not tolerate a long-term mowing height less than 3/16ths of an inch (0.5 cm) and is susceptible to sting nematodes and spring dead spot (Plate 1.3). Its use as a golf green grass is becoming less important but it is still often used on collars, approaches, and tees.

Tifdwarf

This cultivar is believed to be a natural mutant from Tifgreen and was released in 1965 and grows in the latitudes approximately 32° north and south of the equator. Tifdwarf resembles Tifgreen except for its shorter leaves and internodes. It is a high maintenance grass used primarily on golf greens where a very low cutting height is desired for fast putting conditions (Plate 1.4). It develops a very dark green turf with high shoot density and a low, slow growth habit. Tifdwarf has few seedheads, but it is susceptible to caterpillar and mole cricket damage. Tifdwarf turns a purple color when chilled and normally requires overseeding for winter color. Problems with off-types or contaminants in recent years have led to impure stands. Tifdwarf is still the standard by which all other golf green grasses are compared and remains a viable golf green grass for lower-budgeted facilities, and for collars, approaches, and tees.

FloraDwarf

FloraDwarf bermudagrass was released from the University of Florida in 1995. It was selected from a previously planted Tifgreen bermudagrass golf green located in Hawaii but is genetically different from Tifgreen and Tifdwarf. FloraDwarf growth characteristics appear similar to Tifdwarf except for its much finer leaf blade, denser stand, shorter internodal spacing, and extremely low growth habit. Due to finer leaf blades and prostrate growth habit, FloraDwarf is often labeled as an "ultra-dwarf." If left unmowed,

Figure 1.4. Growth characteristics of unmowed "ultra-dwarf" cultivar, FloraDwarf (left), compared to Tifdwarf (right) bermudagrass. Note the lower-growing, denser growth habit of the ultra-dwarf cultivar (Courtesy A.E. Dudeck).

it grows only to about 1/2 inch (1.3 cm) high (Figure 1.4). FloraDwarf produces no viable seeds but does turn the characteristic purple color in cold weather and is thatch-prone. FloraDwarf should be considered on golf greens, tennis courts, and bowling greens.

TifEagle (TW-72)

A 1997 release developed as an induced mutant by cobalt radiation from Tifway II bermudagrass, it resembles other 'dwarfs' in its extremely fine leaf texture and excellent density and appears to have similar maintenance requirements with the major exceptions of being able to tolerate extremely close (1/8 inch, 0.3 cm) mowing heights and tends to rapidly produce thatch/mat layering (Plate 1.5). Only golf courses with adequate maintenance and labor budgets should consider one of the ultra-dwarf bermudagrasses such as TifEagle. TifEagle, however, just like all bermudagrasses used on golf greens, has relatively poor shade tolerance, is thatch/mat prone, and must receive full-day sunlight, year-round to be successful.

Champion, Classic, Florida Dwarf, MS Supreme, MiniVerde, Reese-grass, and Other 'Ultra-Dwarf' Selections

These triploid hybrids are low-growing grasses for closely mowed areas such as putting greens and lawn bowling (Plate 1.6). These are believed to be somatic mutations from Tifdwarf or Tifgreen and possess a low growth habit and are frequently maintained at a 1/8 inch (0.3 cm) mowing height. They have good density with cold tolerance similar to Tifdwarf. Their fertility requirements appear less than Tifdwarf or Tifgreen bermudagrasses to maintain their appearance and vigor. These produce no viable seed and must be vegetatively propagated. Due to tight density, these grasses are thatch-prone, thus requiring periodic vertical mowing, grooming, and topdressing. They tend to be slower growing and develop a purplish color during cool (50°F, 10°C) temperatures, similar to Tifdwarf.

Section II

Bermudagrass Golf Green Construction and Establishment

2. Site Selection; Green Establishment and Grow-In

2 Site Selection; Green Establishment and Grow-In

SITE SELECTION

Golf greens typically experience heavy use throughout the year. Many public courses receive as many as 400 rounds of golf per day, or over 100,000 rounds of golf per year. Although putting greens represent approximately 2% of the total course area, 50% of the game is actually played on them. This concentrated traffic combined with daily mowing almost guarantees a problem with soil compaction, especially if the greens are poorly constructed.

Years ago, turf was usually grown on native soils, but as traffic and maintenance intensities increased, soil structure began to deteriorate (Figure 2.1). A golf green must accept and drain away excess water rapidly and yet retain enough moisture to not require frequent irrigation. Root zones constructed from native soil frequently turned into mud baths. The objective of this chapter is to discuss the proper sequence for the decision-making and construction processes for a high-quality putting green.

Shade

Bermudagrass has poor shade tolerance. This is especially true for bermudagrass maintained under putting green conditions since close mowing reduces the leaf surface responsible for photosynthesis (Figure 2.2). Bermudagrass maintained at putting green height requires full sunlight for a minimum of six to eight hours per day, year-round. Morning sun is most important as this helps dry the leaf surface, which reduces algae and diseases, warms the soil, and provides brightest light, especially during summer when afternoon clouds often reduce light penetration. To ensure this light penetration, it may be necessary to remove all sources of moderate to heavy shade surrounding the putting surface. Although golf courses are often noted for their beautiful landscaping, trees and healthy golf greens do not mix as the trees and their roots will always outcompete the grass.

Planning should take into account that the sun is lowest on the horizon during fall and winter months. Trees to the south and southwest of greens will cast longer shadows during the cooler months and may cause shade problems even though the trees may be some distance from the green. Shade also may increase the potential for cold damage to grasses, since shade-covered greens stay cold longer than greens in full sunlight. It is suggested that during the planning stage, summer (June) and winter (December) shade patterns for proposed golf green sites be sketched every two hours starting at 8:00 A.M.

Figure 2.1. Thin, undesirable turf (top) due to excessive traffic on greens constructed with unamended native soil (bottom).

until dark. These sketches will indicate which trees may need to be removed, or if trees cannot be removed, whether the putting green may need to be relocated. If tree removal is not possible, light can be increased by pruning, and air movement improved with fans.

Size

The size of a golf green should be large enough to allow for adequate selection of pin placement but not so large as to become a maintenance burden. In general, golf greens range from 5,000 to more than 7,500 square feet (465 to 698 m²), averaging about

Figure 2.2. Weak, thin bermudagrass resulting from exposure to excessive shade.

6,000 sq ft (558 m^2). Greens on par 3s are usually larger whereas longer holes have smaller putting surfaces, therefore requiring a more accurate shot.

In order to provide challenge and interest to the player, good putting green design should incorporate unique characteristics in size, shape, contour, and location of bunkers or other hazards. The placement of bunkers and the shaping of contours surrounding a green should prevent concentrated traffic in any one area, and also allow adequate room for efficient turfgrass maintenance practices. The outline of the green should avoid any sharp turns as the pressure exerted by mowers will cause compacted, worn areas. Severe contours or mounds also are not necessary to produce a good test of putting. Instead, they limit cup placement and produce droughty, easily scalped areas.

Profile

The modern putting green consists of two to four distinct components, including (from top to bottom) the root-zone medium, choker sand layer, gravel layer, and drain lines. The root-zone medium is the finest textured, the choker layer is intermediate, and the gravel layer is the coarsest textured component. This profile creates a perched water table in the finer textured layer. This is because water will not move (or percolate) readily from the small pores of the finer textured layer into the large pores of the coarser layer unless the finer layer is saturated with water to some depth. There are several successful putting green construction systems, each using some or all of these components.

USGA Specifications

The best known and most widely used system is that adopted by the United States Golf Association (USGA) which is a tiered or layered system (Figure 2.3). Twelve to 14

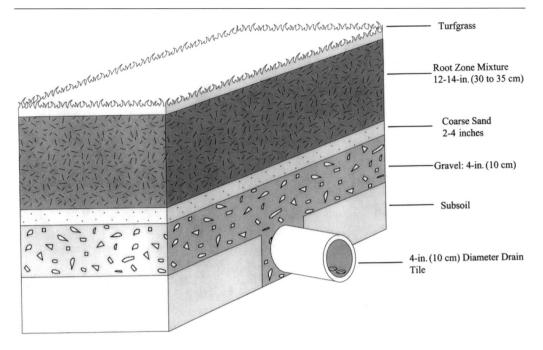

Turfgrass

Root Zone Mixture
12-14-in. (30 to 35 cm)

Coarse Sand
2-4 inches

Gravel: 4-in. (10 cm)

Subsoil

4-in. (10 cm) Diameter Drain
Tile

Figure 2.3. Cross section of the current USGA-adopted golf green profile with proper-sized pea gravel and without the traditionally used 2- to 4-inch (5 to 10 cm) 'choker' layer. Note: for this profile to be successful, strict adherence to specific particle size restrictions are needed for the root-zone mixture and the gravel layer. If appropriate materials and construction procedures are used, this type green profile provides the best construction option for the cost (McCarty, 2001).

inches of root-zone medium overlay a 2- to 4-inch (5 to 10 cm) coarse sand layer (choker) which in turn covers a 4-inch layer of gravel. Drainage is provided by drain lines embedded in the gravel at 15 to 20 foot (4.5 to 6 m) spacings. The gravel blanket helps move water rapidly to the drainage lines and out of the green. The physical textural difference between the gravel and root-zone mix creates a capillary break, where water will not move freely into the gravel unless the root-zone mix above it is saturated.

A modification to the USGA system allows the intermediate choker layer to be eliminated if very specific criteria, as determined by laboratory analyses, are met by the root-zone medium and the gravel. Typically, gravel between 1/4 and 3/8 inch (0.6 to 1 cm) diameter is required to meet this bridging criteria with the root-zone media, thus eliminating the choker layer requirement. USGA greens, if constructed properly, have a history of providing many years of satisfactory service. However, appropriate sands and gravel may be difficult and expensive to obtain and the expertise and care required in construction are demanding.

Sand Greens

Figure 2.4 offers a profile with the minimum construction standards for pure sand golf greens (often referred to as the 'California Method'). It consists simply of 12 to 14

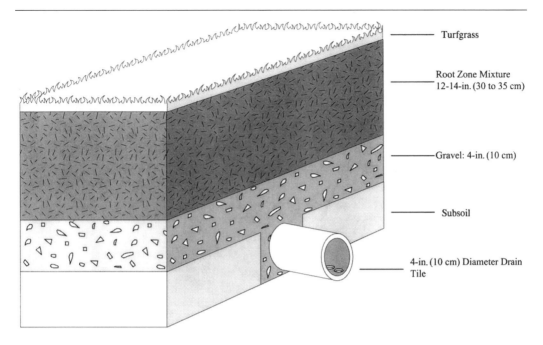

Turfgrass

Root Zone Mixture
12-14-in. (30 to 35 cm)

Gravel: 4-in. (10 cm)

Subsoil

4-in. (10 cm) Diameter Drain
Tile

Figure 2.4. Profile of an alternative method of green construction that eliminates the 4-inch (10 cm) pea gravel layer and 2- to 4-inch (5 to 10 cm) coarse sand (e.g., choker) layer. Note that pea gravel is used to fill drainage line trenches and a plastic barrier may be necessary between the root-zone mix and the subsoil. If pure sand is used as the root zone and the 4-inch (10 cm) gravel layer eliminated, this is referred to as the California method. Although less costly to construct, the California method requires more water and fertilizer to grow in and often is less efficient in removing excessive subsurface moisture due to the lack of gravel layer (McCarty, 2001).

inches (30 to 36 cm) of an approved root-zone sand overlaying the native soil. Drain lines are trenched into the subgrade and backfilled with gravel. Unlike the previous profiles, the 4-inch gravel layer is deleted as is the 2- to 4-inch (5 to 10 cm) choker layer. This type of green is simple and relatively inexpensive to construct. It can perform quite well if the native soil underlying the root zone is either impermeable, or a layer of plastic (e.g., 6-mil) is placed on the subsoil before adding the root-zone mix, to prevent downward movement of water. However, if the native soil drains readily, moisture will be literally sucked out of the root-zone medium and the green will be extremely droughty and difficult to manage.

Sand greens are most difficult to grow in as they tend to remain droughty and lack nutrient holding capabilities. Slower drainage usually results as the water must transverse to the drain tile to be removed instead of simply dropping from the soil mix into the gravel drainage bed. Drainage line spacing should be based on the permeability of the root-zone sand, average rainfall rate, and the amount of water wanted removed or retained. A qualified laboratory should be consulted to help determine this. The planning committee should consider all three green profiles and weigh the benefits of each against their negative points. Generally, better results can be expected from those greens depicted in Figure 2.3; however, under financial restraints, Figure 2.4 may be a suitable alternative.

GREEN ESTABLISHMENT AND GROW-IN

Following golf course construction, golfers are eager to play, owners, developers, and/or financial partners want to start receiving a return on their investment while the general contractor worries about soil erosion from wind or water, hoping they will not have to perform any reshaping. These expectations place much pressure on the golf course superintendent and/or general contractor. Newly established turfgrass is very vulnerable to the elements and must receive adequate time to develop and mature sufficiently to withstand the wear and stresses associated with golf play.

Green Construction

Once the proposed green site is "shelled out," drain lines are installed (Figure 2.5). This most often involves a herringbone design with lines spaced 10 to 15 feet (3 to 4.5 m) apart. Circular perimeter drains (often referred to as "smile" lines) should be considered in the entrance/exit low point into the green to prevent excessive soil moisture which leads to soil compaction and turf thinning (Figure 2.5).

It is also recommended that a plastic barrier be placed between the root zone and surrounding soil (Figures 2.6 and 2.7). In many instances, the surrounding soil is finer than the root-zone mix and will therefore pull moisture from the green, causing dry, bare zones between the green and adjacent soil.

Root-zone mixing of sand with amendments such as peat, fertilizer, and lime should be performed off-site. Otherwise, shallow, uneven distribution of soil amendments occurs (Figure 2.8) and once established, the turf appears mosaic and has uneven growth characteristics (Plate 2.1).

Final grading should ideally be performed with a laser leveling system. A reference grade is established and a laser beam is used to adjust the elevation of the leveling blade to produce a high-quality, precise grade (Figure 2.9). Otherwise, a drag level is repeatedly used over the area until a smooth, somewhat compacted surface grade is achieved.

Once installed, the root-zone mix is settled and compacted by excessive irrigation and by various mechanical means (Figure 2.10). Following grading, fumigating with a plastic-covered fumigant reduces pests such as weeds, diseases, nematodes, and off-type or common bermudagrasses (Figure 2.11).

Plant Material Quality

The components of turfgrass quality reflect its genetic makeup, environmental influences on the turfgrass plant, and the expressed characteristics from biochemical and physiological processes. The characteristics of turfgrass quality have traditionally been established by the personal preferences and needs of the end user. In addition, turfgrass quality characteristics can vary with vegetative materials.

To ensure quality, one should personally inspect all turfgrass materials (sod fields) from which planting stock will be utilized. It is imperative to utilize the same source of turfgrass planting stock over time to minimize contamination of the initial planting stock with off-types or mutations. This not only includes the same grower but also the same

Figure 2.5. Herringbone design for subsurface tile drainage installation. Drain lines are typically 10 to 15 feet (3 to 4.5 m) apart. An additional perimeter drain line, referred to as a "smile" drain, is installed in the entrance/exit point(s) of sloping greens to prevent excessive moisture where soil compaction and turf wear is often greatest. Drain lines are backfilled with gravel to facilitate drainage.

Figure 2.6. Greens should be encircled by a heavy-ply plastic material to prevent unwanted soil moisture movement from the coarser root-zone mix to the surrounding heavier soil. This causes dry green perimeters which are difficult to maintain satisfactorily.

fields or blocks, as variations often occur between these. Most states have turfgrass certification programs to provide a paper trail to ensure quality, but these are not standardized or monitored across state lines. Use reputable producers and sellers because once the turf is established, it becomes very expensive, difficult, and time-consuming to con-

Figure 2.7. Installing the root-zone mix where heavy equipment is restricted to those areas where the soil has previously been placed. This helps prevent damage to the underlying drainage lines and minimizes grade deviations of the gravel layer. Plywood also is often placed in the entrance/exit points of constructed greens to prevent rutting. Note the grade stakes which are marked to indicate the appropriate levels of each root-zone component.

vert grasses. Proceed with extreme caution on lowest bid or lowest cost sources when dealing with golf green grasses.

Sprigging

Sprigging utilizes both rhizomes and stolons as vegetative sources of turfgrass planting material. Sprigging is simply the process of broadcast planting these rhizomes and stolons (sprigs) or planting them in narrow-spaced furrows (Figure 2.12). These rhizomes and stolons have little to no soil associated with them. Sprigging is considered to be the most economical means of vegetative turfgrass establishment.

Sprigs can be purchased by the bushel, or sod can be cut and shredded apart into sprigs. Other harvesting methods include rototilling of sod into sprigs and then raking them up. Tall grown bermudagrass is sometimes verticut to remove the rhizomes and stolons. This method generally requires a higher planting or sprigging rate because the roots and crowns of the turfgrass are missing. The goal is to plant sufficient material so no more than 3 inches (7.6 cm) occurs between sprigs. Refer to Table 2.1 for the vegetative planting rates of sprigs and/or plugs for the various turfgrasses. Using planting rates above those listed in Table 2.1 generally provides diminishing returns since higher rates do not quicken grow-in.

Ideally, sprigs should average at least six inches in length and contain at least two vegetative nodes with only a few green leaves. If sprigs contain excessive leaves they tend to dry out more rapidly, often within hours after their harvest, leaving an aesthetically displeasing brown turfgrass cover. Excessive leaves also increase transportation and storage problems associated with sprigs. Turfgrass sprigs often appear brown and lifeless to

Figure 2.8. Mixing of root-zone amendments such as peat, fertilizer, and lime is highly recommended to be performed off-site where special blending machines provide the appropriate ratios of the soil mix. Attempts to place amendments such as peat (top) on the soil surface and rototilling in produces only soil mixing in the top layer of the root zone (right), often resulting in excessively wet surfaces and uneven distribution of amendments (bottom).

those unfamiliar with the sprigging process; however, these brown sprigs soon are rejuvenated and grow if properly planted and cared for (Figure 2.13).

Turfgrass sprigs need to be freshly harvested for best survival. If sprigs are allowed to dry out or overheat, their survival greatly diminishes. Best survival is by planting sprigs within 48 hours of harvest. Sprigs not planted within two days may experience more damage from respiration and appear moldy and smell musty. To increase survival, turn or rotate the sprigs if possible to allow airflow through them, keep them moist (not wet), and place them in shade to minimize heat buildup. Sprigs also can be covered with a wet tarp or cloth or placed under a mist system to extend their time of survival. Ideally, sprigs should be stored in a layer not more than 8 inches (20 cm) in depth.

There are generally two methods of sprigging: (1) broadcast sprigging, and (2) row planting. Row planting is best suited for larger areas such as fairways since the equipment is large and bulky. The soil should be moist (not saturated) prior to planting to prevent root tip burn when contacting dry, hot soil.

21

Figure 2.9. Final (or finishing) surface grades should ideally be performed by laser leveling (top). Leveling equipment automatically adjusts as the tractor encircles the green to produce the most precise grades. Otherwise, a leveling drag such as the one shown (bottom) must be repeatedly used to provide a desirable smooth, somewhat compacted surface grade.

Broadcast sprigging involves spreading sprigs over the area (like mulch) either by hand or by specialized mechanical equipment. Sprigging rates for various turfgrasses are listed in Table 2.1. After spreading, sprigs are then cut (or pressed) into the soil with a light disc, covered with 1/2 inch (1.3 cm) of topdressing, and then rolled to firm the seedbed to ensure sprig to soil contact. Sprigs are then watered immediately. This method of sprigging provides very fast coverage and establishment of the turfgrass. However, since the sprigs are planted at a shallow depth, they are susceptible to drying out. Light, frequent irrigation (4 to 6 times daily) should be provided until the turfgrass roots be-

Figure 2.10. Mechanically settling the surface of a newly constructed golf green.

Figure 2.11. Fumigating greens to control pests such as nematodes, diseases, and weeds.

come established (2 to 4 weeks). Do not sprig more area than can be watered immediately. Generally, turfgrass sprigs will cover and become established within 6 to 8 weeks after planting. The length of time for establishment depends on the sprigging rate, time of year of planting, and maintenance practices implemented after planting.

Timing of planting is critical as enough time is needed before overseeding. Bermudagrass will not grow aggressively until night temperatures consistently remain in the mid-60°F (15.6°C) or higher. Construction delays, weather, and improper planning often delay proper planting timing. Ideally, in most areas of the southern United States,

Figure 2.12. Broadcast sprigging where sprigs are evenly spread over the area (top) and then are cut (or pressed) into the soil with a light disc, topdressed, and rolled (bottom).

late May through mid-July is optimum for sprigging. If planted after July, overseeding is not recommended the first year as the overseeded grass can outcompete and weaken the immature bermudagrass.

Sodding

Sodding provides 'instant greening' and excellent soil erosion control. Sodding, however, is more expensive initially, and has the possibility of introducing different types of turf (Plate 2.2), soil, or pests such as nematodes, weeds, or fire ants from the harvested

Table 2.1. Vegetative planting rates for various grasses and uses.

Area	Variety	Planting Rate (1 bushel is from 1 sq yd of sod)
Putting greens	Tifdwarf, Tifgreen (328), FloraDwarf, Champion, Classic, TifEagle, plus others	15 to 30 bu/1,000 ft^2 (568 to 1,135 L/ha)
Tees	Tifgreen (328), Tifway (419), plus others	10 to 20 bu/1,000 ft^2
Fairways/athletic fields	Tifway (419), FloraTex, TifSport, Quickstand, GN-1, Vamont, Midiron, plus others	400 to 800 bu/acre (348 to 696 L/ha)
Roughs	Tifway (419), FloraTex, plus others	200 to 400 bu/acre (174 to 348 L/ha)

Figure 2.13 Immediately following sprigging, greens often appear brown and lifeless. These soon begin to grow, producing roots and leaves, eventually turning green again. Note the sodded perimeter to prevent erosion.

field into the root zone. As a minimum specification, sodding should be utilized for areas prone to soil erosion, such as steep slopes and areas surrounding bunkers, tees, and greens (Figure 2.14).

Before installing sod, the seedbed should be watered. The rooting rate and establishment will be significantly increased if the underlying soil is moist and cool, thus receptive for rooting to occur. The sod should be installed soon, preferably within 48 hours after harvest. When sod remains stacked or rolled on pallets for longer periods, respiration of the turfgrass plants creates heat that can dry out and injure the grass.

Start laying the sod along the straightest line possible. Edges of the sod should butt against each other tightly without stretching. Avoid gaps or overlaps by using machetes or sharp knives to trim around corners and edges. Joints between the sod should be staggered in a brick-like fashion so none of the edges of adjacent pieces of sod are parallel. It is important to handle the sod with care to avoid tearing or stretching. If the sod is stretched it will shrink as it dries out, leaving gaps between the edges. On slopes and

Figure 2.14. Planting the perimeter of greens and sand bunkers with sod (top) to prevent undesirable erosion of native soil into the root-zone mix (bottom). Similar sodding or other erosion techniques should be performed around drain basins and other highly erodible sites.

bunker faces, place the sod across the slope and anchor the pieces with sod staples or wooden pegs until the roots have become established. To help avoid indentations or air pockets, refrain from walking on the newly laid sod. Sometimes the sod is installed by using plywood boards to ensure that the sod is installed evenly. This also ensures good sod to soil contact. After installation, the sod should be rolled to ensure evenness and smoothness and immediately watered heavily to wet the entire depth of the sod and top portion of the root zone. Topdressing should be implemented to fill in creases and low pieces and to help conserve moisture. Although sodding produces an almost instant green-appearing turf, it should be allowed to knit-down (or root) before being subjected to traffic and play. Four weeks is generally the minimum time necessary for this during periods of active turfgrass growth with longer periods needed when turf growth is slowed.

TURFGRASS GROW-IN

Immediately after planting, turfgrass requires special attention and maintenance to ensure survival and healthy growth. This grow-in phase is the most overlooked expense of any golf course construction or renovation project. The grow-in period is the time between planting until the time the golf course opens for play. Labor is generally the greatest expense but fertilizer is the greatest material needed during this period. It is important to recognize that the cost of grow-in cannot be offset by income since the golf course is not open for play.

Irrigation

Besides proper timing, proper irrigation or watering becomes the most important step in achieving successful turfgrass establishment. Turfgrass establishment from sprigging, stolonizing, or plugging requires constant moisture due to the lack of soil and roots associated with these vegetative materials. In contrast, sod requires the least amount of water because soil associated with sod provides moisture to the turfgrass plants.

It is critical for newly sprigged, stolonized, or plugged turfgrasses to be irrigated or watered immediately after planting to avoid losses due to desiccation or drying out. Timing is not as critical with plugging due to some soil being associated with the plugs. This maintains a certain level of soil moisture; however, establishment is still best if irrigation occurs as soon as possible. Irrigation or watering should continue on a frequent basis to maintain a moist soil surface for the vegetative plantings. Frequent surface irrigation should be continued for a two- to three-week period or until establishment occurs.

Fertilization

Prior to planting, a starter fertilizer should be applied to the site to encourage good rooting and quicker turf cover. Phosphorus and potassium are essential nutrients often low in high sand-content greens. When soil test results are unavailable, a complete fertilizer such as 10-20-20 should be added at 2-1/2 to 3 pounds per cubic yard (1.5 to 1.8 mg/cm^3) of mix. An organic fertilizer such as processed sewage sludge should also be added to high sand-content greens at 1 lb of a 6-2-0 or equivalent per cubic yard (0.6 mg/cm^3) of mix. These should be performed during off-site mixing to encourage uniform distribution throughout the soil profile. Some prefer to mix fertilizers to the surface and rototill twice into the top 6 to 8 inches (15 to 20 cm). In this case, 100 lb of 10-20-20 or equivalent and 35 lb 6-2-0 or equivalent are added and rototilled twice per 1,000 sq ft (4,880 and 1,709 kg/ha). A granular micronutrient package and a humate or carbohydrate soil conditioner also may be added according to label directions. These become especially important if sand-only (e.g., no peat) greens are constructed.

After planting, turfgrasses established by vegetative means should be fertilized on a frequent basis with a nitrogen-containing fertilizer to promote rapid turfgrass growth. It is recommended to fertilize vegetatively planted turfgrasses with an equivalent rate of 1 pound of water-soluble nitrogen per 1,000 sq ft (49 kg/ha) of turfgrass every 5 to 7 days for greens and tees. A quick-release fertilizer such as ammonium sulfate (21-0-0) or ammonium nitrate (45-0-0) should be alternated with each application with a 1-2-2 ratio fertilizer (such as 5-10-10 or equivalent) at an equivalent rate of 3/4 to 1 pound of nitrogen per 1,000 sq ft (37 to 49 kg/ha) of turfgrass. If additional color is needed or if growth slows, supplement these fertilizations as needed with a liquid nitrogen application at a rate of 1/5 lb nitrogen per 1,000 sq ft (9.8 kg/ha). Each granular fertilization should be irrigated or watered in immediately after application to avoid foliar turfgrass burn.

Mowing

Mowing should be initiated after the vegetatively planted turfgrass has become established and stolons have reached a growing height or length between 1/2 and 1-1/2 inches (1.3 to 3.8 cm). It is recommended to mow during midday when the turfgrass is dry. Turfgrass clippings should be returned to the soil surface for the first couple of mowings to promote rooting of any stolons that may have been cut during mowing. Mowing is usually initiated 10 to 14 days after sprigging. For Tifdwarf and Tifgreen, initial mowing height should be 3/8 to 5/8 inch (1 to 1.6 cm). For ultra-dwarf cultivars, initial mowing height can be lower, approximately 3/16 inch (0.5 cm). This is lowered gradually until 1/8 inch (0.3 cm) height is reached. If lowered prematurely or if the sod surface is uneven, scalping often results (Plate 2.3). Use only a sharpened mower blade because dull ones shred and pull sprigs from soil. Walk-behind units reduce soil compaction and generally provide a cleaner, smoother cut.

Topdressing and Rolling

Frequent topdressing and rolling during turfgrass establishment from vegetative planting of putting greens is recommended to achieve a smooth playing surface and enhance turfgrass establishment. Topdressing amount and frequency is dependent upon the existing smoothness of the surface. Topdressing also serves as a covering for vegetatively planted sprigs, stolons, or plugs; thereby enhancing their establishment. Sodded areas should also be rolled throughout the grow-in period to push roots into the soil and to smooth the surface to prevent mower scalping. Weekly rolling should be performed until the eventual permanent mowing height is achieved.

Initial Surface Firmness

Most golf greens, regardless of construction technique or material used, retain a firm (hard) playing surface the first 6 to 12 months after construction. Once the turf begins to mature and the superintendent is able to aerify and topdress the green and a desirable 0.5- to 1.0-inch mat/thatch layer develops, which acts like a cushion, the surface firmness (hardness) will eventually subside.

Section III

Managing Bermudagrass Golf Greens

3 Cultural Practices

MOWING

Bermudagrass greens are maintained at heights between 1/8 (0.125, 0.32 cm) and 3/16 (0.188, 0.48 cm) inch and are mowed daily. Older bermudagrass cultivars such as Tifgreen are mowed routinely between 3/16 (0.188, 0.48 cm) and 1/4 (0.250, 0.6 cm) inch. Tifdwarf is routinely mowed at approximately 5/32 (0.156, 0.4 cm) and 3/16 (0.188, 0.48 cm) inch, while newer dwarf cultivars such as TifEagle, Champion, and FloraDwarf tolerate routine mowing heights between 1/8 and 5/32 (0.156, 0.32, and 0.4 cm) inch. Mowing heights stated may be misleading since these heights are set on level surfaces (called bench setting) and may vary depending on turf conditions and mower weights.

Mowing height alone, however, should not be the only means of providing a smooth, quick putting surface. Numerous techniques are available besides mowing height to provide the desired putting surface and should be integrated into a total green management plan. Walk-behind mowers are often used, especially with mowing heights below 3/16 inch (0.48 cm) because it becomes difficult to set triplex mowers at these low heights without scalping and excessive compaction (Figure 3.1). Walk-behind mowers also are lightweight, reducing compaction and turf thinning, which can occur on the perimeter of greens when using larger and heavier triplex mowers. Triplex mowers, however, require less labor and time to operate. Clippings are normally removed and the mower pattern changed or rotated daily to reduce grain.

IRRIGATION/WATER MANAGEMENT

Good water management is a key component of any golf course management plan (Figure 3.2). Maximizing the time between irrigations without producing significant moisture stress encourages a deeper root system. Fortunately, bermudagrass is not as sensitive to precise water management as bentgrass, because bermudagrass does not require routine hand-watering and extra labor to check for 'hot spots' hourly during summer months. As stated, the recommended philosophy is heavy and infrequent applications, allowing the grass/soil to dry down between irrigations. Most superintendents prefer to keep their greens slightly on the dry side to minimize disease occurrence and to encourage deeper rooting and to avoid algae. Drier greens also absorb summer thunderstorms and other rainfall events better than saturated greens. It generally is easier to apply water when needed rather than trying to remove it when excessive.

Figure 3.1. Walk-behind mowers (top) reduce compaction and provide desirable striping. Triplex machines (bottom) require less labor and time to operate but may cause more soil compaction and turf damage and periodically leak hydraulic fluids.

Steps in formulating an irrigation strategy include:

1. Calibrate an irrigation system's output and distribution pattern (or DU).
2. Determine daily evapotranspiration (ET) rates or soil moisture status.
3. Accurately track daily rainfall and ET rates so a water budget can be set up and followed.
4. When irrigation is needed, use the appropriate crop coefficient percent (0.75 to 0.85) of daily ET rate and adjust for distribution uniformity (DU) of the irrigation system.
5. Make adjustments for rainfall, varying microclimates, and forecasted weather.

Figure 3.2. Golf green irrigation involves proper coverage with quality water applied deeply (e.g., ½ to ¼ in. 1.2 to 0.6 cm) infrequently (e.g., every three to five days during heat and moisture stress).

Table 3.1. Conversions and calculations for determining turfgrass irrigation needs.

1 acre-inch (amount that covers 1 acre to the depth of 1 inch)			=	27,154 gal	=	102,778 L
			=	43,560 cu in	=	0.71 m^3
			=	3,630 cu ft	=	103 m^3
1 acre-foot (amount that covers 1 acre to the depth of 1 foot)			=	325,851 gal	=	1,233,346 L
			=	43,560 cu ft	=	1233 m^3
1 inch/1,000 sq ft	=	620 gal	=	2,347 L	=	83 cu ft
1 gallon	=	0.134 cu ft	=	3.785 L	=	8.34 lb
7 1/2 gallon	=	1 cu ft	=	28 L	=	231 cu in
1 million gallon	=	3.07 acre-feet	=	3787 m^3		
1 pound of water	=	0.1199 gal	=	454 mL		
1 psi	=	2.31 ft of head	=	6.9 kilopascal (kPa)		
1 foot of head	=	0.433 psi	=	3 kPa		
volume of water	=	7.48 gal/cu ft	=	1,000 L/m^3		

Determining Irrigation Rates and Frequency

In addition to the application rate and uniformity, the turf manager should know how much water the turf is using. This can be determined using reference ET from a weather station/computer system plus a crop coefficient specific for the turf species or with data from an atmometer or other devices. Historical weather information may also provide reasonable estimates of average water use. Managers also need to know where the roots are in the soil profile and approximately how much available water is held by the soil. Table 3.1 lists water conversion and calculations for turfgrass irrigation needs.

The amount of water needed to moisten the soil to a given depth depends on soil type, water infiltration and percolation rates, and surface slope. Soils that are severely sloped, compacted, or clayey in nature may have low infiltration rates. As a result, the

Figure 3.3. Washout of a green side bunker due to improper bunker design and construction and the lack of a separate irrigation system for greens and the surrounds.

soil may not be able to absorb the required amount of irrigation at one time. Managers may have to irrigate using multiple cycles until the desired amount is applied (Figure 3.3). After an irrigation, managers should double-check the depth of moisture penetration using a soil probe so they can fine-tune their timing.

Evaporation during hot, windy, and dry periods can reduce irrigation efficiency. Superintendents can avoid this by irrigating early in the morning before the temperature rises and humidity drops. Early morning irrigation also removes dew from the leaves, and helps prevent diseases that are favored by irrigating in the evening.

Water Quality

Another potential problem with all greens is a gradual buildup of salinity from the use of high pH or bicarbonate-containing irrigation water, effluent sources, or brackish water. This is magnified when highly soluble fertilizer sources are used at relatively light but frequent rates and there is a lack of frequent, heavy rainfall to periodically leach the salt below the root zone.

To combat potential salinity buildup, superintendents have modified their watering practices from light, frequent applications in summer to heavier, infrequent ones. Greens also must drain relatively well so salts can be leached below the root zone by heavy rainfall or by heavy hand-watering. Using low salt-containing water sources also helps. Coastal courses or those using effluent water sources should closely monitor their salt levels, especially during summer.

In recent years, fertigation and foliar feeding (or spoon-feeding) by liquid fertilizer sources have become popular to help better regulate grass color and growth during summer. Fertigation allows many frequent fertilizer applications at low rates. Fertigation may be used as a primary source of fertility or may be used to supplement a dry fertilizer program. Fertigation also allows a turf manager to spoon-feed the turf without weighing fertilizers and driving over the area multiple times during the year. Leaching of nutrients is minimized because of the low application rate. A potential problem is having to irrigate in order to fertilize the greens, whether or not irrigation is needed. Spoon-feeding then becomes an alternative.

There are many materials that can be added to the fertilizer holding tank without negative results. Micronutrients are often added through fertigation systems. Due to solubility problems, micronutrients are often chelated to help them stay in solution. Surfactants, which may aid in water utilization and therefore nutrient efficiency, are often added directly to the fertilizer mixture. Before adding anything to the tank, test the compatibility of materials using the jar test. To do this, take some fertilizer solution from the holding tank and put it into a jar. Then add the material in question at a recommended rate to the fertilizer solution. Observe for any change in composition for a least a few days. If no change occurs, it is most likely safe to add the material to the fertilizer holding tank at a similar concentration.

Fertigation and foliar feeding also reduce the salinity load on the grass. Buffering the water pH to 6.0 to 6.5 and periodic light use of gypsum also help reduce the salinity stress. High bicarbonate water is also commonly treated by artificially acidifying it, often by sulfur injection. This technology is rapidly evolving and dramatic effects can be realized. The following tests provide information concerning soil and water quality:

- total salt content (EC)
- sodium level (SAR or ESP)
- toxic ion levels, especially boron, chloride, and fluoride
- bicarbonates (RSC)
- pH

Also influencing water quality use are soil water infiltration rates, differential salinity tolerance of the turfgrass species, and nutrient content (e.g., N, P, and K). Refer to Chapter 5 for additional information on water quality.

FERTILIZING

To promote recovery from traffic and clipping removal, and to fulfill clientele color expectation, bermudagrass requires ample nutrients. Furthermore, many courses are located in areas with extended growing seasons, high annual rainfall, and predominately sandy soils which increases the precision of using the right amounts and ratios of nutrients.

Questions to ask when developing a turfgrass fertility program include:

- What fertilizer analysis and source is best?
- What application method(s) are best for my course?
- What rate of this fertilizer should be used?
- What timing and frequency will provide optimum results?

Timing

Fertilization programs should provide adequate levels of essential nutrients to sustain growth and acceptable turf quality and color. Improper timing and/or rates of fertilizer influence turfgrass stress tolerance and recuperative ability. In addition, disease occurrence and severity often are closely linked to the amounts and the timing of fertilization programs. For example, dollar spot (*Moellerodiscus* and *Lanzia* spp.) and Helminthosporium leaf spot (*Drechslera* and *Bipolaris* spp.) diseases often are correlated with periods of inactive or slowed turf growth. A fertilizer application containing soluble nitrogen often promotes the turfgrass to outgrow these disease symptoms, eliminating the need for fungicide applications. In contrast, excessive fertilization of overseeded ryegrass, roughstalk bluegrass (*Poa trivialis*), and bentgrass often promotes the occurrence of brown patch (*Rhizoctonia* spp.) and pythium (*Pythium* spp.) diseases.

Proper fertilization, along with providing healthy disease- and stress-free turf, is important for providing an acceptable playing surface. As a rule, excessive fertilization with nitrogen will not only be agronomically detrimental to the turfgrass, but will drastically slow ball roll and draw complaints from players. Exceptions, such as certain high-traffic greens and tees (e.g., par 3) or newly constructed greens, require higher nitrogen fertilization to promote turf recovery or grow-in.

Timing is partially based on minimum and optimum temperatures necessary for turfgrass growth. Table 3.2 lists growth temperatures for cool- and warm-season turfgrasses. If temperatures are outside the growth range of the grass, fertilizer applications will be inefficiently utilized.

Nitrogen Rates

As mentioned, many factors will determine the fertilization rates needed for a particular golf course. A general yearly range of nitrogen needs for bermudagrass golf greens is from 8 to 24 lb N per 1,000 sq ft (1/2 to 2 lb N/1,000 sq ft per growing month, 24 to 98 kg/ha). Courses with sufficient resources, excessive traffic, sandy soils, older bermudagrass cultivars, and elevated demands from players would use the higher rate range. Those courses interested in maintaining a less intensive playing surface, or those that have ultra-dwarf cultivars, or limited labor and financial resources, should use nitrogen rates in the lower range. Exceptions to these values may occur. For example, courses recovering from excessive traffic, pest, or low temperature stresses, or those establishing new greens may require higher (approx. 25% more) nitrogen rates than listed until their grass is sufficiently reestablished.

Frequency

Bermudagrass

The percentages of nitrogen fertilizer applied to warm-season turfgrasses during the year are listed in Table 3.3. In general, to maintain optimum color and density during periods of active growth, highly maintained bermudagrass golf greens need approxi-

Table 3.2. Air temperatures affecting turfgrass shoot growth and soil temperatures at 4 inches (10 cm) affecting root growth (McCarty, 2001).

	Shoot Growth		Root Growth	
Turfgrass	Minimum	Optimum	Minimum	Optimum
	— — — — — — — — — °F[a] — — — — — — — — —			
Warm-season grasses	55°	80 to 95°	50 to 60°	75 to 85°
Cool-season grasses	40°	60 to 75°	33°	50 to 65°

[a] C = F-32° (5/9).

Table 3.3. Percentages of nitrogen fertilizer applied to bermudagrass during the year.

Season	Overseeded	Nonoverseeded
Fall (Sept., Oct., Nov.)	15	10 to 15
Winter (Dec., Jan., Feb.)	15	0
Spring (Mar., Apr., May)	25	35
Summer (June, July, Aug.)	45	50 to 55

mately 1/2 lb soluble N per 1,000 sq ft (24 kg/ha) every 7 to 14 days. For those courses without these resources and for those that have lower expectations, adequate bermudagrass can be maintained with 1/2 lb N per 1,000 sq ft (24 kg/ha) applied every 14 to 21 days during periods of active growth. On intensively maintained courses, higher rates (e.g., 1 lb N per 1,000 sq ft [49 kg/ha] every 7 to 14 days) may be necessary to encourage quicker turf recovery during times of heavy play. However, these higher rates can lead to other problems. Excessive thatch can quickly accumulate, putting speeds will be slower since more leaf area will be produced, and a decrease in turfgrass rooting often occurs.

As discussed later, fertilizer rates for ultra-dwarf cultivars are reduced to approximately 1/2 lb N/1,000 sq ft (24 kg/ha) for granular fertilizer per growing month with slow-release sources. This is usually supplemented with 0.1 to 0.25 lb N/1,000 sq ft (5 to 12 kg/ha) of a liquid source every 7 to 14 days. This program helps maintain consistent color and growth rates, reduces scalping, and minimizes thatch/mat accumulation. Due to their density, miniprilled or greens-grade granular fertilizer should be used on greens to allow better penetration through the turf canopy and not to be removed by mowing.

Overseeded Bermudagrass Greens

Once established, overseeded greens should be fertilized every two to three weeks with 1/2 pound soluble nitrogen (plus potassium) per 1,000 ft² (24 kg/ha) during the fall and winter months. The objective is to provide enough nitrogen to maintain desirable color but not be so excessive as to weaken the overseeded grasses and promote premature growth of bermudagrass. In addition, highly soluble nitrogen use on overseeded grass often leads to excessive turf growth, slower putting speeds, and disease (e.g., brown patch and pythium) occurrence. Many superintendents have discovered that application of manganese, and possibly iron, can often substitute for a nitrogen application. Two to three ounces (56 to 84 g) of an iron source (such as ferrous sulfate) or 1/2 ounce (14 g) manganese sulfate in 2 to 5 gallons of water applied per 1,000 sq ft (8 to 20 L/100 m^3) provides 10 to 21 days of desirable dark green color without undesirable flush of growth. These elements are only foliarly absorbed by plants, hence the relative short color response time.

Nitrogen Sources

The source of nitrogen used to fertilize golf greens affects the amount applied at one time. Usually, a combination of soluble and insoluble nitrogen sources is recommended to provide uniform grass growth. Ureaformaldehyde (Nitroform), IBDU, SCU, and polymer-coated materials often are used to provide slow-release, residual nitrogen while a soluble source is used for quicker turf response. During cold temperatures, IBDU or soluble sources provide the fastest turf response because they are less dependent on microorganisms for nitrogen conversion and release.

Spoon- (also called foliar) feeding with liquid fertilizer programs is often used on high sand content areas to help regulate turf growth and color and to provide a continuous supply of elements such as N or K which are often easily leached (Figure 3.4). Nitrogen rates in a foliar-feeding program typically range from 0.1 to 0.25 lb N/1,000 sq ft (5 to 12 kg/ha) on a 7- to 14-day interval. Phosphorus (as phosphoric acid or P_2O_5) is applied at about one-third the rate of nitrogen, while K rates will be equal to one-half the rate of nitrogen. Other elements such as magnesium or iron also may be added by foliar-feeding to help regulate and maintain desirable turf color.

Other Elements

Potassium

Potassium often is called the 'health' element and without a relatively available supply, turfgrasses will be more susceptible to environmental and pest stresses. Root growth also is related to potassium availability. Research and experience indicate that N:K ratios on greens should be 1:0.5 to 1:0.75. Excessive potassium may increase the soil salinity levels, especially if the leaching capability is limited, and also compete with the soil exchange sites at the expense of other essential elements such as calcium, magnesium, and iron.

Phosphorus

Soil phosphorus levels tend not to fluctuate as readily as nitrogen or potassium. Soil-test results should be used to determine the amount needed for a particular course. Usually 0 to 4 lb phosphorus per 1,000 sq ft (0 to 195 kg/ha) are needed yearly. Phosphorus is generally not very water soluble, therefore, if needed, its efficiency is increased if applications follow aerification. This allows the material to be placed more directly in the root zone. Phosphorus levels can become limiting during a grow-in situation. A N:P ratio

Figure 3.4. Spoon- (or foliar) feeding involves applying light (e.g., 0.25 lb N/1,000 sq ft, 12 kg/ha), frequent (e.g., every one to four weeks) soluble nutrient sources.

of 1:2 has proved best for bermudagrass sprig grow-in and is normally applied at 1 lb N/ 1,000 sq ft (49 kg/ha) every 7 to 14 days until complete coverage is achieved.

Plant deficiency symptoms of P are purple discoloration of leaf blades. However, this can be easily confused with purpling that often occurs during cool periods when anthocyanins (bluish pigments) are exposed. Applying a small area or strip with P fertilizer is an easy way to determine the cause of purpling. If the purpling disappears after P fertilization, then an application across the entire green is probably warranted. Cool-season turfgrasses often have more of a color response to phosphorus fertilization than warm-season grasses. To take advantage of this, turf to be overseeded should have its yearly phosphorus fertilizer applied during the cool-season months.

Micronutrients

Regular soil and tissue testing is the best preventative approach to solving many of the nutrient deficiency problems. Iron and manganese are two of the most common micronutrient deficiencies turf managers experience. However, **if excessive or indiscriminate amounts of micronutrients are applied or soil pH is excessively low (<5.0), plant toxicity can occur.** An example involves growing turf on old vegetable or fruit production fields. These were often sprayed with fungicides containing copper, zinc, and/or sulfur. Because of their relative immobility (with the exception of sulfur) in soils, residues have become toxic to turfgrasses in some cases.

Golf greens, due to their high sand content, typically have low cation exchange capacities (e.g., ≤5.0 meq/100 g or cmol/kg). This, along with soil pH, are two key components of a soil test report important to understand the availability of micronutrients. By default, soils low in pH are saturated with hydrogen ions and are low in calcium, magnesium, potassium, phosphorus, and other cations necessary for plant growth. Thus, low-

Table 3.4. Solution used to spot treat for micronutrient deficiencies (McCarty, 2001).

Deficient Micronutrient	Fertilizer Source	Rate	
		oz/gal	lb element/1,000 sq ft (kg/ha)
Fe	iron sulfate	0.66	0.025 (1.2)
Mn	manganese sulfate	0.5	0.025 (1.2)
Zn	zinc sulfate	0.5	0.010 (0.5)
Cu	copper sulfate	0.5	0.003 (0.15)
B	borax	0.1	0.001 (0.05)
Mo	sodium molybdate	0.01	0.001 (0.05)

CEC and low-pH sand soils often experience magnesium deficiency, especially during grow-in of low organic matter containing greens. Conversely, soils low in CEC but high in soil pH (>7.0) may experience iron deficiency. Tissue testing and experimenting with small areas of a green by applying the suspected element are the two best means to determine if this is a problem.

Micronutrient deficiency symptoms can easily be confused with pest occurrence or other stresses. These problems, however, usually are more localized and appear as irregular spots or in circular patterns. Table 3.4 offers a starting guideline for spot treating of micronutrients when sprayed on the foliage to the drip point.

Chelates

In an effort to reduce turf burn (Plate 3.1) and to maintain a solution, chelated forms of many micronutrients have been developed. Chelates, chelating agents, or sequestering agents are cyclic structures of a normally nonsoluble metal atom and an organic component that, when held together, become soluble in water. The chelation process allows nutrients to move through the soil solution to the plants without being tied up with other soil chemicals. However, the activity of the metallic ion decreases in the aqueous solution.

Commercially available sequestered metallic ions are iron, copper, zinc, and manganese. Organic compounds which have the ability to chelate or sequester these metallic ions include: ethylenediaminetetraacetic acid (EDTA); diethylenetriaminepentaacetic acid (DTPA); cyclohexanediaminetetraacetic acid (CDTA); and ethylenediaminedi (o-hydroxyphenylacetic acid) (EDDHA), citrate, and gluconate. These range from 5 to 14% iron. Their stability fluctuates with various soil pH levels. For example, EDDHA is best for soil pH from 4 to 9, EDTA at soil pH <6.3, and DTPA at soil pH <7.5.

Nonessential Elements

Sodium, aluminum, and arsenic are nonessential elements for turfgrass growth and development. These, in general, become toxic when levels are excessive and should not be applied in supplemental fertilizers.

SOIL ANALYSIS

Soil testing is one of the basic practices of turfgrass management. Soil analysis provides information on relative levels of nutrients, organic matter, pH, soluble salts, and cation exchange capacity. However, variations occur between testing laboratories because of different extraction and analysis techniques. The ranking of the nutrient level, however, should be similar regardless of the extractant. It is recommended that turf managers pick a particular laboratory and stick with it, as chances of the lab switching analysis techniques are minimized. In most cases, these laboratories use university extraction and analysis techniques and fertility recommendations. Managers should be careful the laboratory chosen uses information on calibration of soil test results for the plant material being grown. Recommendations based on responses of plants other than turfgrass may provide inaccurate results since turfgrass needs differ from most crops. For example, laboratories not specializing in turfgrass tend to overestimate phosphorus recommendations and underestimate potassium requirements. Also, laboratories use various extraction techniques, depending on its geographical location (soil type). Table 3.5 lists various extraction techniques used for specific nutrients and soil types.

Soil Analysis Report

Cation Exchange Capacity

Soil cation exchange capacity (CEC) measures a soil's capacity to hold the positively charged cations calcium (Ca^{+2}), magnesium (Mg^{+2}), potassium (K^+), copper (Cu^{+2}), manganese (Mn^{+2}), zinc (Zn^{+2}), and iron (Fe^{+2}) and their relative ability to displace other cations. For example, one meq of potassium is able to displace exactly one meq of magnesium. The unit of measure meq/100 g serves this purpose. Cation exchange capacity (CEC) and the total amounts of individual cations may be expressed using these units. Higher values usually represent better soils in terms of fertility because at high values, the soil acts like a sponge and can hold more nutrients. Soil constituents which attract cations, such as organic matter and clay, have higher CEC values than sandy soil, which are least fertile (Table 3.6).

Base Saturation (or Cation Saturation)

The degree to which the total CEC sites are saturated with the cations calcium, magnesium, and potassium as opposed to the acid cations hydrogen and aluminum is referred to as the base saturation of a soil (Table 3.7). In general, the pH and fertility of a soil increase as the percentage base saturation increases. Higher base saturation generally increases the ease with which cations are absorbed by plants. Greatest availability of most nutrients to plants is in the soil pH range 6 to 7. In highly acidic soils (pH <5.5), exchangeable aluminum may be present and, along with magnesium and/or hydrogen ions, can suppress plant uptake of calcium or potassium. However, toxic aluminum becomes less prevalent, therefore less detrimental to the plant, as the base saturation increases.

Table 3.5. Extraction techniques used to determine soil nutrients levels for various locations and soil types.

Extraction Techniques	Comments
Ammonium acetate (NH$_4$OAc), pH 7.0	Widely used in the Midwest and far western United States; used to determine CEC and K. At pH 4.8, extracts more Ca and Mg.
Ammonium bicarbonate (NH$_4$HCO$_3$) or Sodium bicarbonate (NaHCO$_3$)	Used in central western US States on calcareous soils.
Ammonium acetate + acetic acid	Used to extract sulfate (sulfur)
Bray P1	Extracts relatively soluble CaP, FeP, and AlP; some organic P.
Mehlich I (diluted double acid method; HCl + H$_2$SO$_4$)	Used in the clayey soils of the southeastern United States for relatively soluble CaP, FeP, and AlP; excessive P in calcareous soils. Also used to extract micronutrients Cu, Mn, and Zn.
Mehlich II	Extracts relatively soluble CaP, FeP, and AlP; some organic P; superior on volcanic ash or loess-derived soils.
Mehlich III	Used to extract P and cations.
Morgan	Used in northeastern and northwestern United States; extracts P dissolved by carbon dioxide.
Olsen	Extracts CaP fractions and some FeP. Better on calcareous soils than acid extractants.
Water	Used to extract sulfur in arid and semiarid regions.
Dilute acid or salt	Used to extract sulfur in humid regions.
DTPA-TEA	Most widely used extractant for the micronutrients Fe, Mn, Zn, and Cu.

Nutrient Listing

Most soil analysis reports list nutrients levels by one of two methods: parts per million (ppm) or milliequivalent (meq) per 100 grams of soil. Results for the major elements and micronutrients are most commonly reported in ppm on an elemental basis. An acre of mineral soil, six to seven inches deep, weighs approximately two million pounds. Therefore, to convert ppm to approximate pounds per acre, multiply by two.

From these reported nutrient levels, most soil test readings are given a fertility rating index of very low (VL), low (L), medium (M), high (H), or very high (VH). Usually, the division between medium and high is the critical value. Above this point there is no expected plant response to added fertilizer while below this, increasing amounts of fertilizer are needed with decreasing levels. Table 3.8 summarizes recommended ranges for nutrients levels using the Mehlich-I extractant procedure. The reader should note that differences occur between plants, soils, locations, management practices, and laboratory extraction techniques. Time and experience are required to establish a baseline where superintendents can then gauge specific nutrient level fluctuations according to the specific extraction technique used by a particular laboratory (Table 3.5)

Table 3.6. Cation exchange capacity (CEC) examples of various soils.

Soil	CEC (meq/100 g)	Relative Level
Sand	0–6	Very low
Sandy loam	6–12	Low
Loam	12–30	Medium
Silt loam	10–50	Medium
Clay loams	15–30	Medium
Clays	18–150	High
Organic (e.g., muck)	150–350	Very high

Table 3.7. Desired cation exchangeable capacities (CEC) and percent base saturation range in soils.

Cation	% Cation Exchange Capacity	% Base Saturation
Calcium (Ca^{+2})	60 to 70	50 to 80
Magnesium (Mg^{+2})	10 to 20	8 to 22
Potassium (K^+)	5 to 10	1 to 9
Sodium (Na^+)	0 to 1	0 to 1
Hydrogen (H^+)	0 to 10[a]	0

[a] A hydrogen percentage above 15% may indicate a nutrient imbalance.

Various Ratios of Elements

Ratios of various elements can be important for specific chemical reactions. For example, the carbon to nitrogen ratio of amendments influences decomposition and utilization of organic matter, and generally ranges between 10 and 12 to 1 for soil organic matter. Ratios greater than 20 to 1 may result in inefficient breakdown of organic matter due to the lack of nitrogen necessary to sustain soil organisms. Certain sawdust sources have as high a C:N ratio as 400 to 1. Turf managers who use these as soil amendments should add some nitrogen to the mixture, since sawdust can raise the carbon to nitrogen ratio above 20 to 1. Similar results also could occur if the nitrogen to sulfur ratio exceeds 20 to 1. Guidelines for Mg:K and Ca:K ratios based on saturation percentages on the soil CEC include:

Ca:K	<10:1	Ca deficiency may occur
	>30:1	K deficiency may occur
Mg:K	<2:1	Mg deficiency may occur
	>10:1	K deficiency may occur
Ca:Mg	<3:1	Ca deficiency may occur
	>3:1	Mg deficiency may occur

LEAF ANALYSIS

Tissue or leaf analysis can be an additional tool to help determine those inputs in maintaining the turf. Leaf analysis, along with turfgrass appearance and soil analysis,

Table 3.8. Relative response range of soil elements analyzed by Mehlich-I extractant[a] (modified from McCarty, 2001).

Analysis	Acceptable Ranges	Comments
Nitrogen/Organic Matter	≤ 5%	Due to its readily changing status in soils, nitrogen availability is hard to predict. Many times the percent organic matter serves as a reserve for many essential nutrients, especially nitrogen. Labs, therefore, list an Estimated Nitrogen Release figure based on the percentage of organic matter present to estimate the nitrogen that will be released over the season in pounds per acre.
Phosphorus	5–30 ppm	Phosphorus absorption is greatest between a soil pH of 5.5 to 6.5. Values for other extractant procedures include:
Potassium	5–60 ppm	Generally, higher K levels are required in high clay or organic matter containing soils. Soils with high levels of Mg may also require higher K applications. Sandy soils require more frequent, light K applications compared to heavier ones. Values for other extractant procedures include:

Extractant Technique	Very low	Low	Medium	High
		ppm P		
Bray P1	0–4	5–15	16–30	>31
Mehlich III	0–12	13–26	27–54	>55
Olsen	0–6	7–12	13–28	>29

Extractant Technique	Very low	Low	Medium	High
		ppm K		
1 M NH$_4$OAc (pH 7.0)				
Sands/most soils	0–40	41–75	76–175	>176
Fine-textured (>35% clay)	0–55	56–100	101–235	>235
Mehlich III				
Sands/most soils	0–25	26–50	51–116	>116
Fine-textured (>35% clay)	0–40	41–75	76–175	>176
Mehlich I				
Sands/most soils	0–30	31–60	61–140	>140
Fine-textured (>35% clay)	0–45	46–90	91–200	>201

Calcium	5–50 ppm (see comment)	With most soils, liming with dolomite to ensure an adequate soil pH for proper plant growth will provide more-than-adequate concentrations of Ca and Mg. Their deficiencies are more common in sandy, acidic, and/or low organic matter containing soils. Ca deficiencies are uncommon, however, Mg deficiencies often occur in acidic soils low in CEC and subject to frequent leaching. Heavy liming with calcium carbonate (also called calcite) lime or heavy use of K also may induce Mg deficiency. Apply magnesium sulfate (Epsom salts) to test for Mg deficiency.
Magnesium	5–20 ppm (see comment)	
Soil pH	5.5 to 6.5	Soil pH less than 5.5 becomes highly acidic and can produce toxic elements to the turf. Alkaline soil pH (>7.0) often limits availability of many minor elements.
Cation Exchange Capacity (CEC)	5 to 35 meq/100 g	CEC measures a soil's ability to hold the cations Ca, Mg, K, H, and Na. Increasing CEC generally occurs with increasing soil organic matter or clay content. Generally, the higher the CEC value, the more productive the soil. A suggested range of the total makeup of a soil's CEC is 65 to 75% Ca, 12 to 18% Mg, and 3 to 5% K.
Percent Base Saturation	(see comment)	Percent base saturation refers to the proportion of the CEC occupied by the cations Ca, Mg, K, H, and Na. With sandy soils, base saturation percentages have little value when determining nutrient levels.
Iron	12–25 ppm	Soil pH and relative levels of other elements such as P are important when interpreting Fe soil test. Generally, Fe becomes less available in alkaline or extremely acidic soils, and soils with excessive P or moisture levels. Levels <2.5 ppm and < 50 ppm are deficient as per the DTPA and Mehlich III extractant techniques, respectively.
Manganese	2–10 ppm	Levels where a plant response to applied Mn may occur include: 3-5, 5-7, 7-9 ppm for mineral or organic soils with pH 5.5 to 6.0, 6.0 to 6.5, 6.5 to 7.0, respectively. Deficiencies are more prone on coarse, sandy, acid soils that receive excessive water.
Zinc	1–3 ppm	Levels where a plant response to applied Zn may occur include: 0.5, 0.5 to 1.0, 1-3 ppm for soils with pH 5.5 to 6.0, 6.0 to 6.5, 6.5 to 7.0, respectively. Zinc interactions with P and soil pH can alter needed application rates.

Table 3.8. (Continued)

Analysis	Acceptable Ranges	Comments
Copper	0.1 to 0.5 ppm	Levels where a plant response to applied Cu may occur include: 0.1 to 0.3, 0.3 to 0.5, 0.5 ppm for mineral soils only with pH 5.5 to 6.0, 6.0 to 6.5, 6.5 to 7.0, respectively. Copper deficiencies can occur on alkaline soils, high organic matter (peat and muck) soils, soils fertilized heavily with N, P, and Zn, and when flatwood soils are first cultivated. Toxic conditions may exist when Cu levels exceed 2-3, 3-5, and 5 ppm in mineral soils with pH of 5.5 to 6.0, 6.0 to 6.5, and 6.5 to 7.0, respectively.
Boron	1–1.5 ppm	Boron deficiencies occur more commonly on sandy, low organic matter soils, and alkaline soils. Boron is most soluble (available) under acid soil conditions.
Sulfur	(see comment)	Soil S levels, like N, are dependent on soil organic matter levels and are erratic to measure and often results are meaningless. Soils which are low in organic matter, well drained, have low CEC values, and are fertilized with excessive nitrogen, can develop low S levels. Foliar application of magnesium sulfate (Epsom salt) will indicate if S deficiencies exist by greening up within 48 hours after application.

[a] Acceptable ranges represent typical values generated by the Mehlich-I soil nutrient extractant procedure. Values may vary if other extractant procedures are used which are typically performed for various soil types and geographical regions. Refer to the specific soil testing facility and report to determine which nutrient extractant procedure was used and what the generated values actually represent.

Table 3.9. Adequate or sufficiency ranges for nutrients from tissue analysis.

	Element	Amount
Primary Nutrients	Nitrogen (N)	27–35 g/kg
	Phosphorus (P)	2–5.5 g/kg
	Potassium (K)	10–25 g/kg
Secondary Nutrients	Calcium (Ca)	5–12.5 g/kg
	Magnesium (Mg)	2–6 g/kg
	Sulfur (S)	2–4.5 g/kg
Micronutrients	Iron (Fe)	35–100 mg/kg (or ppm)
	Manganese (Mn)	25–150 mg/kg (or ppm)
	Zinc (Zn)	20–55 mg/kg (or ppm)
	Copper (Cu)	5–20 mg/kg (or ppm)
	Boron (B)	6–30 mg/kg (or ppm)
	Molybdenum (Mo)	2–8 mg/kg? (or ppm)
	Chlorine (Cl)	unavailable

can be used as a means of diagnosing the problems and the effectiveness of fertilization programs, especially for micronutrient deficiency. Soil analysis for some nutrients does not always adequately indicate their availability to plants. Therefore, potential nutrient deficiencies can be detected with leaf analysis before visual symptoms appear. Leaf analysis also provides information on nutrient levels available to turf plants compared to soil test levels and possibly determines what may interfere with nutrient uptake to create a deficiency in the plant.

Primary and secondary nutrients occur in relatively large quantities within plants—their concentrations are usually expressed in grams (g) of the element per kilogram (kg) of plant dry weight. Micronutrients occur in relatively small quantities—their concentrations are usually expressed in milligrams (mg) of the element per kilogram of plant dry weight which is also parts per million (ppm) (Table 3.9).

Fertilizer Sources

Golf courses in the past have relied predominantly on granular fertilizer sources for the majority of their fertilization. However, improved technology and availability of liquid fertilizers have changed this trend. More liquid sources are being used, especially during stress periods. Liquid sources allow superintendents to more precisely control the rate being applied and application uniformity without the need of watering-in like granulars, which becomes important during rainy seasons or on poorly drained greens.

Typically, granular fertilizers are used most months for bermudagrass greens, especially for potassium and phosphorus needs. Liquid materials are used to boost or maintain uniform color. Many courses spoon-feed the greens as needed, e.g., when soil and tissue tests indicate nutrient needs, when color is needed, or when growth dramatically slows. Liquid fertilizers are typically applied during this time every 2 to 4 weeks at approximately 0.2 lb N/1,000 ft^2 (9.8 kg/ha).

Figure 3.5. Worn areas on the perimeter of greens from using heavy mowing equipment at excessive speeds (top). Severely worn, compacted rings (called triplex rings) can develop (bottom) when heavy mowers are continuously used when soils are excessively wet and/or compacted.

AERIFICATION STRATEGIES AND TECHNIQUES

Many golf facilities are not constructed with desirable soil (Plate 3.2). Turf built with "native" soil and exposed to heavy traffic and improper management practices often deteriorates due to compacted soil, thatch or mat development, and excessive use (Figure 3.5). Unlike annual row crops which are periodically tilled to correct these problems, turf managers do not have the opportunities to provide such physical disturbances without destroying the playing surface. Soil related problems are usually confined to the upper 3 inches (7.6 cm) of the turf and once formed, may not be completely corrective, especially where improper site preparation occurred prior to establishing the turf. How-

Figure 3.6. Golf green soil compaction is relieved best by core aerification with plugs (or cores) removed afterward.

ever, over the years a number of mechanical devices that provide soil cultivation with minimum turf surface disturbance have been developed. Cultivation is accomplished by core aerification, vertical mowing, spiking, slicing, and topdressing.

Frequency and Timing of Core Cultivation

Frequency of core cultivation should be based on intensity of traffic the turf is exposed to, soil makeup, hardness of the soil surface, drainage capability, and degree of compaction (Figure 3.6). Areas receiving intense, daily traffic such as golf greens, approaches, landing areas, aprons, and tees require a *minimum* of three to four core aerifications annually. Typical timings are in spring, summer, late summer, and late winter. This should be followed with medium to heavy topdressing with desirable sand (Figure 3.7). If followed for four to five consecutive years, this method will help relieve the undesirable condition of many native soil greens.

Additional aerifications may be needed on exceptionally small greens where traffic is more concentrated, areas consisting of heavy soils high in silt and/or clay that do not drain well, greens established with one of the newer dwarf bermudagrasses, or soils exposed to saline or effluent water use. Such areas may need aerification with smaller diameter tines (3/8 inch or less, 1 cm) every four to six weeks during active growing months in additional to at least twice yearly with layer ($\geq$1/2 inch, 1.3 cm) diameter tines. Heavier (e.g., "native") soil greens should be aerified at least four times yearly with one or two of these with a deep-tine or deep-drill aerifier. Some clubs opt to double aerify to obtain the benefits of two aerifications without having to wait twice as long for the holes to heal even though double the amount of sand and time are needed to perform this. Failure to maintain an aggressive aerification program in such situations will result

Figure 3.7. Holes from aerifying should be filled with desirable sand to reduce soil compaction and to improve soil oxygen and surface drainage.

in a gradual reduction in turf quality from poorly drained soils, thin grass stands, mat accumulation, and continued problems with algae and moss.

Another means to determine how much to aerify is based on the amount of turf surface impacted by aerification. A 15 to 20% surface area being impacted on an annual basis is a reasonable routine goal for many well-established golf courses. A percentage basis is sometimes easier for nonagronomists to understand instead of trying to comprehend tine diameters and spacing. Courses that have been neglected may need a more aggressive aerification program. As outlined in Table 3.10, using various tine sizes and hole spacings will determine the surface area of turf impacted. For example, a fourfold increase in surface area impacted occurs when using 1/2 inch (1.3 cm) tines instead of 1/4 inch (0.6 cm) tines. An approximately 50% increase in surface area impacted occurs when using 5/8 inch (1.6 cm) tines instead of 1/2 inch (1.3 cm). Another example involves changing tine spacing. Changing tine spacing from 2 x 2-inch (5 x 5 cm) to 1 x 2-inch (2.5 to 5 cm) (with 3/8-inch diameter tines, 1 cm) increases the surface area impacted by 100%.

Spiking and Slicing

Two other cultural practices available to help relieve surface compaction, break up algae layers, and promote better water penetration and aeration are spiking and slicing. These generally are pull-type, nonpowered units consisting of a series of blades mounted

Table 3.10. Aerfication tine size diameter and hole spacing effects on the turf surface area displacement.

Tine Diameter (in.)	Tine Hole Spacing (in.)	No. of Holes per sq ft	Surface Area Impacted per Tine (sq in.)	Surface Area Displacement (%)	No. of Aerifications Needed to Impact 20% of Surface Area
1/4 (0.25)	1 x 1	144	0.049	4.9	4
	1.25 x 1.25	92		3.1	6.5
	1 x 2	72		2.5	8
	2 x 2	36		1.2	16.7
	2.5 x 2.5	23		0.8	25
3/8 (0.375)	1 x 1	144	0.110	11	1.8
	1.25 x 1.25	92		7.1	2.8
	1 x 2	72		5.5	3.6
	2 x 2	36		2.76	7
1/2 (0.5)	1 x 1	144	0.196	19.6	1
	1 x 2	72		9.8	2
	2 x 2	36		4.9	4
	2.5 x 2.5	23		3.1	6.5
5/8 (0.625)	1 x 1	144	0.307	30.7	0.7
	1 x 2	72		15.3	1.3
	2 x 2	36		7.7	2.6
	2.5 x 2.5	23		4.9	4
	5 x 5	5.8		1.2	0.8
3/4 (0.75)	2.5 x 2.5	23	0.44	7.1	2.8
	5 x 5	5.8		1.8	11
1 (1.0)	5 x 5	5.8	0.79	3.16	6.5

51

Figure 3.8. A slicer has thin, V-shaped blades that cut into the soil. This improves soil drainage, air exchange, turf stands, and reduces algae.

on a horizontal shaft. A slicer has thin, V-shaped knives bolted at intervals to the perimeter of metal wheels that cut into the soil (Figure 3.8). Turf is sliced with narrow slits about 1/8 to 1/4 inch (0.3 to 0.6 cm) wide, 2 to 4 (5 to 10 cm) inches deep.

A spiker has solid tines mounted on a horizontal shaft. It provides an effect similar to a slicer but the penetration is limited to approximately 1 inch (2.5 cm) and the distance between perforations along the turf's surface is shorter. Because of these reasons, and since spiking causes less surface disruption than coring, spiking is practiced primarily on greens and tees. Slicing and spiking are performed to: (a) break up soil surface crusting, (b) break up algae layers, and (c) improve water penetration and aeration by relieving shallow soil compaction. Solid tines are associated with a spiker and holes are punched by forcing soil downward and laterally. This results in some compaction at the bottom and along the sides of the holes. Since only minor disruptions of soil surfaces occur, spiking and slicing can be performed more often (e.g., every 7 to 14 days) than core aerification (e.g., every 4 to 8 weeks).

Vertical Mowing

A vertical mower is a powered unit with a series of knives vertically mounted on a horizontal shaft. The shaft rotates at high speeds and the blades slice into the turf and rip out thatch and other debris (Figure 3.9). Depending on the task, the shaft can be raised or lowered to cut shallowly or more deeply into the turf. Vertical blade thickness varies between 1/32 and 1/4 inch (0.08 to 0.6 cm) according to use. Vertical blade spacing varies from 1/2 to 1 inch (1.3 to 2.5 cm), depending on desired results. Golf greens require thinner blades to prevent excessive surface damage, while fairways require the heavier, thicker blades. The surface area impacted by various vertical mowing blade widths are listed in Table 3.11. For example, as simple math demonstrates, using 9/64-

Figure 3.9. A vertical mower (also referred to as a verticutter) physically removes thatch to aid in turf establishment and growth.

Table 3.11. Turf surface area impacted by vertical mowing blade widths.

Vertical Mower Blade Width (in.)	Spacing (in.)	Surface Area Impacted (%)	No. of Vertical Mowings Needed to Impact 25% of Surface Area
5/64-inch	0.5	15.6	1.6
	1	7.8	3.2
9/64-inch	0.5	28	0.9
	1	14.1	1.8

inch (0.4 cm) wide blades almost doubles the surface area impacted compared to 5/64-inch (0.2 cm).

Depth

Different objectives can be met with vertical mowing, depending on the depth of penetration. Grain is reduced when knives are set shallow enough to just nick the surface of the turf. Shallow vertical mowing also is used to break up cores following aerification, which provides a topdressing effect. Deeper penetration of knives stimulates new growth of creeping species when stolons and rhizomes are severed and also removes accumulated thatch (Figure 3.10). Seedbed preparation prior to overseeding also is accomplished by deep vertical mowing.

When dethatching is the objective, the depth of thatch will determine the depth of the blades. The bottom of the thatch layer should be reached by vertical mowing, and preferably the soil surface beneath the thatch layer should be sliced. However, there is a limit to the depth blades should be set or excessive removal of turf roots, rhizomes,

Figure 3.10. Grooves remaining after aggressive, depth verticutting in an attempt to remove accumulated thatch.

stolons, and leaf surface may occur. For example, blades should be set at a depth to just cut stolons and no deeper if new growth stimulation is the objective. Vertical blade spacing for thatch removal should be between 1 and 2 inches (2.5 to 5 cm). This range provides maximum thatch removal with minimal turf damage.

Deep vertical mower penetration requires the use of a heavy-duty machine which can penetrate 1-1/2 to 3 inches (3.8 to 7.6 cm). Deep vertical mowing grooves the turf surface, so subsequent topdressing and rolling is often required to smooth the surface and cover exposed stolons. Shallow-rooted or immature turf can be severely damaged or torn out by deep vertical mowing. Preliminary testing at the site to be verticut should be done by hand pulling to measure if favorable rooting of the grass exists. Irrigation and topdressing should follow such deep vertical mowing to prevent quick desiccation of exposed roots, rhizomes, and stolons and to help smooth the turf surface and encourage turf recovery.

Frequency

Rate of thatch accumulation dictates the frequency of vertical mowing. Vertical mowing should begin once the thatch or mat layer on golf greens exceeds 1/4 to 1/2 inch (0.6 to 1.3 cm) (Figure 3.11). Areas prone to thatch accumulation may require heavy vertical mowing several times per year. For bermudagrass, the first is during mid- to late-spring when bermudagrass is actively growing. This removes thatch and encourages turf spread by slicing stolons and by warming the soil surface quicker than if the thatch is allowed to remain. The second vertical mowing should be timed one to seven days before anticipated fall overseeding. This discourages late-season bermudagrass growth which can compete with the overseeded grasses, and exposes the soil surface so grass seed can reach the soil better and have optimum germination. However, fall vertical mowing will result in a degree of surface damage which may not be masked until the overseeding has time to become established.

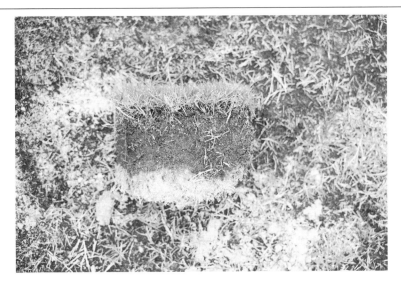

Figure 3.11. Thatch layering greater than 0.5 inch on golf greens should be removed by mechanical (e.g., verticutting) and biological means (e.g., aerifying and topdressing).

Soil and thatch should be dry when deep vertical mowing is performed or turfgrass injury will be more extensive since moist conditions encourage excessive plant material to be removed. Following verticutting, debris should be removed and the area immediately irrigated. Approximately five to seven days following heavy vertical mowing, one pound of nitrogen per 1,000 sq ft (49 kg/ha) should be applied to encourage rapid recovery. Quick-release nitrogen sources are preferred.

Interchangeable vertical mower units are now available for many of today's triplex greensmowers. This equipment allows for frequent vertical mowing and simultaneous debris collection. The vertical blades on greensmowers should be set to only nick the surface of the turf so the surface is not impaired. By conducting frequent, light vertical mowing, severe vertical mowing needed for renovation may be avoided.

Grooming and Conditioning

The grooming mower (also called turf conditioners) is a recent advancement in vertical mowing. Grooming keeps greens smooth and fast by reducing grain and removing excessive top growth. In front of the reel cutting unit of greensmowers is an attached miniature vertical mower (often referred to as vertical grooming) with blade spacing typically 1/4-inch (0.6 cm) that rotate through slots in the front roller (Figure 3.12). Traditionally, a solid roller was used in place of grooved rollers. Each time turf is mowed with this unit, the turf is lightly vertically mowed (groomed or conditioned). This unit improves the playing surface by standing up leaf blades before mowing, thus removing much of the surface grain. New shoot development is also stimulated by slicing stolons, and thatch near the surface is removed. Weekly grooming, along with timely topdressing and aerification helps eliminate the need for traditionally performed turf renovation by severe vertical mowing. The height of the groomer is usually adjustable and is indepen-

Figure 3.12. Vertical mower units on a greensmower where a slotted (or grooved) front roller allows for a closer cut or grooming.

dent of the mowing unit, allowing the superintendent to adjust the groomer height higher or lower than the mower, depending on how aggressive one wants to be.

Other groomers use a rotary brush which rotates in the direction opposite to the mower blade. The brush stands up the grass prior to mowing, reducing grain and providing a smooth surface. A stiff brush is also often attached in front of mowers to accomplish these goals.

TOPDRESSING

Topdressing adds a thin layer of soil to the turf surface which is then incorporated into the turf by dragging or brushing (Figure 3.13). Frequency and rate of topdressing depend on the objective. Following coring and heavy verticutting, moderate to heavy topdressing is used to help smooth the surface, fill coring holes, and cover exposed roots resulting from these two processes. Irregular playing surfaces or gradual soil profile modification will require frequent and relative heavy topdressing. Rates ranging from 1/8 to 1/4 inch (0.4 to 0.8 cubic yards of soil per 1,000 sq ft, 0.33 to 0.66 $m^3/100\ m^2$) are suggested, except if the capacity of the turf to absorb the material is limited, as grass smothering would result.

If the objective of topdressing is to change the characteristic of the underlying soil, then a heavy topdressing program following numerous core removal operations is required. But even following a rigorous coring and topdressing program, adequate modification of underlying soil may take several years to accomplish. Deep tine aerification and core removal should be performed as much as possible prior to topdressing.

If thatch control is the main objective of topdressing, the amount and frequency are governed by rate of thatch accumulation. A suggested amount of a medium rate of topdressing when thatch is not excessively (1/4 to 1/2 inch, 0.6 to 1.2 cm) thick is ap-

Figure 3.13. Topdressing with sand adds a thin layer of soil at the turf surface to improve putting characteristics and reduces thatch development.

proximately 1 cubic yard per 5,000 sq ft (0.17 m³/100 m²). If this relatively light rate does not adequately enhance the decomposition of the thatch layer, then frequency of application and topdressing rate should be increased.

If the objective of topdressing is just to provide routine smoothing of the playing surface, then light, frequent topdressings are suggested. Matting or brushing the green following topdressing results in the material being dragged into low spots (Figure 3.14). Surface irregularities of the green are reduced and the area is somewhat leveled. Topdressing with 1/2 to 1 cubic yard per 5,000 sq ft (0.09 to 0.17 m³/100 m²) of green surface every two to four weeks provides a smoother, truer playing surface. Light topdressing is also performed approximately 10 to 14 days prior to major club tournaments to increase speed of greens and provide a smoother putting surface. Frequent, light topdressing should also be applied on newly planted bermudagrass greens to cover stolons and to smooth the surface. This should be performed every two to four weeks until complete cover or desired smoothness is achieved. Putting speed on a freshly topdressed green will be much slower initially but will increase in several days following irrigation, incorporation, and several mowings.

When attempting to reduce thatch and mat layering of the newer ultra-dwarf bermudagrass cultivars, a "frequent dusting" is often strongly recommended. With this light (1 to 3 ft³ /1,000 ft², 0.03 to 0.09 m³/100 m²) rate, topdressing is usually applied weekly. This is followed by light brushing or irrigation to incorporate the sand. Dry, bagged sand is becoming popular as a topdressing source.

Plant Growth Regulators

Plant growth regulators or retardants (PGRs) are tools which provide superintendents opportunities for smoother putting surfaces. PGRs used on golf greens promote

Figure 3.14. Mechanically incorporating topdressing sand into aerification holes by continuously circling with a brush attachment. Light topdressing is often incorporated by irrigation.

lateral and root growth instead of top or horizontal growth. This encourages thicker, more laterally growing bermudagrass, often simulating grass that is mowed at much lower heights. Regular PGR use provides the desired smoother putting surface for courses not able to replant to one of the newer ultra-dwarf bermudagrasses. PGRs also help regulate or delay top growth when regular mowing scheduling is disrupted due to weather conditions or when seeking putting characteristics in the afternoon to more reflect that following morning mowing. PGR use prior to overseeding slows bermudagrass growth competition, allowing a smoother transition to the overseeded grass, although these benefits are less dramatic.

During periods of active growth, PGRs are used every three to four weeks to achieve these desirable traits. Current PGR examples include paclobutrazol (Turf Enhancer), trinexapac-ethyl (Primo), flurprimidol (Cutless), and mefluidide (Embark). Not all of these are used on greens or tees. Each have their own precaution statements to be read before using them. Currently, the most popular for smoothing greens is trinexapac-ethyl. Light rates (~4 oz/acre, 0.3 L/ha) are applied every three to four weeks during periods of active growth and/or just prior to anticipated rainy weather. Other PGRs are used to help regular *Poa annua* growth and development. Refer to the Weed Control and Plant Growth Regulators Use section for more information.

OVERSEEDING

Overseeding is performed in late summer through early fall to provide green color to the bermudagrass, which turns brown when temperatures drop below 50° F (10° C) for an extended period. In addition, golf course fairways also are overseeded to clearly mark suggested landing areas for golfers. Overseeding is an important economic aspect of golf because many resort courses enjoy their heaviest play from tourists during the fall, winter, and spring months, and this helps attract golfers. Overseeding also improves winter and spring play conditions.

Overseeding, however, requires various degrees of seedbed preparation in the form of aerifying, verticutting, and topdressing. Extensive watering is needed until the overseeded grass becomes established. Spring transition from the overseeded grass back to the bermudagrass also can be unpredictable, erratic, and undesirably extend into summer. Chapter 4 of this publication covers overseeding practices.

MANAGING ULTRA-DWARF CULTIVARS

Cultivation Practice Summary for
Ultra-dwarf Bermudagrasses

The newer dwarf-growing bermudagrass cultivars such as TifEagle, FloraDwarf, Champion, and others are noted for their tight, horizontal growth habits. In fact, unless these are mowed below 3/16 inch (0.48 cm), their effectiveness and desired qualities for a putting surface are diminished. These characteristics have allowed ultra-dwarf bermudagrass to rival bentgrass in terms of putting speed and smoothness with much less input in terms of heat and water management and disease control. However, the ultra-dwarf bermudagrass, like many of the newer bentgrass cultivars, characteristically develops an extensive thatch (or mat) layer in a relatively short period of time. This mat layer holds approach shots, provides better traffic tolerance, and allows quick recovery from divots and ball marks. It should, however, not be allowed to accumulate excessively (e.g., >1/2 inch thick, 1.2 cm) or the green becomes puffy, scalps easily, is difficult to water efficiently, and provides a poor seedbed for overseeding. This mat layer, therefore, must be aggressively controlled through core cultivation, vertical mowing and grooming, and topdressing techniques.

During periods of active growth, this mat layer should be lightly vertical mowed or groomed on a weekly basis. Additional events may be needed if weekly frequency does not control the mat layer. Core cultivation or aeration will be needed with small tines every six to eight weeks with the cores removed. Light, frequent topdressing should also be incorporated. Light topdressing every one or two weeks will help control this mat layer along with the coring and vertical mowing.

It should be noted that the ultra-dwarf bermudagrasses require intensive maintenance, thus cost more to maintain and are not suited for all courses. However, for those courses desiring premium putting greens, these grasses should be considered. The following is a summary of management practices that have to date been shown beneficial in managing these newer grasses.

Fertilization

For Tifdwarf of Tifgreen bermudagrass, the rule of thumb for nitrogen fertilization has been 1 to 2 lb of nitrogen per 1,000 sq ft (49 to 98 kg/ha) per growing month. These rates are considered essential in maintaining lateral growth to help recover from traffic and ball marks, recover from spring transition, and are necessary to maintain a desirable green color. Most of this fertilizer is in granular form from various nitrogen sources.

Due in part to their extremely tight (high) density, the need to water-in granular products, and desire not to encourage thatch/mat development, fertilization practices for the ultra-dwarf bermudagrass have changed. For example, granular fertilizers, even greens-grade or mini-prill, often do not adequately penetrate the high shoot density of the ultra-dwarf grasses, thus are easily removed by the mowing process. Granular products also need to be incorporated by being watered-in even during wet weather and/or on poorly draining greens. Bermudagrass courses, therefore, have adopted a practice from many southern United States bentgrass growers where spoon-feeding with liquid fertilizers has become more widely used. Spraying with low rates (e.g., 0.1 to 0.25 lb N/1,000 sq ft, 4.9 to 12 kg/ha) of nitrogen of readily available nutrients on a frequent basis (e.g., 7 to 14 days) during the growing season has become commonplace. This enables superintendents to better control growth levels, thus minimizing thatch/mat layering, and also providing desirable green color without the need to water-in (Table 3.12).

A fertilizer program combining granular and spoon (or liquid) feeding is suggested. A mini-prilled fertilizer containing a slow-release nitrogen source should be applied monthly at approximately 0.5 lb N/1,000 sq ft (24 kg/ha) during the growing season. This is supplemented with spoon-feeding at 0.1 to 0.25 lb N/1,000 sq ft (4.9 to 12 kg/ha) every 7 to 14 days to provide a total of approximately 1 lb of N/1,000 sq ft (49 kg/ha) per growing month. This or any fertilization program should be backed with regular tissue and soil testing to monitor and track nutrient levels to ensure adequate levels are being absorbed.

Topdressing

Like fertilization programs, topdressing programs have changed with the introduction of the ultra-dwarf bermudagrasses. Topdressing has long been recognized as the main cultural practice which smooths the putting surface, allows better root-zone management, and prevents (or reduces) thatch/mat buildup. A rule of thumb is to match topdressing rates and frequencies with the growth rate and density of the turf. With the higher shoot densities of the ultra-dwarf bermudagrass cultivars, traditional heavy and infrequent topdressing has evolved to lighter, more frequent events. This has been accented with newer topdressing techniques and equipment as well as the ability to purchase dried sand in bags. These light topdressings (a.k.a. "dusting") are quicker to perform, less intrusive to players and playing surfaces, and easily incorporated by light brushing or irrigation. Walk-behind fertilizer applicators are often used to quickly apply these dustings of topdressing.

With the ultra-dwarf bermudagrass cultivars, expect to topdress frequently but lightly. This is performed on a 7 to 14 day schedule during the growing season with 1 to 2 cubic feet of sand per 1,000 square feet (0.03 to 0.06 m^3/100 m^2) or 0.012 to 0.024 inches (0.03 to 0.06 cm) in depth, respectively. Light verticutting or grooming is often performed prior to topdressing to open the turf canopy for better incorporation of the topdressing sand. Superintendents should experiment with their conditions at this rate and frequency and be aware of the extra wear and tear this may place on mowing units.

Table 3.12. Summary of cultural practices for bermudagrass golf greens.

Practice	Description
Fertilization	
Optimum timing for N fertilization	April through September
Damaging response to excessive nitrogen fertilizer	November through March
Yearly N requirements (lb N/1,000 sq ft)	8–18 (391 to 879 kg/ha)
Monthly N requirement (lb N/1,000 sq ft)	0.5 to 1.5 lb N/1,000 sq ft
Acceptable pH range	5.5 to 7.0
Acceptable phosphorus levels	Low to high
Optimum potassium levels	Medium to high (improves low temperature tolerance). Usually applied at one-half to equal amounts of nitrogen.
Cultural Requirements	
Overseeding	Necessary in temperate and most subtropical areas for winter color.
Irrigation requirements	Moisten full root zone depth, rewetting just prior to wilting.
Air circulation requirement	Not normally required.
Aerification/cultivation	Minimum of two to four times yearly. Shallow and deep aerifying are used.
Cultivation timing optimum	May through September
Fertilizer application	Slow-release (primarily) granular + liquids for color
Mowing height	0.100 to 0.25 (1/10 to 1/4) in. (2.54 to 6.35 mm)
Mowing frequency	Daily
Mowing pattern	Changed (rotated) daily
Clippings	Removed
Thatch/mat control	Frequent topdressing, light vertical mowing and grooming, regular aerification
Compaction control	Use a predominately sand-based root zone during construction, routine aerification, limit play (traffic) during wet conditions.
Topdressing	Light (0.2 cu yd/1,000 sq ft, 0.17 m³/100 m²) but frequent (weekly) during active growth. Monthly at 0.3 to 0.5 cu yd/1,000 sq ft (0.25 to 0.4 m³/100 m²) during slowed growth.
Aerification (coring)	Performed two to six times annually with at least one deep-tine yearly. Stop within 30 days of overseeding.
Regular (deeper) verticutting	Once or twice yearly, once in spring and another just prior to overseeding.
Grooming/brushing	Performed weekly (grooming) or daily (brushing) with ultra-dwarf cultivars.
Slicing	Performed weekly in two directions to reduce surface compaction and algae and to facilitate soil air exchange and infiltration.

Grooming, Verticutting, and Brushing

Due to relatively quick buildup of thatch/mat layering, frequent grooming, brushing, and/or verticutting are necessary with the ultra-dwarf bermudagrasses. Frequency and timing will vary depending primarily on the fertilization and topdressing program used by a particular course. Weekly grooming or light verticutting is suggested during growing months. This is supplemented with one or two relatively heavy vertical mowings, often following aerification in mid- to late spring and again in mid- to late summer just prior to overseeding. Brushing is performed 4 to 7 days weekly during the bermudagrass growing season to reduce grain and smooth the playing surface.

Like the newer trend of light but frequent topdressing, light and frequent grooming, brushing, or verticutting often go unnoticed by players, yet help prevent or maintain thatch/mat layering. These techniques have proved extremely beneficial, yet less disruptive than previous practices.

Aerification

The introduction of the ultra-dwarf bermudagrass cultivars has not decreased the need for or frequency of core aerification. In addition to soil compaction relief, core aerification penetrates the thatch/mat layering, creating a more favorable environment for soil organisms to naturally decompose this. Two to four core aerifications are still the norm for most bermudagrass greens. At least two of these are typically performed with ½-inch (1.2 cm) diameter tines, especially when performed in conjunction with topdressing. Greens that are heavier in composition (e.g., more silt and clay content) and courses with heavy yearly play would consider the more frequent aerification schedule with one or two of these using the deep-tine or deep-drill units (Figure 3.15). When used in conjunction with heavy topdressing, green soil composition can slowly be improved as well as improving deep soil aeration and compaction. Topdressing cores brought to the soil surface can be hand or mechanically removed (Figure 3.16) or reincorporated by lightly verticutting or dragging-in (Figure 3.17).

Additional Considerations

PGR Use

Plant growth regulators (PGRs) are often used on Tifgreen and Tifdwarf bermudagrass to promote lateral growth (e.g., surface tightening) over vertical growth. PGRs also help to produce consistent putting surfaces during periods of growth surges, provide more consistent putting throughout the day, promote a darker blue-green color, and provide those greens with "off-types" of bermudagrass patches with an illusion of having only one type of grass present. The most popular PGR product currently for these purposes is trinexapac-ethyl (trade name: Primo 1EC). Used on a three to four week interval at light rates (e.g., 4 to 6 oz product per acre [0.29 to 0.44 L/ha] of the 1EC formulation) it has proved beneficial during the growing months. PGRs, however, do not necessarily increase putting speeds (or distances) but help maintain those current playing conditions.

Double Cutting and/or Rolling

A popular practice rediscovered in the 1990s was double cutting and/or rolling greens to help provide smoother playing surfaces without having to mow at extremely low

Figure 3.15. Deep drill aerifiers (top) help penetrate into the soil profile to relieve compaction, increase surface drainage, and provide the opportunity to reincorporate desirable sand (bottom). Limitations of such machines are efficiently and effectively removing soil brought to the surface and relative slowness by current machines (right).

heights, which often proved detrimental to Tifgreen and Tifdwarf greens. Double cutting, due to costs, is still used but mostly prior to and during tournament play. Rolling is also provided then, but more courses provide this two to four times weekly, especially when bermudagrass mowing heights are raised during periods of cloudy/rainy weather and/or when days become shorter (late summer). Courses, obviously, must weigh the benefits of double cutting and/or rolling greens compared to increased equipment needs, costs, and wear and tear as well as the possibility of increased soil compaction or turf wear, especially on cleanup passes.

On ultra-dwarf bermudagrass, double cutting is used only during tournament play (for most courses, due to costs), while rolling may be used more routinely. However, due to their normal close mowing heights, these practices are less beneficial for the ultra-dwarf cultivars than for higher mowed Tifgreen or Tifdwarf. However, as mentioned, during periods of overcast weather and/or shorter days, the mowing height of the ultra-dwarf bermudagrass should be raised. These practices, along with PGR use, help to maintain more desirable putting characteristics without overly damaging the grass.

Figure 3.16. Aerification cores are often removed by hand (top) or mechanically (bottom).

Overseeding

Due to their high shoot densities, several traditional overseeding practices are altered to accommodate the ultra-dwarf bermudagrasses. First is grass (or seed) selection. The smaller seeded *Poa trivialis* and/or bentgrass are the current grasses used to overseed ultra-dwarf bermudagrass greens. These smaller seeded varieties require less aggressive seedbed preparation compared to using larger seeded grasses such as ryegrass. Even with these smaller seeded varieties, aggressive seedbed preparation will be needed prior to overseeding greens where an excessive (e.g., >1/2-inch, 1.2 cm) thatch/mat layer has developed. This should begin three or four weeks prior to seeding by aggressive coring,

Figure 3.17. Aerification cores also are reincorporated by dragging, verticutting (top), or vacuuming (bottom). Dragging and verticutting of cores should be performed only if the underlying soil is desirable.

followed by weekly vertical mowing (Figure 3.18). Topdressing both before and after overseeding is ideal but at a minimum, topdressing following overseeding is suggested to increase soil contact with the seed.

In areas where no or only light and infrequent frost occurs, overseeding the ultra-dwarf bermudagrasses may not be necessary. Due to their close proximity to the normally warmer soil surface, short periods of cool or cold weather may not cause browning of these grasses. However, if heavy frosts are normally experienced, overseeding is generally required. In areas which only occasionally experience cold weather, temporary removable covers are available which can be placed on the greens to protect them from frost. These, however, should be removed daily if temperatures are forecasted to be

Figure 3.18. Golf green following aerification verticutting and topdressing with desirable sand to remove thatch, increase soil oxygen and moisture exchange, and improve soil-to-seed contact when overseeding.

above 50°F. Spraying greens with charcoal also helps to prevent discoloration due to temporary cool temperatures. Charcoal should be applied at a rate of 2 to 5 lb of product per 1,000 sq ft (98 to 244 kg/ha), and preferably when the sun is shining so heat can be absorbed and retained during cool periods.

4 Overseeding

BENEFITS

Bermudagrass growth stops when temperatures drop below 60°F (15.6°C) and discoloration (browning) can be expected if temperatures drop at or below 50°F (10°C) for an extended period (Plate 4.1). This browning continues until spring, when soil temperatures warm sufficiently to promote a gradual greenup of the previously dormant bermudagrass (Plate 4.2). Bermudagrass, therefore, is often overseeded with cool-season grasses to provide a green playing surface with desirable color (Plate 4.3) and for suggested landing areas in fairways during fall and winter months (Plate 4.4). Optimum overseeding performance is a sequential procedure requiring proper seedbed preparation and timing. Proper winter management and spring turf species transition also ensure optimum playing conditions during tournament play periods. Luck, mostly in terms of favorable weather, also is as important as sound agronomic procedures.

DETRIMENTS

Overseeding does increase maintenance costs in terms of fertilizer needs, watering, pesticides, soil preparation, labor, and equipment wear. Weeds, most notably annual bluegrass (*Poa annua*), gradually increase with consecutive yearly overseeding. Overseeding also unfavorably competes with the bermudagrass in late spring and early summer, delaying greenup of the bermudagrass (Plate 4.5). Overseeding also does not "dry-out" wet areas or spots, and normally does not "protect" the bermudagrass from traffic damage or low temperature damage (or kill).

TIMING

There are several available means for determining when to overseed. A general indicator of optimum overseeding time is when late summer/early fall night temperatures consistently are within the 50°F (10°C) range. Cool-season grass seed germination is favored by temperatures between 50° and 70°F (10° and 21°C). Other timing indicators include overseeding when soil temperatures at a four inch depth are in the mid-70°s (21°C), or the average midday air temperatures remain in the low 70°s (21°C). Overseeding also should be timed at least 20 to 30 days before the first expected killing frost. This timing minimizes bermudagrass competition, and optimizes seed germination and estab-

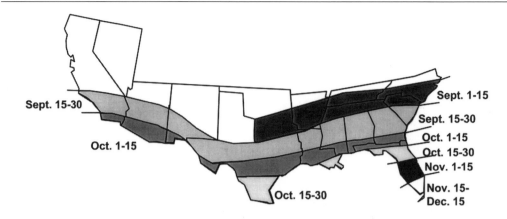

Figure 4.1. Typical overseeding timing for most bermudagrass regions in the mainland United States.

lishment of the overseeded grasses. It also will reduce seedling diseases. Figure 4.1 indicates typical overseeding timings for various regions of the United States.

Other factors, such as tournament play and golf course usage, may dictate that seeding dates be altered. For example, light frosts can occur in subtropical areas such as southern Florida and California, but deep freezes are rare. Bermudagrass normally does not completely go dormant in these areas. Soil temperatures in these subtropical areas remain in the 80°F (26.7°C) range through November, thus temperature-based indicators are not always applicable. Overseeding timing then becomes a management decision based primarily on the timing of play intensity, demands of customers, availability of seed, and the level of aesthetics desired.

PREPARATION

Overseeding preparation actually is a year-long process and not just two weeks prior to overseeding. Planning should take place several months before the actual overseeding operation to ensure a seed source and a seed type. Purchasing of seed and its timely delivery also will allow flexibility for overseeding scheduling if done in advance. A healthy bermudagrass base also is needed to withstand harsh cultural practices and turf competition associated with overseeding. This can only be accomplished by careful management of bermudagrass throughout the year.

An erroneous practice often seen involves heavily overseeding newly established bermudagrass areas or bermudagrass that is thin and weak. Bermudagrass produces few rhizomes its first year, thus cannot recover as effectively as during subsequent years. As a result, late summer-established bermudagrass that is heavily overseeded often suffers through long transition the following spring and early summer. Clubs should time bermudagrass grow-in in late spring or early summer to allow a full season before overseeding. Those greens established in late summer should skip overseeding the first year or use considerably lower overseeding rates. As the saying goes, "bermudagrass weak going into overseeding will be as weak or weaker coming out."

Figure 4.2. Thin overseeding stands due to insufficient preparation of the overseeding seedbed.

Proper seedbed preparation ensures seedling roots will be in contact with the soil which reduces susceptibility to drought and temperature stress (Figure 4.2). Thatch greater than 1/2 inch prevents this good seed-to-soil contact and therefore should be reduced before overseeding. Proper seedbed preparation to minimize thatch and allow optimal germination and growth includes the following procedures:

Twenty to Forty Days Prior to Overseeding

1. Quick-release granular nitrogen fertilization should be reduced or completely stopped three to four weeks prior to overseeding to minimize competitive bermudagrass growth. Excessive growth at the time of overseeding will provide competition for the germinating seed and also may predispose the grass to winter injury. Iron or foliar nitrogen feeding will help provide color during this period without excessive bermudagrass growth.
2. Cultivate the soil by coring four to six weeks prior to overseeding to alleviate soil compaction and to open the turf. Allow the cores to dry and pulverize them by verticutting, power raking or dragging. Coring is performed in advance of the actual overseeding date to allow coring holes to heal over, thus preventing a speckled growth pattern of winter grass. The overseeded grasses typically grow faster with a darker green color in and around cores holes than between them.
3. Following coring, verticut in several directions to reduce thatch and to open the soil surface to allow better soil-to-seed contact (Figure 4.3). Verticut debris should be removed by raking, blowing, or mowing with catcher basket attachments. Depth of verticutting depends primarily on the depth of thatch. Thicker thatch layering requires deeper verticutting. Other parameters, such as algae formation however, may dictate how severe this verticutting is. If algae is a problem, light, frequent grooming may substitute for verticutting greens.
4. Topdress with approximately 1/2 cubic yard per 1,000 square (0.4 m³/100 m²) feet following the removal of the verticut debris in order to provide a smooth seedbed and to minimize effects

Figure 4.3. Areas to be overseeded should be vertical mowed, especially if excessive thatch is present.

Figure 4.4. Topdressing before and/or following overseeding improves seed-to-soil contact, a condition necessary for optimum seed establishment and prevention of desiccation.

of the remaining thatch (Figure 4.4). Best overseeding stands occur when the seedbed is topdressed before and immediately after seeding to provide desirable seed-to-soil contact. Use desirable topdressing mix; e.g., containing <10% of particles smaller than 0.1 mm and none above 1 mm in diameter.

5. Apply phosphorus (P_2O_5) and potassium (K_2O) at a suggested rate of 10 pounds of 0-9-27 (or equivalent) per 1,000 square feet (488 kg/ha), or at the rate suggested by a soil fertility test. The soil should be tested approximately four weeks prior to overseeding. Phosphorus and potassium will enhance overseeding rooting without promoting excessive bermudagrass top growth.

Ten to Fourteen Days Prior to Overseeding

1. Approximately 10 days to 14 days prior to overseeding, reduce the mowing height and verticut lightly in two directions (just touching the soil surface) to open the turf and to allow the seed to fall into the turf canopy. This practice provides good seed-to-soil contact, minimizes wind and water from carrying seed away, and provides sufficient time for verticut slits to recuperate before overseeding.
2. Next, use a power sweeper, a mower with basket attachments, or blower to remove remaining debris, and then irrigate thoroughly. On sloped areas, if possible, discontinue mowing two or three days prior to overseeding, or raise the mowing height 1/4 or 5/16 inch (0.6 to 0.8 cm) one week prior to overseeding to provide an upright framework of grass to prevent seed from washing. Spiking or slicing in several directions just prior to seeding also enhances seed-to-soil contact. Care, however, might be taken to evenly distribute seed without concentrating it in spiked holes to prevent a speckled appearance.

Overseeding with small-seeded species such as fine fescue or *Poa trivialis* often does not require as extensive seedbed preparation as larger seeded grasses like ryegrass. However, some seedbed preparation is needed for all species, with the last two steps listed above being minimum requirements for all overseeding. The greater the thatch layer and the use of larger seeded species, the more seedbed preparation (Figure 4.5).

Annual Bluegrass Weed Control

Annual bluegrass (*Poa annua* L.) is an undesirable bunch-type winter annual weed because of its clumping growth habit, its early spring dieback and its prolific seedhead production (Plate 4.6). Due to its prolific seed production, occurrence of herbicide resistant biotypes, and increased use of the closely related species, *Poa trivialis*, as an overseeding grass, *Poa annua* has become the most troublesome winter weed in turf. Control of annual bluegrass with traditional herbicides is difficult due to potential injury of germinating overseeded grasses.

There are several herbicide options for preemergence control of annual bluegrass in overseeded bermudagrass golf greens. One, fenarimol, is actually a fungicide that also has preemergence herbicidal activity on annual bluegrass. Fenarimol (Rubigan 1AS) can be used as a single application, although multiple applications of two or three treatments are preferred. If only one application of fenarimol is made, 8 ounces per 1,000 square feet (0.58 L/ha) is applied. If two applications are planned, they must occur 10 to 14 days apart at a 4 ounce (0.29 L/ha) concentration each. If three applications are made, apply three treatments of 2.75 ounces (0.2 L/ha) each at 10 to 14 day intervals. In both multiple applications the last application should be timed two weeks prior to the expected overseeding date if the overseeding is perennial ryegrass. Bentgrass and *Poa trivialis* overseeding requires the last fenarimol application be at least 30 days prior to overseeding. In heavy *Poa annua* infestation areas, a follow-up fenarimol application in early winter (e.g., mid-December through early January) at 2 to 4 oz product per 1,000 sq ft (0.15 to 0.29 L/ha) is suggested. Fenarimol only has preemergence herbicidal activity and becomes relatively ineffective once annual bluegrass germinates and emerges.

Dithiopyr (Dimension) at 0.5 lb ai/acre (56 kg/ha) 45 to 60 days prior to overseeding followed by another 0.5 lb ai/acre (56 kg/ha) in January or February has also provided

Figure 4.5. Close-up of an appropriately prepared overseeding seedbed which has been core aerified and vertical mowed. Topdressing should be considered before and/or following overseeding to provide beneficial seed-to-soil contact.

Figure 4.6. *Poa annua* control in overseeding with appropriately timed pronamide (Kerb) application. Note the *Poa annua* seedheads where skips in application occurred.

good control. A granular formulation of Dimension tends to provide more consistent control than liquid formulations.

Pronamide (Kerb 50 WP) also is used for annual bluegrass preemergence control (Figure 4.6). However, there are several precautionary measures to follow when using pronamide, with timing being the most important consideration. Pronamide should be applied 60 days before the expected overseeding date. For most areas this will require a late July or early August treatment. This early application allows for germination of the overseeded grass, but not annual bluegrass germination. The application rate is two pounds of the 50WP product per acre or 0.73 ounce per 1,000 square feet (0.053 L/ha). **Do not apply pronamide (Kerb) to established cool-season grasses such as ryegrass, fescue, or bentgrass unless their control is desired.** Follow all label directions.

Charcoal has been used in conjunction with pronamide when pronamide was applied less than 60 days prior to overseeding to negate its effect on germination of overseeded grasses. Activated charcoal should be applied at 2 to 5 pounds per 1,000 square feet (98 to 244 kg/ha). At least 14 days should be allowed between herbicide and charcoal applications. Overseeding should occur no sooner than seven days following charcoal application. There is an inherent chance that the charcoal application may not totally work due to the difficulty of application. Charcoal also might negate the herbicidal effect of the pronamide on annual bluegrass germination. Available activated charcoal sources include: 'Clean Carbon' from Aquatrols, 'Gro-Safe' from American Norit Company, and '52 Pickup' from Parkway Research Corporation.

Other herbicides and prior to overseeding fairways for *Poa annua* control include oxadiazon (Ronstar 2G) and rimsulfuron (TranXit GTA). Ronstar is applied at 2 lb ai/A 60 days before overseeding while TranXit is applied at 2 oz product/A 10 to 14 days prior to overseeding. Overlap should be minimized when using oxadiazon.

OVERSEEDING GRASS SELECTION

The primary grasses used for overseeding are perennial ryegrass, annual ryegrass, intermediate ryegrass, roughstalk bluegrass or *Poa trivialis*, creeping bentgrass and fine (chewings, creeping red, or hard) fescue (Plate 4.7). Improved cultivars of perennial ryegrass seeded alone or in mixtures with roughstalk bluegrass or fine fescue, are grasses and mixtures most widely used on golf greens and tees (Plate 4.8). For golf courses wishing for greatest chance of success on overseeding greens, perennial ryegrass should be the major component of the blend or mix chosen. With ultra-dwarf bermudagrass, overseeding is performed with smaller seeded grasses, mainly *Poa trivialis*, fine fescue, and/or bentgrass. Each grass has advantages and disadvantages. Table 4.1 illustrates and describes each of these.

Blend and Mixtures

Blends (two or more cultivars of the same grass species) of perennial ryegrass, or mixtures (two or more cultivars of different grass species) of bentgrass and *Poa trivialis* (roughstalk bluegrass), or mixtures of perennial ryegrass and fine fescue are commonly utilized as a measure of protection against disease and environmental stresses. They also are used to enhance fine texture and smoothness. If late or extended spring transition is a problem, reducing or eliminating the ryegrass component may be considered, while roughstalk bluegrass is typically mixed with perennial ryegrass and bentgrass to enhance their performance and to provide a more desirable spring transition. A typical seed weight formula is 85% perennial ryegrass plus 15% bluegrass, 60% bentgrass plus 40% bluegrass, or 80% roughstalk bluegrass and 20% bentgrass. Since no one grass provides all

Table 4.1. Characteristics of selected grasses used for winter overseeding (modified from McCarty, 2001).

Grass Species	Green Color	Texture	Density	Establishment Rate	Winter Performance	Spring Performance	Spring Transition	Wear Tolerance	Shade Tolerance	Putting Quality	Leaf Fraying	Disease Resistance
Perennial ryegrass (turf-type)	Dark	Med.-fine (2-4 mm)	Good	Fast (3-4 weeks)	Good-excellent	Good-excellent	Slow	Fair-excellent	Fair-good	Fair-excellent	Moderate-minimum	Fair-good
Annual ryegrass	Light	Coarse (3-5 mm)	Poor	Very fast (2-3 weeks)	Fair-good	Poor	Medium	Poor-fair	Fair	Poor	Heavy	Poor
Intermediate ryegrass	Intermediate	Coarse-med. (3-4 mm)	Fair	Fast (2-4 weeks)	Fair	Fair	Medium	Fair-good	Fair	Poor-fair	Moderate	Fair
Fine fescue	Light-dark	V. fine (1-2 mm)	Excellent	Slow (4-6 weeks)	Fair	Good	Fast	Fair	Very good	Good	Minimum	Fair
Roughstalk bluegrass (Poa trivialis)	Light to intermediate	Fine (1-4 mm)	Excellent	Slow (4-6 weeks)	Fair	Excellent	Fast	Poor	Good	Excellent	Minimum	Poor-fair
Creeping bentgrass	Intermediate	V. fine (1-2 mm)	Excellent	Very slow (6-8 weeks)	Fair	Fair	Slow	Fair	Fair	Excellent	Minimum	Fair

optimum characteristics necessary for overseeding, turf managers often choose different mixtures or blends to suit their needs. It is suggested that you contact your local university Turfgrass Extension Specialist to determine what works best in your area.

The grass species selected to be used for overseeding will depend on a number of considerations including:

1. **Budget**. Budget often will limit the availability of options. For those with limited financial resources, annual ryegrass is usually the cheapest; however, turf quality is sacrificed. More expensive perennial ryegrasses or bentgrass, *Poa trivialis*, and/or fine fescue should be chosen for a high quality surface.

2. **Intended Quality**. A quality blend of grasses should be considered for those areas receiving heavy traffic. For example, on many golf greens where uniformity, putting quality, and species transition are of prime importance, combinations of bentgrass, fine fescue, perennial ryegrass, or roughstalk bluegrass will enhance the turf's fine texture and smoothness. In fairways, where color and appearance are less important than on golf greens, perennial ryegrass is most often used.

3. **Planting Date**. At times, the expected planting date may affect grass selection. If major tournaments should occur during optimum overseeding periods, then the grasses chosen should reflect earlier or later planting dates. If seeding occurs late in the fall, ryegrasses may be the only option since it germinates and establishes itself quickly. Roughstalk bluegrass and bentgrass may not have sufficient time to become established if they are seeded in late fall. Early overseeding of fine fescue should not be planned because it generally is more heat-sensitive than the other grasses. In spring, if tournaments are scheduled during transition the superintendent must carefully select the overseeding grass species. For example, if a tournament occurs in the earlier portion of spring transition then a greater amount of annual ryegrass, intermediate ryegrass, and *Poa trivialis* can be used. If the tournament is later, or during the transition period, then more heat-resistant varieties of perennial ryegrass or bentgrass should be considered.

4. **Traffic or Play Intensity**. Resort or municipal courses that depend on heavy play during fall, winter, and spring months should carefully select their overseeding grass(es). Perennial ryegrass offers quickest establishment and best tolerance to intense or heavy traffic. Bentgrass, fine fescue, and *Poa trivialis* generally make a better putting surface but at the cost of sacrificing establishment rate and traffic tolerance. Blends containing perennial ryegrass plus bentgrass and/or *Poa trivialis* or fine fescue are often used to try to take advantage of each grass. Other resort clubs use bentgrass or *Poa trivialis* exclusively but buy enough additional seed to periodically 'dust' weak or excessively damaged areas. Shady or excessively wet greens also perform better if a percentage of their overseeding blend contains *Poa trivialis* and/or fine fescue.

Seed Quality

Only certified (blue tag) seed should be used when selecting species and cultivars for overseeding. Maximum percent purity and acceptable germination should be specified at the time of purchase. Seed also should be certified free of hard-to-control weeds such as annual bluegrass.

Fungicide-treated seed should be requested to reduce potential seedling loss due to *Pythium* and *Rhizoctonia* diseases. Metalaxyl (Apron), or etridiazole (Koban), are fungicides commonly used for this purpose. Bentgrass used for overseeding normally is not treated with a fungicide. Extra seed (approximately 10%) also should be purchased for repairing small areas that may be lost from pests, weather, or traffic. All stored seed should be protected from rodents and placed in a cool, dry place to retain seed viability.

Seeding Rate

The grasses being used and the desired turf density will dictate seeding rate. Small seeded grasses, such as bentgrass and roughstalk bluegrass, can be seeded at lower rates when compared to large seeded grasses such as annual and perennial ryegrass. They will provide a comparable number of plants per given area. Areas receiving heavy traffic require a higher seeding rate than those areas where winter color is the main objective. Table 4.2 lists suggested overseeding rates. If either of these high or low seeding ranges are exceeded, thin, open, and disease susceptible turf can be expected (Figure 4.7). Applying split applications of seed is a common practice to compensate for early season losses. Apply at least 2/3 of the final seeding rate initially followed by the remainder two to three weeks later.

OVERSEEDING PROCEDURE

Golf Greens and Tees

Before overseeding, steps listed in 'Seedbed Preparation' should be implemented to provide a desirable seedbed. Following this, a uniform application of seed is needed to provide a smooth and uniform playing surface. Seed should be applied when the surface is dry. Drying can be hastened by dragging a hose across the turf surface.

Spreaders should be carefully calibrated to deliver the appropriate amount of seed. Another method is to preweigh seed for a known area, such as a putting green, and carefully meter it out over the area. This usually requires numerous passes over the area to ensure uniform seed coverage and at least two directions should be used when broadcasting the seed (Figure 4.8). Apply half of the seed in one direction and the other half while moving at right angles to the first pass (Figure 4.9).

Boundaries of the overseeded areas should be defined by using a drop spreader. The remaining seed is applied with a drop, or centrifugal, spreader within the outer fringe of the seeded area. Avoid seed spread to nontarget areas such as collars, fringes, and other nearby turf areas. Wind speed should be less than five miles per hour and heavy irrigation and rainfall avoided to minimize seed movement onto adjacent areas. Unwanted seed will reduce aesthetic value and create the need for additional maintenance (Figure 4.10). Clumps of ryegrass are most noticeable the spring following application and tend to remain visible into early summer (Figure 4.11). Control of these clumps, once they are established, is difficult and slow. When trying to reduce the amount of unwanted ryegrass drift, carpets and mats should be placed in the areas used to fill and empty spreaders. Mats also can be placed around the perimeter of seeding area to minimize escaped seed. Worker shoes and dragging equipment should be cleaned before and after entering the perimeter area surrounding the green. If ryegrass drift is suspected outside the intended overseeded area, a preemergence herbicide should be applied after overseeding. A short

Table 4.2. Suggested overseeding rates for various grasses and mixtures (by seed weight) used on golf courses (McCarty, 2001).

Grass	Greens	Tees	Collar/Aprons	Fairways
	─── lb per 1,000 sq ft[a] ───			lb/acre[b]
Perennial ryegrass	25–40	15–20	10–20	250–450
Italian (annual) ryegrass	35–50	15–25	15–25	250–400
Chewings (fine) fescue	25–30	10–20	5–20	—
Bentgrass	2–5	2–3	2	—
Poa trivialis	8–12	5–7	4–7	—
Typical mixture for enhanced performance and better spring transition: 75% Perennial ryegrass + 25% Chewings fescue	30–40	10–20	10–20	150–250
Typical mixture for enhanced performance and better spring transition: 75% Perennial ryegrass + 25% P. trivialis	30–40	10–20	10–20	150–250
Typical mixture for better performance in shady or wet areas: 60% bentgrass + 40% P. trivialis	5–7	3–4	2–4	—
Typical mixture: 60% Perennial ryegrass + 25% chewings fescue + 15% P. trivialis (widely adaptable to poorly drained or shady areas)	25–30	10–15	10–15	150–250
Typical mixture for enhanced fall establishment and better spring transition: 80% Chewings fescue + 20% P. trivialis	20–25	8–10	8–10	150–200

[a] kg/ha = lb/1,000 ft^2 × 48.83.

[b] kg/ha = lb/acre × 1.12.

Figure 4.7. Thin overseeding stand showing dormant bermudagrass where insufficient seeding rate was used.

Figure 4.8. Poor overseeding pattern from not using multiple passes when seeding.

boom, backpack sprayer, or drop spreader are used to treat areas not accessible by tractor-drawn or self-powered sprayers.

If nonfungicide-treated bentgrass seed is used, a fungicide is needed for disease control. For best seed coverage, fungicides should be applied before the green is topdressed. Fresh seed also should be used because good seedling vigor is necessary for plants to quickly develop past the susceptible seedling stage. Proper seeding rates should also be

Figure 4.9. Overseeding in multiple directions to increase uniformity of seed distribution.

Figure 4.10. "Trails" of overseeded grass where the seed hopper leaked during the seeding operation.

Figure 4.11. Escaped "renegade" ryegrass clumps from an intended area of overseeding.

adhered to because higher rates should not be used since this could produce weak, succulent plants.

Once the seed have been applied, light topdressing of greens and tees at 1/3 to 1/2 cubic yard per 1,000 square feet (0.27 to 0.4 m³/100 m²) encourages desirable seed-to-soil contact and turf establishment. Seed and topdressing material is then incorporated by dragging a carpet across the seeded area. A steel mat may need to be placed on the carpet to provide sufficient weight. Topdressing should be dry before dragging to minimize seed pickup on shoes and equipment. A cover on the ground also should be used when entering and leaving overseeded areas to prevent unwanted seed movement.

Pregerminated Seed

If bare areas result from excessive play or diseases, reseeding with ryegrass through early spring is possible. It always is a good idea to order an extra 10% of seed in the event of thinning. Ryegrass seed (5 to 10 lb per 1,000 sq ft, 244 to 488 kg/ha) may be pregerminated by soaking in water for 24 to 48 hours and mixed with topdressing prior to dispersal. The soil in these areas should first be loosened by spiking or aerifying.

POSTPLANTING MAINTENANCE

Irrigation

Following seeding, irrigate lightly to carefully moisten the soil surface without puddling or washing the seed into surrounding areas. Three to four light irrigations per day may be needed until all seedlings are established. Once germination begins, the seed cannot be allowed to dry out or the stand will thin. If seed washes into concentrated

Figure 4.12. Poor overseeding stand due to insufficient draining greens.

drifts following intense rains or heavy irrigation, a stiff-bristled broom should be used to redistribute it. Once grass is established, gradually reduce watering frequency to decrease disease potential. Areas overirrigated and/or poorly drained often have poor stands of overseeding, excessive damage from traffic, and/or high occurrence of diseases (Figure 4.12).

Disease Management

After seedling emergence (5 to 7 days for ryegrass, 10 to 14 for bentgrass and for roughstalk bluegrass), apply a preventative fungicide to help protect against Pythium root rot and Rhizoctonia brown patch, which can destroy overseeding stands. These diseases are encouraged by:

- unseasonably warm weather;
- using excessive seeding rates which produces young, succulent plants;
- prolonged periods of high, free moisture on leaf and stem surfaces, such as extended foggy conditions; and
- bermudagrass aggressiveness.

Proper timing and application rate of seeding, minimum use of nitrogen, efficient irrigation scheduling, and the use of pretreated fungicide seed are methods to reduce disease potential. Many areas often experience warm, foggy mornings in the fall. Turf managers especially should be on the lookout for diseases during these conditions since they are ideal for rapid fungal reproduction and spread (Plate 4.9). To prevent development of resistant strains of *Pythium*, always follow the label instructions and alternate between chemical groups.

Mowing

When overseeding greens with ryegrass, mow at a 1/2 (1.3 cm) inch height when the new stand reaches 2/3 (1.7 cm) to 3/4 (1.9 cm) inches. Gradually lower the cutting height to 1/4 (0.6 cm) to 5/16 (0.8 cm) inch over a two to three week period at 1/32 (0.08 cm) inch increments and skip the cleanup mowing lap the first few mowings to minimize traffic and wear on the tender seedlings. Continue this gradual reduction in height for four to six weeks until 3/16 (0.48 cm) inch height is reached. Use a sharp mower that will not pull up seedlings. Do not use catch baskets the first few mowings if the seedlings are not well rooted. Once well established, mowing heights gradually can be reduced to the desired height and the heavier triplex mowers then can be used (Plate 4.10). On tees and fairways, initiate mowing when the grass reaches one or two inches. This will allow time for seedlings to root. Tees and fairways usually are permanently mowed at 3/8 (0.95 cm) inch to 3/4 (1.9 cm) inch.

With *Poa trivialis*, fine fescue, or bentgrass, begin mowing at 1/4 to 3/16 inch (0.6 to 0.48 cm) when the overseeded grass reaches 3/8 to 5/8 inch (0.95 to 0.8 cm) in height. Gradually reduce these in height over a three week period to the final height of 5/32 to 3/16 inch (0.4 to 0.48 cm). Again, always use sharpened mowers to prevent seedling damage.

Fertilization

Do not fertilize with nitrogen during overseeding because this may encourage excessive bermudagrass competition. Adequate levels of phosphorus and potassium, however, should be maintained for good plant rooting. Begin to fertilize shortly after significant shoot emergence (two to three weeks after seeding for perennial ryegrass and three to five for *Poa trivialis*, bentgrass, and fine fescue) and continue until cold weather halts bermudagrass growth. Normally, 1/4 pound to 1/2 pound nitrogen per 1,000 sq ft (12 to 24 kg/ha) every two to three weeks with a soluble nitrogen source (e.g., ammonium nitrate/sulfate), or 1 pound per 1,000 sq ft per month with a slow release nitrogen source (e.g., IBDU, milorganite, SCU), is adequate to promote desired growth without over-stimulating growth and encouraging disease. Traffic during grass establishment should be minimized whenever possible. Cups in greens and tee markers should be moved daily.

WINTER MANAGEMENT

Maintaining an acceptable turf appearance during winter involves proper watering and fertilization practices, proper traffic control, and proper disease management. In addition, areas that become damaged or do not provide an acceptable stand after the initial seeding may require additional seed applications (Plate 4.11). Oftentimes, following a hard frost or freeze, overseeded grasses leak some chlorophyll, thus turn off-colored (Plate 4.12). These recover with warm temperatures, which are more conducive for growth.

Irrigate regularly during the dry winter months to prevent plant desiccation. In addition, light, midday irrigations may be necessary if the overseeded grass begins to wilt. Do not overwater since this may promote algae and disease occurrence.

Plate 1.1. When properly maintained, bermudagrass produces a desirable dark green, dense turf that withstands traffic and many pests.

Plate 1.2. Patches of off-type bermudagrasses have plagued the industry in recent years. It is thought these are chance mutations, expressions of normally recessive genes and/or contamination.

Plate 1.3. Tifdwarf (left) compared to Tifgreen (right) bermudagrass. Tifdwarf typically tolerates mowing heights to approximately 5/32 to 3/16 (0.4 to 0.5 cm) inch while Tifgreen tolerates 3/16 to 1/4 (0.5 to 0.6 cm) inch.

Plate 1.4. Tifdwarf bermudagrass as a putting green surface, overseeded with *Poa trivialis*.

Plate 1.5. Tifgreen (left) compared to TifEagle bermudagrass (right) when mowed below 5/32 (0.4 cm) inch.

Plate 1.6. Classic dwarf (left), an ultra-dwarf bermudagrass, compared to Tifdwarf (right) when mowed at 9/64 (0.36 cm) inch.

Plate 2.1. When amendments are incorporated on-site as shown in Figure 2.8, turf often possesses uneven color and growth character-istics.

Plate 2.2. Sodding of closely mowed turf areas such as greens generally is not recommended due to the difficulty in obtaining grass identical to that currently on the green.

Plate 2.3. It is difficult to evenly lay sod so scalping does not occur, or edges of seams dry out. Extensive rolling and topdressing are required following sodding to provide the desired smooth, seam-free playing surface.

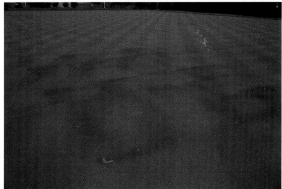

Plate 3.1. Turf burn from using a soluble iron source when temperatures were excessive (>85°F, 29°C).

Plate 3.2. Golf greens constructed with native soil (middle and right) often drain poorly, become compacted, and quickly fail. Greens constructed with a tested sand (left) provide at least 20 years (or more) of desirable turf.

Plate 4.1. Brown, dormant nonoverseeded bermudagrass following frost/freeze.

Plate 4.2. Mixed stand composition of dormant and partially green bermudagrass during spring greenup.

Plate 4.3. Overseeded bermudagrass golf green with *Poa trivialis*.

Plate 4.4. Overseeded bermudagrass fairway with perennial ryegrass to provide desirable year-round color and suggested landing areas for players.

Plate 4.5. Thin turf stand as overseeding competes with the permanent bermudagrass during spring. Premature death of the overseeding often leaves a bare soil surface until temperatures are warm enough to promote bermudagrass recovery.

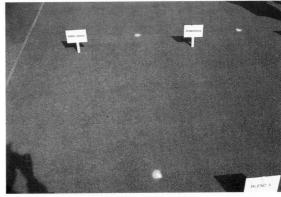

Plate 4.6. Seedheads of annual bluegrass (*Poa annua*) in an overseeding stand.

Plate 4.7. *Poa trivialis* (left) compared to creeping bentgrass (right) as overseeding grasses.

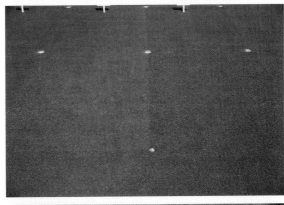

Plate 4.8. *Poa trivialis* (left) compared to perennial ryegrass (right) as overseeding grasses.

Plate 4.9. Erratic overseeding stand due to excessive seeding rate which encourages Pythium disease, resulting in eventual stand thinning.

Plate 4.10. Scalping of overseeding grass from premature lowering of the mowing height on an uneven surface of new greens.

Plate 4.11. Erratic fairway overseeding stand due to late overseeding date, insufficient irrigation coverage, and excessive thatch.

Plate 4.12. Off-colored perennial ryegrass following a heavy freeze/frost.

Plate 4.13. Poor bermudagrass recovery in spring following heavy overseeding. The bermudagrass green was established in late summer of the previous year and was not well established when overseeded.

Plate 4.14. Accidental runoff of a herbicide onto a overseeded green showing insufficient greenup of bermudagrass.

Plate 4.15. Overseeding damage from application of an improper preemergence herbicide.

Plate 4.16. *Poa annua* seedhead control (left) in overseeded ryegrass with appropriate use of a plant growth retardant.

Plate 5.1. Spotty stands of grass from exposure to irrigation containing high salinity and bicarbonate levels. This is most acute in poorly drained, low-lying areas.

Plate 5.2. Purpling of bermudagrass in fall following cool nights and bright, sunny days. No disease problems or nutritional disorders are involved.

Plate 5.3. Patches of bermudagrass off-types from chance mutations, expression of a normally recessive gene, or grass contamination.

Plate 5.4. Algae formation on closely mowed turf. This is most common in turf areas thinned by excessive shade, premature overseeding transition, effluent water use, or overwatering.

Plate 5.5. Moss formation, a condition often indicative of excessive low mowing heights and of conditions which thin the turf stand.

Plate 5.6. Localized dry spots on greens that form when organic acid coats sand particles during the normal breakdown of soil organic matter.

Plate 6.1. Mature weeds require multiple herbicide applications for control, increasing costs and potential of turfgrass phytotoxicity. Shown is mature goosegrass, which is very difficult to selectively control.

Plate 6.2. Bermudagrass phytotoxicity from spot treatment of herbicides for goosegrass control.

Plate 6.3. Although effective in selectively controlling annual bluegrass in ryegrass-overseeded bermudagrass, timing of ethofumesate (trade name: Progress) treatments are critical. It should only be used in areas where bermudagrass goes completely dormant in winter and only in fall and early winter months. Shown is delayed spring greenup of bermudagrass from ill-timed late winter/early spring applications.

Plate 6.4. Kyllinga weed occurrence in bermudagrass is rapidly spreading. These nutlet-less sedges can thrive under almost any bermudagrass growing condition, including golf greens.

Plate 6.5. Plant growth regulators provide a management tool for turf managers to regulate vertical growth and clipping production. Shown is a skip in the application of trinexapac-ethyl (trade name: Primo) where on either side, the bermudagrass has less vertical growth, thus less clipping production.

Plate 6.6. Bermudagrass damage from improper timing, tank mixture, and application method of postemergence herbicides.

Plate 8.1. Nematode damage to a golf green. Note the thinning, chlorotic patches of grass.

Plate 8.2. Nematode damage to turf root (right) compared to healthy roots (left). Nematode damage typically involves feeder (or secondary) roots being reduced and the roots eventually turning black in color.

Plate 8.3. Some nematicides are slit-injected into the soil for improved control. Minor, short-term yellowing to the bermudagrass may occur following this process.

Plate 9.1. Tifgreen bermudagrass showing symptoms of bermudagrass decline (*Gaeumannomyces graminis* var. *graminis*) (Courtesy of Monica Elliott).

Plate 9.2. Patches of bermudagrass decline disease (*Gaeumannomyces graminis* var. *graminis*) (Courtesy of Monica Elliott). Note the green turf recovery in aerification holes.

Plate 9.3. Brown patch disease (*Rhizoctonia solani*) affecting bermudagrass.

Plate 9.4. Brown patch disease (*Rhizoctonia solani*) in overseeded ryegrass.

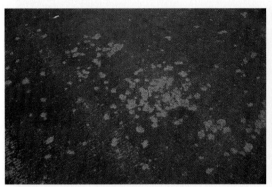

Plate 9.5. Dollar spot disease (*Sclerotinia homoeocarpa*) on a golf green.

Plate 9.6. Large fairy ring in overseeded bermudagrass with darker green rings of turf due to increased nitrogen available from decomposition of organic complexes in the soil.

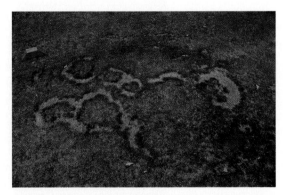

Plate 9.7. Type I edaphic fairy ring with a narrow zone of dead grass (necrotic ring) adjacent to darker green turf. Typically, a layer of hydrophobic (water-hating) mycelium mat often forms under fairy rings, causing the turf to die from moisture stress.

Plate 9.8. Type II edaphic fairy (right) with a band of dark green turf.

Plate 9.9. Type III edaphic fairy ring with only a circle of mushrooms present and no dead grass zone or a stimulated dark green zone.

Plate 9.10. Helminthosporium leaf spot (*Bipolaris* and *Drechslera* spp.) on bermudagrass golf green. Note the turf thinning and characteristic reddish color associated with the disease.

Plate 9.11. Lesions of Helminthosporium leaf spot (*Bipolaris* and *Drechslera* spp.) on bermudagrass leaves.

Plate 9.12. Thinning of bermudagrass from Helminthosporium leaf spot (*Bipolaris* and *Drechslera* spp.) disease but not affecting the overseeded ryegrass.

Plate 9.13. Pythium diseases can totally destroy turf areas quickly. Most susceptible are highly fertilized cool-season grasses grown on poorly draining soils with excessive moisture.

Plate 9.14. Initial symptoms of Pythium blight on overseeded grass where small, distinct reddish-brown patches of grass appear dark and water-soaked. Later the grass shrivels and turns straw-colored.

Plate 9.15. White cottony mycelium associated with Pythium diseases sometimes observed in early morning before mowing when moisture is present.

Plate 9.16. Yellowing of overseeded bermudagrass from Pythium root rot where excessive soil moisture is present.

Plate 9.17. Spring dead spot disease (*Gaeumannomyces graminis* var. *graminis*) of bermudagrass.

Plate 9.18. Early spring symptoms of spring dead spot (*Gaeumannomyces graminis* var. *graminis*) on an ultra-dwarf bermudagrass green.

Plate 9.19. Spring dead spot in overseeded bermudagrass. Note the darker green color of the overseeded grass presumably from the disease organisms breaking down soil organic matter, releasing nitrogen.

Plate 9.20. General browning and thinning of bermudagrass due to fall outbreak of anthracnose (*Colletotrichum graminicola*).

Plate 9.21. Anthracnose (*Colletotrichum graminicola*) on bermudagrass often resembles dollar spot disease (*Sclerotinia homoeocarpa*).

Plate 9.22. Anthracnose (*Colletotrichum graminicola*) black fruiting bodies (acervuli) and setae protruding from leaf tissue.

Plate 9.23. Curvularia blight (*Curvularia geniculata*) can cause yellowish-colored spots on greens. This rarely kills grass and occurs on bermudagrass mostly during periods of inactive growth.

Plate 9.24. Orange-colored rust (*Puccinia* spp.) on turf. This disease occurs most often on slow-growing, nitrogen-deficient turf in shade.

Plate 9.25. Pink snow mold, or Fusarium Patch (*Microdochium nivale*), on dormant, nonoverseeded bermudagrass. No permanent damage occurs to the bermudagrass.

Traffic control in winter reduces injury to the bermudagrass crowns and stolons. Ways to control this include not allowing traffic during frost events or when the soil surface is frozen, frequently alternating or changing mowing patterns, cleanup laps regularly skipped, and pin placement changed daily to distribute traffic.

Nitrogen fertilizer influences the appearance of the overseeded grass and spring recovery of the bermudagrass. Excessive nitrogen should be avoided to prevent unhealthy grass competition and to prevent succulent overseeding growth. Nitrogen applications either as a granular, sprayable, or combination every two to three weeks with 1/2 pound nitrogen per 1,000 sq ft (24 kg/ha) usually is sufficient. More frequent applications may be needed if the recovery time from traffic or weather damage is slow.

Applications of phosphorus, potassium, manganese, and iron should be considered during winter. All of these provide desirable color without stimulating excessive shoot growth. In addition, potassium helps in carbohydrate formation. These, along with iron, also prevent grass desiccation. Soil phosphorus and potassium levels and rates can be determined by soil testing. Iron generally is applied every three to four weeks as ferrous sulfate at 2 ounces per 1,000 sq ft (0.15 L/ha). Iron sulfate or a chelated iron source usually can be tank-mixed with most fungicides. Manganese can be applied as manganese sulfate at 1/2 to 1 ounce in 3 to 5 gallons of water per 1,000 sq ft (0.04 to 0.07 L/ha).

Once the overseeded grass becomes established, the chances of severe disease are reduced. Dollar spot usually develops when nitrogen levels are low or when *Poa trivialis* or bentgrass is used as an overseeded grass. Its occurrence usually is suppressed with sufficient nitrogen levels. Brown patch and pythium blight generally are the exception and not the rule for today's overseeded grasses. Greens, however, which drain poorly, or during continuous wet periods, can trigger outbreaks of these diseases. Excessive amounts of soluble nitrogen also can trigger disease. Turf managers constantly should check the weather forecast and be ready to use a fungicide if extended warm, moist (foggy) conditions are forecasted.

In addition to these diseases, the overseeded grass and the nondormant bermudagrass base grass can develop Helminthosporium leaf spot during the fall, winter, and spring months when temperatures slow grass growth. Leaf spot is similar to dollar spot in that maintaining adequate nitrogen levels usually keeps the grass growing aggressively enough to outgrow the disease symptoms. Fungicides, however, may be required during extended periods of cool weather which prevents adequate bermudagrass shoot growth.

SPRING TRANSITION

The main objective in spring is the gradual and smooth transition from overseeded grasses back to bermudagrass turf. Dormant bermudagrass shows signs of greenup when soil temperatures reach the 60°F (15.6°C) range. Some overseeded grasses, especially the new and aggressive heat-tolerant perennial ryegrasses, can successfully compete with bermudagrass through the spring and often result in a poor transition. Golf greens seeded with mixtures containing bentgrass often experience the same problem. On the other hand, mixtures high in *Poa trivialis* or fine fescue are difficult to maintain once temperatures reach the 80°F (26.7°C) range or when other drying conditions exist. During these times, these grasses become very sensitive to management practices designed to encourage bermudagrass recovery (Plate 4.13). As early spring approaches, a cultural program is initiated using increased fertility levels, lower mowing heights, brushes, topdressings, and the use of other reel implements such as grooved rollers. The following procedures have proved beneficial in encouraging bermudagrass at the expense of overseeded grasses with minimal disruption to the turf (McCarty, 2001):

1. **Use the appropriate seed or mixture.** Reducing the amount of perennial ryegrass or bentgrass in an overseeding mixture tends to aid in spring transition. Intermediate ryegrass, fine fescues, and roughstalk bluegrass are less heat-tolerant and therefore tend to transition earlier than perennial ryegrass or bentgrass. A 75% to 85% perennial ryegrass plus 15% to 25% roughstalk bluegrass, or 60% bentgrass to 40% bluegrass mixture transitions better in spring, yet provides a desirable putting surface. For those greens with good drainage and less traffic, an 80% fine fescue plus a 20% roughstalk bluegrass provides a quicker, smoother spring transition.

2. **Time transition according to temperatures.** Temperatures (both day and night) are the most important criteria influencing overseeding. Unfortunately, turf managers have little direct control over this. However, management practices can be timed around traditional temperature patterns and short-term weather forecasts. Probably the most important temperature range to remember is that bermudagrass will not aggressively begin to grow laterally until night temperatures consistently reach the mid 60°s F (15.6°C). Bermudagrass shoots will greenup much sooner when daytime temperatures reach the mid 50°s F (10°C). Members become excited with the first warm spell of the season and this puts added pressure on the superintendent to hasten transition. However, bermudagrass will not aggressively grow (especially laterally) until the high 60°s F (15.6°C) are reached. Therefore, do not begin your transition steps until just before these temperatures are anticipated. If performed prematurely, bare areas may become exposed and will not recover until temperatures are high enough to favor bermudagrass growth. Also, if a late cool snap occurs and night temperatures drop into the 50°s (10°C) or low 60°s (15.6°C), it will require three to seven days of high 60°s F temperatures for the bermudagrass to resume active growth.

3. **Reduced mowing height.** Begin reducing the mowing height several weeks before the expected spring transition period. Begin in mid- to late February by reducing the cut height 1/32 inch (0.08 cm) every two weeks until a height of 5/32 or 1/8 inch (0.4 to 0.3 cm) is reached in late March. Maintain a short mowing height until at least 50% of the overseeded grass has been removed (e.g., early May). The mowing height might be raised back to 5/32 to 3/16 inch (0.4 to 0.5 cm) as the bermudagrass begins to recover, but should not be raised while the overseeded grass still dominates. A lower mowing height reduces overseeding shading of developing bermudagrass, warms the soil, and inhibits the growth of the overseeded grasses. The use of grooved rollers and brushes also improves the putting surface and helps maintain the overseeded grass in an upright growth habit, which then mows cleaner.

4. **Cultivation.** Spike approximately three weeks before bermudagrass normally begins to green up and every week following, to enhance soil warming and turf recovery. Spiking also reduces surface compaction and algae growth. Aerify several weeks before expected spring greenup to promote bermudagrass growth by warming the soil and reduce the competition from the overseeded grass. Small (1/4-inch, 0.6 cm) tines should be used and good soil moisture present. The superintendent and club pro should coordinate spring tournaments around aerification times to minimize play disruption.

5. **Fertility.** Maintain low fertilizer application rates in late winter through early spring to reduce overseeded grass growth. Liquid iron will aid in maintaining desirable green color without excessive flush of growth. When bermudagrass growth is apparent, restore fertilizer applications. Approximately two weeks after initiation of spiking, fertilize with a half pound of soluble

N per 1,000 square feet (24 kg/ha) to help stimulate new bermudagrass growth. Fertilize weekly at this rate until an adequate bermudagrass cover is achieved.

6. **Verticutting.** While overseeded grasses still are actively growing, initiate light and frequent (e.g., weekly) verticuttings to help maintain the overseeded grasses in an upright growth habit which allows increased sunlight and warmth to penetrate through to the soil and thus encourage an earlier and more rapid regrowth of the bermudagrass. Begin verticutting when daytime temperatures are consistently above 70°F. Another method of judging when to initiate verticutting is when the nonoverseeded adjacent fairways green up. *This verticutting should be no lower than 1/16 inch (0.16 cm) below the bedknife.* It should cut above the soil surface and remove only surface leaves and not remove or damage bermudagrass stolons. Light verticutting or grooming, in addition to aiding the bermudagrass, also will improve the putting quality of greens. Light topdressings on a two to three week basis at approx. 1/8 yd^2/1,000 sq ft (0.1 m^3/100 m^2) also aids in maintaining a desirable putting surface. Note: Although traditional light, frequent verticutting and core aerification may promote the gradual transition to bermudagrass, visual turf quality may be reduced until the bermudagrass has had sufficient time to recover. This is especially true if medium to heavy verticutting is implemented. Typically, patches of thin turf form and remain unsightly until the bermudagrass greens up and fills in.

7. **Maintain adequate soil moisture.** Reducing or withholding water in an attempt to encourage the overseeded grass to die from moisture stress is not recommended. Spring is when bermudagrass suffers from natural decline of older roots and initiation of new ones. Withholding water during this root transformation may cause greater damage to the extremely shallow-rooted bermudagrass more than the deeper-rooted winter overseeded species. Water deeply and infrequently to encourage deep bermudagrass rooting at the expense of the overseeded grass.

8. **Use of herbicides or plant growth retardants.** Selective herbicides have proved useful for slow removal of overseeded grasses in spring. This allows the superintendent better control on transition timing. Herbicide use also provides an earlier indication of how well the bermudagrass wintered and allows more time should resprigging or sodding be required. Removal of overseeded grass with herbicides also will remove the competitiveness and therefore will allow quicker bermudagrass recovery. Control of other weeds, such as *Poa annua*, also is possible with some of the herbicides.

Pronamide (Kerb 50WP), metsulfuron (Manor 60 DF), and TranXit GTA are often used with varying success for transition. Kerb is applied from a 1/2 pound to 1 pound product per acre (0.56 to 1.12 kg/ha), while Manor is applied at 3/4 to 1 oz/acre (0.53 to 0.7 g/100 m^2) and TranXit at 2 oz/acre (1.4 g/100m^2). Results are desirably slow. Two to four weeks, depending on temperatures and rates, are typically required to gradually reduce the overseeded grass. Warmer temperatures and the higher rates usually hasten this conversion. However, a weak stand of bermudagrass may result if greens are treated too soon in spring and if the weather remains cool. Thin turf will remain until temperatures are warm enough for bermudagrass to recover (Plate 4.14). Research indicates that April treatments of Kerb 50W at 1 pound product per acre (1.12 kg/ha) or Manor at 1 oz per acre (0.7 g/100 m^2) provide the best timing and rate for transition. Visual injury to ryegrass with this treatment normally lasts from one to three weeks.

Experience suggests that turf managers wishing to use herbicides to enhance transition proceed with caution. Do not begin treatments until one to two weeks after bermudagrass resumes active growth. Lighter rates than listed may be wise if weaker overseeded grasses such as *Poa trivialis* or fine fescue are present (Plate 4.15). Sprayer calibration and application uniformity are extremely critical and once the overseeded grass begins to die from the herbicide, there is no turning back.

Plant growth retardants have also been used to help make a smoother spring transition. Mefluidide (Embark 2S) and trinexapac-ethyl (Primo 1EC) have been used in early spring to help discourage the overseeding without retarding the bermudagrass greenup. Rates appear important since heavy applications may retard the bermudagrass as well as the overseeding. Primo 1EC at 3 to 4 ounces of product per acre (0.22 to 0.29 L/ha) and Embark 2S at 1 quart per acre (2.3 L/ha) are applied every two to four weeks until substantial bermudagrass appears. Rates are often increased to encourage lateral bermudagrass growth instead of vertical growth. Mefluidide is also used to selectively suppress *Poa annua* seedheads (Plate 4.16). Multiple applications may be necessary and must be applied before seedhead initiation.

5 Selected Stresses of Bermudagrass

SHADE, LIGHT, AND PHYSIOLOGICAL ADAPTATION

Adaptation can be defined as an adjustment to environmental conditions and may involve a modification of an organism or its parts to better fit its environmental conditions. Adaptive changes in plants are often fine-tuning adjustments in a physiological process to enable survival. Although differences occur in both geological and morphological characteristics between warm- and cool-season grasses, the most important and profound difference occurs in the physiology of these plants. Why some plants, such as bentgrass, 'prefer' cooler climates was not fully understood until the Calvin-Benson or C_3 and the Hatch and Slack or C_4 cycles for warm-season grasses were discovered in the 1950s and 1960s, respectively. The existence of two different carbon fixation mechanisms provided an understanding of inherent differences between certain plants and has allowed superintendents to manipulate microenvironment to allow certain species to grow outside their naturally adapted areas.

Photosynthesis

Photosynthesis is the process by which light energy is converted into biologically usable chemical energy (carbohydrates) by plants. The end products of this process, which are important to human life, are food and oxygen. The photosynthetic production of oxygen (O_2) by plants is the only natural source of O_2 on earth. Photosynthesis not only provides energy-rich substances for various metabolic reactions (including food), but also the oxygen for oxidative conversion of organic matter. A summary reaction for conversion of CO_2 to a molecule of carbohydrate (glucose) via photosynthesis is as follows:

$$6\,CO_2 \quad + \quad 6\,H_2O \quad \text{(light)} \quad 6\,O_2 \quad + \quad C_6H_{12}O$$

carbon dioxide   water   photosynthesis   oxygen   carbohyd

In 1965 the specific pathway of carbon fixation in warm-season grasses was discovered. It was found in sugarcane that instead of a three-carbon compound, 3-phosphoglyceric acid (or 3-PGA), as the first product of carbon fixation like that in cool-season (or C_3 plants), a four-carbon compound, oxaloacetic acid (OAA) was the first product formed. This gave rise to the designation of C_4 cycle or C_4 plants. Most (but not all) C_4

plants are monocots and presumably evolved from the tropics since high temperatures and light intensities are needed for their optimum performance. All warm-season turf species (bermudagrass, centipedegrass, zoysiagrass, bahiagrass, St. Augustinegrass, seashore paspalum, and buffalograss) are C_4 plants; thus they are adapted to warmer temperatures and higher light intensities. Other C_4 grasses include dallisgrass, crabgrass, and goosegrass, all of which are common weeds in turf. These weeds, when present in C_3 turfgrasses such as fescue, ryegrass, or bluegrass, have the distinct physiological growth edge during warm summer months since they grow faster during warm temperatures.

Light

A major environmental parameter influencing plant growth is light. C_4 plants exhibit a nonsaturating growth curve at light intensities found in nature, meaning they require full sunlight for optimum photosynthesis. C_3 plants, on the other hand, are fully saturated at one-half full sunlight. At conditions beyond one-half full sunlight, photosynthesis decreases in C_3 plants because of photorespiration.

As mentioned, C_4 plants (such as bermudagrass) grow best when exposed to full sunlight. At lower light intensities (<70% full sunlight), bermudagrass responds by developing narrow, elongated leaves, thin upright stems, elongated internodes, and weak rhizomes and stolons. Consequently, bermudagrass develops very sparse turf when grown under shady conditions, and when mowed excessively low, such as on a golf green, is frequently invaded by other pests such as algae or annual bluegrass. This high light intensity requirement is why most C_4 grasses have relatively poor shade tolerance compared to C_3 grasses.

In the field, only a small fraction of the light striking the upper turf leaves is able to filter through to leaves below. The second layer of leaves receives about 10% of the light striking the top layer, and the lower third layer only 1%. The arrangement and angle of the leaves also help determine how much light will pass to lower leaf layers. The more upright the leaves, the more sunlight can reach the lower layers and the more efficiently the plants can utilize full sunlight. This explains why during shorter light duration days as found in late summer and fall, C_4 plants such as bermudagrass become stemmy. This is an attempt by the plant to allow lower leaves to capture as much sunlight as possible to make the plant as efficient in photosynthesis as possible. During longer days as found during late spring and early summer, bermudagrass has more of a prostrate (or decumbent) growth habit. Lower leaves are not as important to the plant during these times since the longer days allow enough sunlight absorption by the upper leaves to adequately sustain growth.

Day length and temperature are known to be the most important environmental parameters influencing bermudagrass growth. Growth declines exponentially when day length hours are decreased. Optimum growth of warm-season grasses occurs when daily solar radiation day length is greater than 13 hours. When solar radiation day length is reduced below 13 hours, growth is gradually slowed regardless of whether adequate irrigation or nitrogen fertilizer is available. The opposite effect occurs with some cool-season grasses. For example, shorter day-length periods, as experienced in spring and fall, promote the greatest tillering of perennial ryegrass and annual bluegrass.

Figure 5.1. Bermudagrass green thin from excessive shade. Bermudagrass golf greens require six to eight hours daily of full sunlight to maintain a healthy stand. As the quality and quantity of sunlight are reduced below these values, increasing stand thinning normally results.

When day length is reduced below six to eight hours of full sunlight, bermudagrass, especially shorter mowed areas such as greens, will thin. Taller mowed bermudagrass such as fairways and approaches can withstand less sunlight and day length due to their higher mowing heights, thus more leaf surface area to capture available light. Golf greens, meanwhile, due to their shorter mowing heights, have less leaf surface area and cannot maintain a strong stand at reduced day length or light quality condition (Figure 5.1). Bermudagrass golf greens, therefore, require six to eight hours minimum full sunlight, year-round to provide satisfactory coverage.

In winter, when days are shortest and the sun lowest on the horizon, excessive shade from trees 30 to 50 feet away from greens often occurs. This is especially true for trees on the south to southeastern direction of greens. As these trees mature and grow larger, golf clubs must maintain an ongoing aggressive selective limb pruning and possible tree removal program.

In addition to reducing light, shaded areas generally have: (a) increased competition to the turf for nutrients and water by trees and shrubs; (b) increased humidity; (c) reduced or restricted air movement; (d) longer periods of dew and frost occurring during the morning before burning-off; and (e) lower temperature.

Optimum growth also is related to having good morning sunlight. By afternoon during summer, cloud and haze buildup naturally reduces the quality and quantity of sunlight reaching the earth's surface. Therefore, preventing morning shade sources and allowing earliest sunlight appears best for most grasses. Early sunlight also reduces time needed for dew evaporation and frost melting.

WATER QUALITY

A potential problem with all greens is a gradual buildup of salinity from the use of high pH-, effluent-, or bicarbonate-containing irrigation water (Plate 5.1). This is magnified when highly soluble fertilizer sources are used at relatively light but frequent rates and there is a lack of frequent, heavy rainfall to periodically leach the salt below the root zone.

To combat potential salinity buildup, superintendents have modified their watering practices from light, frequent applications in summer to heavier, infrequent ones. Greens also must drain relatively well so salts can be leached below the root zone by heavy rainfall or by heavy hand-watering. Using low salt-containing water sources also helps. Coastal courses or those using effluent water sources should closely monitor their salt levels, especially during summer.

In recent years, fertigation and foliar feeding by liquid fertilizer sources have become popular to help regulate grass color and growth during summer. These also reduce the salinity load on the grass. Buffering the water pH to 6.0 to 6.5 and periodic light use of gypsum also helps reduce the salinity stress. High bicarbonate water is also commonly treated by artificially acidifying it, often by sulfur injection. This technology is rapidly evolving and dramatic effects can be realized, especially in coastal and arid regions. The following tests provide information concerning soil and water quality:

- Total salt content (EC), including Ca^{+2}, K^+, Mg^{+2}, Na^+, Cl^-, SO_4, NO_3, NH_3, and HCO_3^-
- Sodium level (SAR or ESP)
- Toxic ion levels, especially Boron, Chloride, and Fluoride
- Bicarbonates (RSC)
- pH

Also influencing water quality use are soil water infiltration rates and differential salinity tolerance of the turfgrass species, and nutrient content (e.g., N, P, and K).

Assessing Soil Salinity

Saline soils are classified based on two criteria: (1) the total soluble salt or salinity content (electrical conductivity or EC), and (2) exchangeable sodium percentage (or, more recently, sodium adsorption ratio). Additional information is also often used such as carbonate content and potential toxic ions. Soils are a key to continued use of saline irrigation water. A potential salinity problem may exist in a poorly drained soil. Good drainage is essential to leach soluble salts through the soil profile. The better the drainage, the better one can keep the soil level of soluble salts within tolerable limits. Sand soils are usually best suited for saline irrigation because of easy drainage, but they must be maintained near field capacity in order to prevent intolerable salt levels.

Soluble salts are measured in soils by a conductivity instrument which measures electrical conductivity (EC) either from a saturated paste extract from a soil or from a soil water dilution ratio. EC readings from these two methods are not comparable. Soil testing laboratories frequently use a 1:2 dilution method with one part dry soil:two parts water. Using this method, soils with EC readings of 2.0 to 4.0 dS/m are considered to

Table 5.1. General guidelines for toxicities of sodium, chloride, boron, and bicarbonate by root absorption and foliar contact (modified from McCarty, 2001; Westcot and Ayers, 1985).

Item		Minor Problems	Increasing Problems	Severe Problems
Soil Permeability/Infiltration				
EC[a]$_{water}$	(mmhos/cm or ds/m)	<0.75	0.75–3	>3
EC[a]$_{soil}$	(ds/m)	2–4	4–12	>12
Sodium (SAR)	(meq/L)	<6	6–9	>9
TDS[a]	(mg/L or ppm)	<450	450–2,000	>2,000
Bicarbonates (HCO$_3^-$)	(ppm)	0–120	120–180	180–600
RSC[a]	(meq/L)	≤1.25	1.25–2.5	>2.5
Turf Toxicity from Root Absorption				
Sodium	(SAR)	<3	3–9	>9
Chloride	(meq/L)	<2	2–10	>10
	(mg/L)	<70	70–355	>355
Boron	(mg/L)	<1	1–2	>2
Turf Toxicity from Foliar Contact				
Sodium	(meq/L)	<3	>3–9	>9
	(mg/L)	<70	>70	—
Chloride	(meq/L)	<3	3–10	>10
	(mg/L)	<100	100–350	>350
Boron	(meq/L)	<0.75	0.75–3	>3
Ornamental Plants Tolerance				
NH$_4$-N (ammonium-N)	(mg/L)	<5	5–30	>30
NO$_3$-N (nitrate-N)	(mg/L)	<5	5–30	>30
Bicarbonate HCO$_3^-$	(meq/L)	<1.5	1.5–8.5	>8.5
Unsightly foliar deposits	(mg/L)	<90	90–520	>520
Residual chlorine	(mg/L)	<1	1–5	>5
pH			normal range is 6.0 to 8.0	

[a] EC = electrical conductivity; TDS = total dissolved salts; RSC = residual sodium carbonates.

have low salt levels (Table 5.1). Soils with EC readings of 4.0 to 12.0 dS/m have medium levels. When soil readings are above 12.0 dS/m, soils are considered to have high salt levels and only salt-tolerant turfgrasses survive above 16 dS/m. Soil in irrigated turf is usually two to five times saltier than the water with which it is irrigated.

Substantial amounts of salt can accumulate in the root zone rapidly during periods of drought when poor-quality irrigation water is the predominant source of water. The application of 1 inch of moderately saline irrigation water of 1.0 dS/m contributes approximately 3.3 pounds of salt per 1,000 sq ft (161 kg/ha). Since turf water use during peak demand is about 0.15 to 0.30 inches/day (0.38 to 0.76 cm), this amount of salt can accumulate in the soil in three to seven days. Compare this amount of salt added via irrigation to routine fertilization which is usually less than two pounds (908 kg) of salt (fertilizer) per application, and is usually avoided when the weather is hot and dry.

Assessing Irrigation Water for Sodium Problems

The potential for irrigation water to have poor infiltration properties is assessed by determining the sodium adsorption ratio (SAR) and the electrical conductivity (EC) of the water. The sodium adsorption ratio relates the concentration of sodium to the concentration of calcium and magnesium. The higher the sodium in relation to calcium and magnesium, the higher the SAR, the poorer the water infiltration, and increased problems with soil deflocculation.

The effects of high SAR on irrigation water infiltration are dependent on the electrical conductivity of the water. For a given SAR, the lower the EC_w, the poorer the infiltration properties, the higher the EC_w, the better the infiltration. For example, irrigation water with an SAR = 15 has poor infiltration properties if the EC_w = 0.5 dS/m but good infiltration properties with an EC_w = 2.0 dS/m. A good rule of thumb is if the SAR is more than 10 times greater than the EC_w, then poor water infiltration is likely to occur.

General guidelines for precautions and management of irrigation water with various SAR values and an EC_w =1.0 dS/m are provided in Table 5.1. Fine-textured soils such as clay can have permeability problems if a water SAR > 9 is used over an extended period. Note: some labs report adjusted SAR values instead of SAR. The adjusted SAR includes the added effects of the precipitation or dissolution of calcium in soils and is related to carbonate and bicarbonate concentrations. Bicarbonates can interact with soil Ca and Mg to precipitate out lime ($CaCO_3$) or magnesium carbonate ($MgCO_3$), causing an increase in sodium hazard.

Assessing Soils for Sodium Problems

Salt-affected soil can be classified as saline, sodic, and saline-sodic soils. Saline soils are plagued by high levels of soluble salts, primarily Cl^-, SO_4^{-2}, and sometimes NO_3^-. Salts of low solubility, such as $CaSO_4$ and $CaSO_3$, may also be present. Because exchangeable sodium is not a problem, saline soils are usually flocculated with good water permeability (Table 5.1). Soil deterioration with poor water infiltration can occur when water with high Na concentrations are used with high HCO_3^- and relatively low Ca^{+2} and Mg^{+2} levels. Sodic soils have high levels of exchangeable sodium and along with low EC, these soil tend to disperse, reducing water infiltration. Sodic soils also have a pH between 8.5 and 10 and are often called black alkali soils because the humus in the soil tends to disperse. Calcium and magnesium ions in sodic soils tend to form lime, leaving soluble Ca and Mg levels low, allowing the sodium problems. Saline-sodic soils have both high contents of soluble salts and exchangeable sodium. Cationic materials such as calcium and magnesium are added to flocculate the soil. The cations hold soil particles and allow the formation of water-stable aggregates which increase porosity, aeration, and infiltration.

A soil SAR >13 indicates a sodic soil where sodium causes soil colloids to disperse and plug the soil's drainage pores, which reduces the permeability of the soil to water and air. Sodic soils become saturated with sodium ions compared to calcium and magnesium ions, especially if bicarbonate ions are present. Symptoms of reduced permeability include waterlogging, reduced infiltration rates, crusting, compaction, disease occurrence, weed invasion, and poor aeration. Sodic soils often have considerable clay which is sticky due to the sodium.

Correcting water or soil due to excess sodium includes: (1) blending good and bad irrigation water sources; (2) applying soil amendments such as gypsum, sulfur, or sulfuric acid to directly or indirectly replace sodium ions with desirable calcium; (3) providing excess moisture to help leach salt out of the root zone; and (4) aerifying, spiking, and slicing frequently to counteract soil deflocculation and surface algae, thus allowing internal drainage and good air/soil gas exchange. These procedures are explained in greater detail later in this chapter.

CARBONATES

Bicarbonate (HCO_3^-) and to a lesser extent carbonate (CO_3^{-2}) are found in high pH water. The primary source of carbonates and bicarbonates in soils is carbonic acid (H_2CO_3) that forms when carbon dioxide from microbial and root respiration reacts with water. As the concentrations of bicarbonates and carbonates increase, more hydroxyl ions are formed, with a corresponding reduction of hydrogen ions (H^+) causing an increase in pH.

When water containing HCO_3^- dries at the soil surface, insoluble salts of Ca and Mg carbonates (lime) are formed. Since Ca and Mg are no longer dissolved they do not counteract the effects of Na, and problems related to high ESP may occur. This results in an increase in the SAR and soil pH and a decrease in water quality and soil infiltration. White lime deposits may also become visible on turf leaves during hot, dry periods because bicarbonates are deposited during evaporation.

There are two measurements used for assessing the carbonate level of irrigation water, the direct measurement of carbonate and bicarbonate and the residual sodium carbonate equation (RSC).

Residual sodium carbonate (RSC) equation reflects alkalinity of water by indicating this potential precipitation of Ca and Mg and resulting increases of effective sodium percentage of water. RSC specifically measures presence of excess carbonates (CO_3^{-2}) and bicarbonate (HCO_3^-) content over calcium (Ca^{+2}) and magnesium (Mg^{+2}) ions each expressed as meq/L. Labs often report values as parts per million (ppm) or milligrams per liter (mg/L). These values should be divided by their equivalent weights (mg/meq) to obtain milliequivalents per liter (meq/L) (Table 5.2).

$$meq/L = \frac{ppm \; or \; mg/L}{equivalent \; weight \; in \; mg/meq}$$

For example, a water sample test reports 1,000 mg/L Na^+, 200 mg/L Ca^{+2}, and 100 mg/L Mg^{+2}. First, calculate the number of milliequivalents per liter for each ion (or refer to Table 5.2):

$$Na^+ = 1,000 \; mg/L \div 23 \; mg/meq = 44 \; meq/L;$$

$$Ca^{+2} = 200 \; mg/L \div 20 \; mg/meq = 4.4 \; meq/L;$$

$$Mg^{+2} = 100 \; mg/L \div 12.2 \; mg/meq = 8.20 \; meq/L$$

Table 5.2. Laboratory analysis to determine water quality and factors for converting ion concentration reported in parts per million (ppm) or milligrams per liter (mg/L) to moles per liter (mol/L) or milliequivalents per liter (meq/L) (McCarty, 2001).

ppm (or mg/L) ÷ molecular weight (g) = moles per liter (mol/L)
ppm (or mg/L) ÷ milliequivalent weight (mg/meq) = milliequivalents per liter (meq/L)
milliequivalents per liter (meq/L) = molecular weight ÷ total valence number

Analysis	Reporting Symbol	Reporting Unit	Molecular Weight (g)	Milliequivalent Weight (mg/meq)
Electrical conductivity	EC_w	mmhos/cm	—	—
Calcium	Ca^{+2}	meq/L	40	20
Magnesium	Mg^{+2}	meq/L	24.3	12.2
Sodium	Na^{+1}	meq/L	23	23
Carbonate	CO_3^{-2}	meq/L	60	30
Bicarbonate	HCO_3^{-1}	meq/L	61	61
Chloride	Cl^{-1}	meq/L	35.4	35.4
Sulfate	SO_4^{-2}	meq/L	96	48
Boron	B	mg/L	10.8	10.8
Nitrate-nitrogen	$NO_3\text{-}N$	mg/L	14	14
Acidity	pH	pH	—	—
SAR	—	meq/L	—	—
Potassium	K^{+1}	meq/L	39.1	39.1
Lithium	Li^{+1}	mg/L	7	7
Iron	$Fe^{+2 \text{ or } +3}$	mg/L	55.8	27.9 or 18.6
Ammonium-nitrogen	$NH_4\text{-}N$	mg/L	14	14
Phosphate phosphorus	$PO_4\text{-}P$	mg/L	31	varies

Conversion Values between mg/L and meq/L for Most Water Constituents

Constituents	Multiply by the following value to convert mg/L to meq/L	Multiply by the following value to convert meq/L to mg/L
Sodium (Na^{+1})	0.043	23
Magnesium (Mg^{+2})	0.083	12
Calcium (Ca^{+2})	0.05	20
Chloride (Cl^{-1})	0.028	36
Sulfate (SO_4^{-2})	0.021	48
Bicarbonate (HCO_3^{-1})	0.016	61
Carbonate (CO_3^{-2})	0.033	30

Assessment for poor water infiltration due to high carbonates and low calcium and magnesium as determined by the RSC equation is listed in Table 5.1.

If hazardous RSC water is repeatedly used, the soil becomes alkaline and likely to become sodic over time. Values greater than 1.5 meq/L may justify irrigation acid injection. Acid injection changes the carbonates and bicarbonates to carbon dioxide and water but does not affect the calcium or magnesium. Normally, if irrigation RSC values are high but SAR values are low, acid injection is unnecessary since insufficient sodium is present to cause a problem. This also is true in areas of high rainfall where sodium is readily leached out of the soil profile.

Bicarbonate levels alone are sometimes used to assess potential limitations of an irrigation water source (Table 5.1). Water containing 2 to 4 meq/L of bicarbonates can be managed by applying ammoniacal fertilizer as part of a regular fertilizer program to help reduce soil pH. Water with greater than 4 meq/L bicarbonates may need to be acidified with sulfuric or phosphoric acid. Blending poor quality water with better quality water and applying soil amendments such as gypsum or sulfur also are means to help manage bicarbonate problems. The negative effects on soil infiltration of bicarbonate and carbonate are negated by high levels of Ca and Mg. Bicarbonate and carbonate are good indicators of hazard when irrigation water calcium and magnesium concentrations are low, but the RSC equation should be utilized when water calcium and magnesium are high. High HCO_3^- and CO_3^{-2} water can have good infiltration properties if Ca and Mg levels are also high.

Nutrient Loads

To determine the amount (lb/acre) of calcium and magnesium supplied in an acre-inch of irrigation water, multiply each element (in mg/L or ppm) by 2.72. For example, an irrigation source containing 75 mg/L calcium and 30 mg/L magnesium would supply the following:

Ca^{+2} = 75 mg/L × 2.72 = 204 lb calcium supplied per acre-foot (75 kg/m^3) irrigation water.

Mg^{+2} = 30 mg/L × 2.72 = 82 lb magnesium per acre-foot (30 kg/m^3) irrigation water.

A similar approach would also be used when total dissolved solids (TSS) are a concern. Lower quality effluent sources often have undissolved solids such as organic material, sand, silt, and clay. Excessive amounts could potentially clog or seal soil surfaces. Use the same manner of calculating nutrients added when irrigating.

pH

Continued use of high bicarbonate and carbonate water also leads to a high soil pH. When Na is the predominant cation in the soil, sodium bicarbonate and sodium carbonate form, causing the pH to be as high as 10 since these ions are water soluble and tend to ionize, which keeps high levels of bicarbonate and carbonate. However, when Ca predominates, usually insoluble calcium carbonate forms which, unlike sodium carbonate, does not ionize to form more carbonate ions, thus the soil pH generally stabilizes around 8.0. High pH can induce iron, manganese, and to a lesser extent zinc, deficiencies by rendering these micronutrients unavailable to turfgrass roots. Unfortunately, simply adding these micronutrients in fertilizers is sometimes ineffective since these elements quickly become unavailable in high pH soils. Using chelates and foliar applications helps to avoid interactions between micronutrients and high pH soils.

With moderate levels of HCO_3^- and CO_3^{-2}, acidifying amendments can be soil-, rather than irrigation-applied to reduce soil pH. Acidifying N fertilizers or elemental S are generally employed. Although N fertilizers containing or generating ammonium (NH_4^+)

Figure 5.2. A sulfureous generator used to lower the pH and bicarbonate levels in irrigation water.

reduce soil pH, it is important to note that nitrate (NO_3^-) fertilizers increase soil pH. Usually, irrigating with water sources containing low bicarbonate concentrations can be managed by using acidifying fertilizers (e.g., ammonium sulfate) or application of granular elemental sulfur.

Irrigation Acid Injection

High bicarbonate-containing water may require acidification (via injection into the irrigation system) with sulfuric acid (H_2SO_4), phosphoric acids (H_3PO_4), or urea plus sulfuric acid (monocarbamide dihydrogensulfate) to correct the problem. This two step process forms carbon dioxide (CO_2) and water (H_2O) from reacting an acid, such as sulfuric acid (H_2SO_4), with bicarbonate (HCO_3^-).

Other acidifying units (often called sulfur generators) dissolve sulfur chips or flakes (Figure 5.2) into stored irrigation water to form sulfite (SO_3). The sulfite then reacts to form sulfurous acid and sulfuric acid which then has the same effect as acid injection. The generator consists of a sulfur chip storage hopper, oxidizing chamber, blower, and absorption tower. Pure elemental sulfur chips or flakes are combusted in the oxidizing chamber to form sulfur dioxide gas. When sulfur dioxide gas mixes with water, sulfurous acid is formed.

Sulfurous acid is a mild acid that is only slightly corrosive and easy to handle. In comparison, sulfuric acid (H_2SO_4) is an extremely strong and corrosive acid and difficult to handle. Sulfurous acid improves water quality by lowering water pH and neutralizing bicarbonates and carbonates. Sulfurous acid reduces pH by dissociating into hydrogen ions and sulfite. The hydrogen ions reduce water pH.

Bicarbonates and carbonates often form lime (calcium or magnesium carbonate), thus increasing soil pH and tending to reduce soil percolation and drainage. These are

Table 5.3. Amounts of bicarbonate, carbonate, calcium, and magnesium in irrigation which can cause soil deflocculation, reducing soil water infiltration.

Element	Levels in Irrigation Water Which May Reduce Soil Water Infiltration, mg/L
Bicarbonate (HCO_3^-)	100 to 400
Carbonate (CO_3^-)	0 to 5
Calcium (Ca)	25 to 200
Magnesium (Mg)	20 to 40

neutralized by the sulfurous acid to form sulfite, carbon dioxide, and water. The carbon dioxide gas escapes to the air.

Sulfur treatment will reduce water pH, bicarbonates, and carbonates. This treatment, however, will not in itself correct water sodium problems. Sodium rich water is usually injected with soluble gypsum and/or gypsum is added to the soil surface. Sulfur treated water, however, helps maintain soluble calcium and magnesium ions, reducing SAR values, thus helping counter the detrimental effects of sodium ions in the water.

Irrigation water high in bicarbonate/carbonate and high in calcium and/or magnesium reacts to form insoluble lime ($CaCO_3 \bullet MgCO_3$) in the upper centimeter of soil. This insoluble lime, called calcite, can eventually coat soil and sand particles, reducing water infiltration. Concentrations of these in irrigation water which can cause reduced water infiltration are in Table 5.3.

Ways to disrupt the calcite layer include physically breaking it up by periodic cultivation or dissolving it into more mobile forms such as gypsum ($CaSO_4$) and magnesium sulfate ($MgSO_4$) by using acidifying fertilizers such as ammonium sulfate, by injecting or dissolving sulfur in the irrigation system, or by applying elemental sulfur to the turfgrass surface. However, it is necessary for lime to be present for gypsum to form.

To determine if water acidification is needed, one should compare the relative concentration of HCO_3^- and CO_3^- to Ca^{+2}, Mg^{+2}, and Na^+ levels. When HCO_3^- levels exceed 120 ppm, residual sodium carbonate (RSC) exceeds 1.25, and SAR is >6meq/L, then acid treatment of irrigation water may be necessary.

MANAGING IRRIGATION WATER QUALITY PROBLEMS

Managing salinity, sodicity, and alkalinity problems requires constant attention. Management practices which aid in remedying these problems on golf greens include:

1. Diluting poor quality water with good quality water
2. Leaching excess salts by applying extra water
3. Modifying soils with various amendments to replace and leach sodium from the soil
4. Amending irrigation water to correct sodium and bicarbonate problems
5. Enhancing soil drainage by using sands and installing subsurface tile drainage
6. Continuously aerifying, spiking, and slicing the turf's surface to prevent soil crusting and algae development—both common results of using poorer quality irrigation water.

Blending Water Sources for Reducing Salinity

High salinity water that is unacceptable for use can be made suitable as an irrigation source by diluting with nonsaline water. Enough nonsaline water must be available to create a mixed water of acceptable quality, e.g., do not end up making a less saline water that is still unacceptable. Quality of a poor water source should improve proportionally to the mixing ratio with better quality water. For example, a water source with an EC_w of 5 dS/m mixed equally with a source with an EC_w of 1 dS/m should reduce a salinity blend to approximately 3 dS/m. A chemical analysis of the blend should be determined to confirm this. The salinity of the mixture can be calculated with this equation:

Mixing of irrigation sources can occur in irrigation ponds or within the irrigation system itself. When mixing water sources in irrigation ponds, the nonsaline water should be added immediately prior to being used so as to reduce evaporative losses. Evaporation of surface water is not only an inefficient use of water, it also increases the salinity of the water remaining in the pond.

Leaching Soils to Remove Salts

The ability to leach soils is the most important management capability needed when managing salts. Salt buildup from salt-laden irrigation water occurs when rainfall is low and evaporative demand is high. As water evaporates from the soil surface, salt deposits are left behind. Determining the EC of the soil is the best way to determine the extent of salt accumulation. When the EC exceeds the tolerance level of the turfgrass, the soil should be leached to move the salt below the root zone.

Frequent flushing of the soil with good quality irrigation water or rainfall is the best method of preventing excessive salt accumulation. Unfortunately, low salinity irrigation sources are not always available and frequently saline irrigation water must be used to manage soil salinity. However, as long as the salinity of the irrigation water is acceptable, it can be used to leach accumulated salts from the turf root zone. The use of soil amendments, such as gypsum, should be considered in conjunction with leaching irrigation applications in saline-sodic soils. However, if excessive soil sodium and poor water drainage is not a problem the use of soil amendments should be avoided since they add to the salinity of the soil.

If saline water is used to reduce the salt level of the soil, irrigation must be applied at rates exceeding evapotranspiration to leach excess salts out of the root zone. To determine the amount of excess water required to leach salt below the root zone, the following leaching requirement equation is often used.

Leaching requirement is the amount of extra water needed to leach salts from the root zone and is defined as:

Figure 5.3. Greens that are candidates for effluent or poor quality water irrigation use must have excellent internal drainage in order to periodically flush these soils.

$$\text{Leaching Requirement} = \frac{EC_{iw}}{EC_{dw}} \times 100\%$$

EC_{iw} equals the electrical conductivity of the irrigation water and EC_{dw} is electrical conductivity of a saturated paste extract that can be tolerated by the turfgrass being grown. For example, an irrigation water source with a salinity level of 2 dS/m used on a turfgrass tolerant of a salinity of 4 dS/m would equal 50% [(2 ÷ 4) × 100%]. In this example 50% more irrigation water than is needed to satisfy normal irrigation requirements is required to leach salt from the root zone (e.g., 50% greater than 2 inches of water applied would equal 3 inches). As the irrigation water becomes saltier, the leaching requirement becomes larger, meaning more water must be added for leaching to avoid salt accumulation.

Good Soil Percolation and Drainage

As previously mentioned, leaching works well only with soils possessing good drainage. If compacted zones or abrupt changes in soil texture exist, less leaching occurs as water movement through the soil is reduced. Pushup greens are often noncandidates for leaching or for the use of sulfur treated irrigation (Figure 5.3). Under anaerobic conditions, black layer formation may occur. Good soil drainage through use of drainage tile is used for carrying away salty water. Tile lines, spaced no more than 20 feet apart, are used on golf greens for this purpose.

Counteracting Excess Soil Sodium with Soil Amendments

Several soil amendments are used to replace sodium in sodic soils in conjunction with leaching to remove salts from the root zone. The amendments counteract sodium by providing calcium either directly (contain calcium) or indirectly (provide acid to dissolve calcium carbonate present in the soil). Calcium arising from the soil amendments reacts with soil sodium to displace it from the cation exchange sites on clay and organic matter particles. The released sodium can then be leached out of the soil profile.

Amendments used for treatment of clay-textured sodic soils include gypsum, sulfur, sulfuric acid, lime sulfur, ferric sulfate, calcium chloride, calcium nitrate, and calcium carbonate.

Because of their expense, calcium chloride and calcium nitrate are not widely used. Sulfuric acid is dangerous to handle and can be corrosive to some types of equipment. Ferric sulfate and lime sulfur also are usually too expensive for practical applications. Ground limestone is effective on acid soils, but its usefulness drops in high pH soils—which includes most sodic soils. Even though gypsum supplies calcium, it is a neutral salt and does not appreciably affect soil pH. Thus for several reasons, gypsum is the material most often used for reclaiming sodic soils.

Gypsum

Gypsum is low-to-moderately soluble in water and supplies soluble calcium to replace sodium. Gypsum, by mass action, drives sodium off the soil exchange complex and replaces it with calcium. It leaves sodium sulfate (Na_2SO_4), which is soluble, and must be removed from the soil profile by leaching.

Gypsum rates required to counteract the effects of sodium can be calculated by two methods: RSC and Eaton's gypsum requirements (EGR). All units are listed meq/L. In general, 1 meq/L calcium is needed per meq/L HCO_3^-.

$$RCS = 234 \, (CO_3^{-2} + HCO_3^-) - (Ca^{+2} + Mg^{+2})$$

$$EGR = 234 \, (a + b + c)$$

$$a = 0.43 \, (Na^+) - (Ca^{+2} + Mg^{+2})$$

$$b = 0.7 \, (CO_3^{-2}) + HCO_3^-$$

$$c = 0.3$$

Results are reports in pounds of 100% pure gypsum needed per acre-foot of water. If a lower grade of gypsum is used, for example 90%, then an extra 10% percent is added to the final value.

In general, on established grass, gypsum is added at rates ranging from 1/2 to 1 lb/1,000 sq ft (24 to 49 kg/ha) and applied monthly when needed. Gypsum, however, should only be applied during mild temperatures (e.g., ≤80°F, 26.7°C). It is slow reacting and does not normally burn foliage. Due to its low water solubility, some time will be required before gypsum will disappear from the soil surface.

Gypsum may also be injected into the irrigation system. Several forms of gypsum are available including natural dihydrate gypsum and the natural anhydrite form. The dihydrate form dissolves quicker because of attached water molecules. The finest grade available should be used.

Sulfur and Other Acid-Forming Amendments

Elemental sulfur and other acid-forming amendments and fertilizers may also be used to provide soluble calcium by lowering soil pH and dissolving calcium carbonate precipitated in the soil. If soil pH is only slightly elevated, routine applications of acid-forming N fertilizers containing or generating ammonium (NH_4^+) may be sufficient to maintain soil pH. Ammonium sulfate is about three times more acidic than other commonly used nitrogen sources and is widely used as a primary nitrogen source where irrigation sources have moderate levels of bicarbonate. However, when irrigation sources have severe bicarbonate problems, elemental sulfur is the most frequently utilized acid-forming amendment. Sulfur is more available and less costly than the other amendments, such as aluminum sulfate. Extreme care should be exercised when using sulfur to lower soil pH. Elemental sulfur has a high potential to burn plant tissue and can lower pH to 3.0 if used unwisely.

Managing Sulfur Applications

Sulfur-oxidizing bacteria are most active in wet, warm, well-aerated soil. No activity occurs when soil temperatures are below 40°F (4.4°C). Sulfur application, therefore, should be limited during cooler fall and winter months. Acidity equal to 3 pounds (1,362 g) of limestone is generated by each 1 pound (454 g) of sulfur.

The acidifying effects of elemental sulfur are slow to move into the soil when sulfur is surface-applied. Therefore, large decreases in pH may occur in the thatch layer and immediate soil surface with little initial impact on soil pH of the root zone. Application rates must be minimal to avoid damage to the crowns of the turfgrass plant. Rates applied to bermudagrass at fairway or rough height may be as high as 5 lb/1,000 sq ft (244 kg/ha), whereas applications to greens should not exceed 0.5 lb/1,000 sq ft (24 kg/ha). Total annual applications should not exceed 10 lb/1,000 sq ft (489 kg/ha) on fairways. Sufficient irrigation water should be applied immediately after each application to wash the sulfur from the turfgrass leaves. Applications are best made when temperatures are warm enough for the bacteria to oxidize the sulfur (70–80°F, 21–26.6°C), but not hot enough to accentuate tissue burn. It is wise to have the soil pH checked before reapplication of sulfur to avoid overacidification. Sulfur application coincident with core aerification minimizes the potential for tissue burn and accelerates the acidification of the root zone.

Figure 5.4. Extensive winter kill (low temperature damage) to bermudagrass fairways. Areas compacted from uncontrolled cart traffic, ridges exposed to winds, low poor draining areas, and shaded areas are most prone to damage.

LOW TEMPERATURE STRESS

Winter turfgrass injury due to low temperature stress on warm-season turfgrasses is commonly referred to as 'winter kill.' The term 'winter kill' in the simplest of terms refers to the loss of turfgrass during the winter or early spring season (Figure 5.4). There are vivid memories of the winters of 1976–77, 1983–84, 1989–90, 1993–94, and 1995–96 where severe losses of warm-season turfgrasses in the southern areas of the United States had superintendents concerned about the proper steps in diagnosing and correcting any turfgrass damage and the appropriate management practices to minimize future losses.

The growth of warm-season turfgrasses slows significantly when the average day-time temperatures decrease to below 60°F (15.6°C) and leaf discoloration (onset of dormancy) begins when temperatures drop below 50°F (10°C). However, warm-season turfgrasses can continue to slowly grow with nighttime temperatures as low as 34°F as long as daytime temperatures increase to near 70°F (21°C). Permanent turfgrass injury to warm-season turfgrasses often occurs if ambient temperatures drop rapidly to below 23°F (–5°C) or drop gradually to below 10°F (12.2°C).

Turfgrass Susceptibility to Low Temperatures

There are several influencing parameters that relate to the susceptibility of warm-season turfgrasses to low temperature stress; however, only a few are controlled by turfgrass managers. Temperature, freeze and thaw frequency, and freeze and thaw rate are outside a turfgrass manager's control. Conversely, several parameters within the control of turfgrass managers include (Table 5.4): (1) degree of shading (Figure 5.5), (2) drainage, (3) fertility, (4) irrigation, (5) mowing, (6) pest control, (7) soil cultivation, (8) thatch level, (9) traffic, and (10) turfgrass selection.

Table 5.4. Parameters associated with turfgrass low temperature kill (modified from McCarty, 2001).

Excessive traffic. Traffic can crush frozen crowns, killing the plant (Figure 5.6). Traffic also reduces soil oxygen levels which weakens the plant, making it more susceptible to low temperature kill. Most often observed on tees, tee and green approaches, and in golf traffic areas in fairways.

Standing water. Poor surface and subsurface drainage results in direct temperature damage to crowns.

Moisture deficiency. Just as excessive moisture may increase low temperature kill, lack of moisture also contributes to injury. A certain amount of moisture is needed in the plant for crown tissue to survive. If moisture deficiency occurs, these tissues are weakened and are more susceptible to damage.

Potassium deficiency. Soil test levels should indicate medium to high levels while leaf tissue analysis should be at least 1.5% K.

Excessive thatch. Excessive thatch elevates crowns and lateral stems above the more insulating soil.

Excessive fall nitrogen fertilization. Late fall nitrogen fertilization promotes succulent green tissue growth and reduced root carbohydrate formation. A 4-1-2 or 3-1-2 ratio of the last fertilization in late summer has shown best results in minimizing low temperature damage.

Excessive desiccation. Excessive wind, especially during periods of low humidity, often can cause massive areas of winter damage (Figure 5.7). If the turf is not covered by snow, managers may have to artificially cover them to minimize the desiccation leading to low temperature kill. In many instances, winter kill is exacerbated by winter desiccation from warm days, low relative humidity, and windy conditions. Cold fronts following such unusual warm conditions dramatically lower the temperature. Without adequate moisture present in turf crowns to help buffer these temperature extremes, plants become very susceptible to winter injury.

Close mowing. Close mowing in late summer discourages deeper rooting and carbohydrate reserve accumulation which can contribute to low temperature kill.

Shade on bermudagrass. Shade reduces the carbohydrate levels in bermudagrass, produces a weaker plant, and keeps soil temperatures lower due to lack of sunlight. Competition from tree roots for nutrients and water also weaken turfgrasses. Slopes facing the north or northeast receive less (or little) direct sunlight in the winter and are more prone to injury.

Grass cultivar. Generally, the common type bermudagrasses are more susceptible to low temperature damage. Cold tolerant cultivars tend to have deeper growing, more dense rhizomes which escape low temperature damage by being better insulated in the deeper soil profiles. Vamont, Midiron, and Quickstand bermudagrasses are cultivars which have increased cold tolerance; however, leaf texture and density of these are less desirable than Tifway or TifSport. Little is currently known about the relative cold tolerance of the new ultra-dwarf cultivars but are assumed to be similar to that of Tifdwarf. The zoysiagrass cultivars—Korean Common, Meyer, Belair, and El Toro—show promise for being more cold tolerant.

Pest or pesticide damage. Pests which damage roots, for example mole crickets and white grubs, and pesticide which may restrict rooting of immature plants (some preemergence herbicides) may add to low temperature damage. Root rotting (*Pythium* spp.) and patch-type diseases (*Rhizoctonia*, *Gaeumannomyces*, and *Leptosphaeria* spp.) also weaken grasses.

Turf Covers. Turf covers may help protect the turfgrass crowns from direct low winter temperatures and desiccation. Snow is probably the best insulator and should remain as long as possible. Covers which use an air layer to insulate the turf from extreme moisture and temperatures are next best. However, turf should not be induced to greenup artificially with covers if temperatures are still likely to drop suddenly. Breathable covers may be helpful when sudden temperature reductions below 25°F (3.9°C) occur.

Diagnosing Low Temperature Injury

Each year, prior to normal turfgrass greenup in the spring, diagnostic measures should be taken by turfgrass managers suspecting possible cold weather injury to determine the extent of turfgrass damage.

Figure 5.5. Bermudagrass winter kill (left) from excessive shade which allowed the soil to remain frozen for extended periods.

Figure 5.6. Damage to frozen ryegrass crowns from unrestricted tire traffic.

Figure 5.7. Bermudagrass winter kill from winds drying out turf crowns prior to the passage of a severe cold front.

Superintendents should anticipate certain areas of turfgrass that may be more susceptible to low temperature injury than other areas. Cultural factors that tend to contribute to low temperature injury and increased susceptibility include poor drainage (soil compaction), excessive thatch, reduced light intensity (shade), north or northeastern facing slopes, excessive fall nitrogen fertilization, and low mowing heights. Any areas that exhibit any one or more of these factors may be more susceptible to low temperature injury.

If any of the aforementioned conditions are present, or have occurred, and low temperature injury is suspected, utilize one of the following methods to determine the severity of the potential damage.

Method One:

1. Remove the individual turfgrass plant crowns near the soil surface.
2. Cut a slice through it with a sharp razor blade or knife.
3. Examine the crown under a 10X magnifying lens. If the tissues of the crown are firm and white in color with turgid cells, the crown should be healthy and the meristematic area has survived the low temperature stress. Crowns that exhibit dark-colored or brownish color with a 'mush' or soft appearance have been injured from the low temperature exposure.

Method Two:

1. Collect representative turfgrass plugs using a cup cutter from suspected low temperature damage areas, such as late planted, shady, or heavy traffic areas, especially areas that tend to be partially shaded.

2. Place or plant these plugs in a suitable container of native soil with drainage holes and properly label the respective plugs and containers.

3. Place the containers in a greenhouse, or in a room beneath a heat lamp or grow light, or as a last resort, in a window facing south.

4. Keep the turfgrass plugs adequately watered.

5. Turfgrass should initiate growth and greening within 7 to 10 days, depending on the growing conditions.

6. Assess the amount of greening after the plugs have been collected for two to three weeks. Suspected areas that exhibit less than 50% greening should be considered extensively damaged from low temperature exposure and will probably require renovation. Lesser damaged areas may recover with proper management practices and extra attention.

7. Repeat the above sampling procedure on a 14- to 21-day interval through the periods of potential cold weather injury.

Proper diagnosis of low temperature injury to warm-season turfgrasses can alleviate the extent of the damage. Take a proactive approach by planning early to reestablish damaged turfgrass areas, and communicate to your membership and/or customers that the action taken now will yield positive results in the future.

Turfgrass samples should be taken during January, February, and March to assay low temperature damage. Assess the amount of turfgrass greening of the samples after a couple of weeks after sampling. Samples that exhibit less than 50% greening should represent areas that are extensively damaged and will probably require renovation.

If initial greenup of the turfgrass in the spring indicates only small areas of turfgrass damage (< 6 inch diameter), then plan to aggressively encourage surrounding turfgrass to grow or fill in these damaged turfgrass areas. Small damaged turfgrass areas on putting greens can be easily repaired by plugging these damaged areas with turfgrass taken with a cup cutter.

For those areas with widespread damage, renovation may be the best and possibly the only alternative. The options for renovation include plugging, sprigging (hand, broadcast, row planting), and sodding. For fairways and roughs, row planting or row sprigging may be the least expensive and best method of renovation. However, approximately six weeks will be required before an adequate stand of bermudagrass will develop. In many instances, turfgrass damage from low temperature stress is most severe on the shoots (leaves and stolons) of the turfgrass plants, and the deeper rooted rhizomes are often healthy and unaffected by the low temperature stress. When soil temperatures reach 75°F (23.9°C) for several consecutive days, these rhizomes will sprout new growth and over time eventually fill in the damaged areas. Therefore, sometimes it may be worthwhile to wait until the soil temperatures warm sufficiently, allowing the growth and development of these deeper rhizomes to occur. In either case, it will be necessary to intensify the management practices and apply additional nitrogen, conduct some form of soil cultivation(s), and irrigate or water to encourage regrowth and/or establishment to occur.

Minimizing Low Temperature Injury

There are few means of preventing low temperature stress from causing damage or injury to turfgrasses; however, there are several management practices that can be implemented that will minimize the probabilities of damage or injury as a result of low temperature stress. Table 5.4 lists and discusses the major means of minimizing low temperature damage.

Documentation

Documentation or record keeping is probably one of the most overlooked aspects of turfgrass management and one of the most important. Historical documentation of factors such as shade patterns, wind movement, and drainage problems can be directly correlated to the risks associated with low temperature stress and turfgrass damage or injury. These factors should be documented for each golf hole and a proactive management plan initiated to improve problem areas. Other maintenance practices should be documented as well, such as irrigation amounts, mowing heights, mowing patterns, rainfall amounts, minimum and maximum temperatures, frost occurrences, length of frost, fertilizer applications, and pesticide applications. All of these and many other factors should be documented in detail and retained for later use if needed.

Frequent Soil Sampling

Soil samples should be taken on a frequent basis until an understanding of the baseline for certain factors is completely documented. Soil samples should be taken and utilized to determine chemical analysis (fertility levels), disease pathogens, nematodes, and physical property analysis (particle size, bulk density, porosity, water infiltration rates). All of the information garnered from these samples could be correlated to low temperature stress tolerance or lack thereof.

There are several other management practices that should be considered to decrease the risk of turfgrass damage or injury as a result of temperature stresses. Mowing heights should be increased in the fall on warm-season turfgrasses prior to the onset of cold to enhance rooting and rhizome growth as well as carbohydrate accumulation. Thatch levels should be monitored and managed with an aggressive soil cultivation and topdressing program. Turfgrass should be scouted on a daily basis for pests and/or other potential problems that may develop. Fertility programs should be based on soil test results for the specific turfgrass species and/or cultivars that are present. Herbicide usage should be limited in the fall and summer to prevent any additional stress to the turfgrasses prior to the onset of temperature stress periods.

GROWTH HORMONES

Unlike mammals, plants lack a nervous system and sensory organs which allow them, among other things, to respond to various environmental stimuli. Plants, however, substitute a nervous system with various growth hormones which are produced in one part of the plant, translocated to other parts, and in low concentrations, cause various growth responses. Growth-promoting hormones include auxins, gibberellins, and cytokinins. Growth-inhibiting hormones include ethylene and abscisic acid (Table 5.5).

Table 5.5. Growth hormones influencing plant growth and development.

Hormone	Examples	Major Growth Influence
Growth Promoters		
Auxins	indole-acetic acid (IAA), phenylacetic acid, naphthalene-acetic acid (NAA), dichlorophenoxy acetic acid (2,4-D)	Stimulates cell elongation, cell division, and cell differentiation. Its presence promotes apical dominance which inhibits lateral bud development, delays leaf senescence and fruit ripening. Produced in meristematic tissue.
Gibberellins	GA_3, GA_4, GA_7, and many others	Promotes cell division and cellular elongation. Produced in plant meristematic tissue in young leaves, developing roots and seeds.
Cytokinins	kinetin and other derivatives of adenine	Stimulates cytokinesis or cell division. Delays plant aging and leaf senescence by delaying chlorophyll and protein degradation. May help plants overcome external stresses. Produced in root tips.
Growth Inhibitors		
Ethylene	ethylene gas	Promotes plant aging and senescence. Inhibits root growth, lateral bud development, and cell elongation. Produced in shoots.
Abscisic acid	ABA	Inhibits coleoptile growth and promotes senescence and abscission. ABA levels increase when plants are exposed to stresses such as drought, flooding, starvation, injury, and salinity. Produced in chloroplasts.

Biostimulants

Biostimulants are materials that promote plant growth when applied in small quantities. Among the application uses of biostimulants, research indicates biostimulants may increase photosynthesis rates, reduce turfgrass senescence, enhance seed germination and root growth, help sod establish faster, and increase salt tolerance and drought resistance after application. They often contain cytokinin as their principal ingredient and tend to help plants withstand harsh environments. They also exhibit other growth regulating actions as found from auxins, gibberellin, and abscisic acid. Seaweed extract (or seaweed kelp) most commonly from the sea kelp species *Ascophyllum nodosum* is a common commercial cytokinin-containing growth material used in turf. A commercially available synthetically produced cytokinin is benzyladenine (or BA).

Products with cytokinin-like properties also are available such as the triazole systemic fungicides—propiconazole, triadimefon, and others. These fungicides inhibit sterol biosynthesis and also cause an increase in ABA synthesis and an inhibition of gibberellin synthesis. Sterols are part of cell membranes and help protect plants and promote growth. When sterol and gibberellin biosynthesis are inhibited, plant ABA levels rise which favor plant stomatal closure, thus an increase in plant water content. Cytokinin levels also tend to decrease when drought stress begins and the ABA level increases, resulting in closed stomata. Further evidence suggests that these triazole fungicides translocate to shoot tips and cause growth reduction of the foliage but not the roots. Therefore, enhanced root development occurs with reduced shoot growth and increased plant water content. In addition, research shows that triazol-treated plants not only inhibit reduced transpiration, increased yields are observed when plants are under moisture stress, senescence is delayed, chlorophyll levels are increased as are carbohydrate levels. These compounds also have protected plants from chilling temperatures, heat stress, and ozone exposure.

The levels of cytokinin in plants regulate, to an extent, the growth response. For example, large applications of cytokinin have been shown to inhibit root formation, but it is known that a small amount of cytokinin is necessary for the formation of rooting. Root growth, therefore, appears to require a certain cytokinin level and a favorable auxin-to-cytokinin ratio.

It appears that the greatest benefit turfgrass has from biostimulant application is when the turf is being grown under a physiological stress. These stresses include cold (or chilling) temperatures, low soil nutrient levels (especially potassium and/or phosphorus), low mowing stress, and periods of rapid growth where these and other resources become limiting. Other possible stresses which may be partially overcome by biostimulant applications include salinity and nematode exposure. Newly planted turfgrasses also may benefit from biostimulant use. If the effects of applied commercial plant growth retardants need reversing, gibberellin-containing biostimulants are beneficial. Several plant growth regulators retard shoot growth through the interference of gibberellin biosynthesis. Cell division and seedhead formation are not greatly influenced, but cell elongation is retarded. The results from using these growth retardants are miniature plants. Examples of gibberellin-inhibiting growth retardants include trinexapac-ethyl (Primo), paclobutrazol (TGR/Trimmit), flurprimidol (Cutless), and fenarimol (Rubigan).

TURF PURPLING

Bermudagrass, when exposed to chilling temperatures in the 50°Fs (10°C) along with high light intensity, may turn a distinctive purple color (Plate 5.2). This is most pronounced in fall just prior to overseeding when an early cool period occurs. Under these conditions, chlorophyll levels are reduced, exposing other purple-colored plant pigments, most notably, the carotenoids and anthocyanins. This phenomenon is similar to deciduous tree leaves turning various shades of orange and yellow in fall with the onset of cooler temperatures where their chlorophyll levels are reduced, exposing these and other plant colored pigments. Tifdwarf bermudagrass is especially sensitive to this fall purpling. Often, this purpling is interpreted as a disease with needless fungicides being applied.

One method of short-term relief from this purpling is the use of plant growth promoters which help retain the chlorophyll, thus preventing expression of the purpling. Commercial formulations of gibberellic acid encourages cell division and elongation to overcome this discoloration. RyzUp (formally, ProGibb) is one commercial gibberellic acid source used just prior to anticipated cool snaps. It should not be used when night temperatures exceed 65°F because turf phytotoxicity may result.

OFF-TYPE GRASSES

In recent years considerable attention has been made toward the occurrence of mutants or off-types of grasses in previously pure bermudagrass stands (Plate 5.3). It is believed that this has arisen from the chance occurrence of mutation of the parent material, expression of a normally recessive gene, or possibly contamination through mechanical means. Mutations are abrupt inheritable changes brought about by alterations in a gene or a chromosome or by an increase in chromosome number. The rate of mutation occurrence can be increased artificially, but the results cannot be controlled. Usually recessive, mutations may be unexpressed for generations.

Mutations are produced by internal disorders, such as inaccurate gene duplication, and by natural external forces, such as severe temperature changes and sunlight radiation. They are induced experimentally by use of atomic radiation, X-rays, chemicals, and sudden temperature changes. Natural mutations appear very infrequently, while artificial ones occur quicker. Tifway II, Tifgreen II, and TifEagle are induced mutations of original grasses by exposing parent material to artificially high levels of radiation. Tifdwarf, FloraDwarf, and Pee Dee 102 bermudagrasses are believed to be natural mutants from Tifgreen bermudagrass. Tifgreen is a first generation hybrid between *Cynodon dactylon* and *C. transvaalensis* and is a completely sterile triploid (2n=27), thus must be propagated vegetatively. Since Tifdwarf is a probable vegetative mutant from Tifgreen bermudagrass, a possibility exists that an original planting of Tifdwarf can undergo another mutation to produce a different grass. Mutations offer breeders new ways of introducing genetic variability into breeding lines but also may cause existing materials to be somewhat unstable, thus may produce undesirable off-types after several years of growth.

A temporary means of masking off-type patches is by the use of the plant growth regulator trinexapac-ethyl (Primo 1EC). Trinexapac applied every three weeks at 3 to 4 oz/acre (0.2 to 0.29 L/ha) provides the illusion that off-types of bermudagrass patches have blended together and only one type of grass is present.

ALGAE

Algae is caused by several organisms including *Nostoc, Oscillatoria, Chlamydomonas, Hantzschia* spp., and others. This is a disease-associated problem. The primary algae are blue-green algae which are actually a type of bacteria called **cyanobacteria**. Depending on their chlorophyll *a* (green pigment), carotenoids (yellow pigments), phycocyanin (blue pigment), or phycoerythrin (red pigment) in their cells, algae can range in color from blue-green to black, brown, yellow, red, and green. Algae are considered primitive plants since they contain chlorophyll. However, they lack roots, stems, and leaves. Algae are most noticeable on close-cut areas such as tees and putting greens.

Algae occurs mostly during warm weather in turf stands that become weak and begin to thin when grown in partially shaded, damp locations. These algae are commonly green or brown in color and can be sheet-like, leaf-like, or cushion-like in appearance. Algae will develop on turf areas where grass is less dense than normal and surface soil moisture is high, resulting in a dark-color "scum" or "mat" forming on the soil surface (Plate 5.4). Black algal scums development often occurs in summer following periods of rainy, overcast, warm days when wet, algal scums feel sticky or rubbery. When dry, a crust that may peel and loosen from the soil may occur. Although erroneously thought to cause algae on golf courses, algae species found in irrigation ponds, lakes, and streams are different species and do not appear to contribute to this problem.

Several agronomic practices or conditions favoring algae dictate its occurrence and severity. Surface water, high light, surface compaction, soil pH and fertility are known contributors to algae development. High surface water, especially on the lower sections of sloping greens, promotes high populations of algae. High levels of sunlight reaching the soil surface also promote algae. Thin areas from excessive mowing heights and/or inadequate fertilization often are the ones most invaded. Although found in shaded areas, this is thought to be from extended surface moisture due to reduced evaporation. Soil compaction and low (or acidic) soils also favor development.

Cultural control begins by correcting those conditions which predispose the turf to algal growth. This involves reducing surface moisture by improving air circulation and light exposure by removing adjacent underbrush and selectively removing trees. Improve drainage and reduce irrigation frequency and amount. Reduce freely available nitrogen at the site. Reduce irrigation and improve growth of the turfgrass where the algae is present so the turf can form a dense area. If the area occupied by algae is large, spiking, verticutting, and topdressing will help to break up and dry the mat and facilitate grass recovery. Applying ground limestone or hydrated lime will help desiccate algae. Diluted bleach, copper sulfate, and chloride also may help reduce algae growth. However, these should not be used during hot temperatures as they may cause varying levels of turf discoloration. Increase the mowing height because low mowing aggravates the problem.

Chemical control includes some fungicides such as mancozeb and chlorothalonil which help to prevent development of algae and prevent its spread when a mat has already formed. They need periodic applications (e.g., every 10 to 14 days) and should be used prior to algae formation. When conditions favor algae growth, high rates of fungicides should be used on a seven-day schedule. Members of the quarternary ammonium chemical group also provide varying controls of certain algae. Control diseases, such as brown patch, to prevent thinning of the turf canopy. In areas with high disease pressure and low turf recuperative potential, such as the transition zone region of the United States, preventative disease control approaches are necessary in the summertime.

MOSS

Moss species include *Selagimella, Byrum, Amblystegium, Brachythecium, Ceratodon, Hypnum, Polytrichum* spp., plus others. *Amblystegium trichopodium* and *Brachythecium* spp. are usually found in higher cut turf and are often referred to as "yard moss." *Byrum argetum* has a silvery appearance, is referred to as silvery thread moss, and is the one found most frequently on greens. Moss are threadlike, branched, primitive plant forms encompassing many species. They are not parasitic and they spread by spores disseminated by wind and water movement. They do not form true roots, but form rhizoids which are filamentous structures that do not provide anchoring. Many mosses are nonvascular plants requiring constant contact with water to prevent drying. Others are able to absorb water through their rhizoids. Mosses are able to photosynthesize and fix nitrogen.

Moss is most noticeable on close-cut areas such as tees and putting greens that are poorly drained (thus remain continuously wet) and heavily shaded. However, moss can rapidly fill a void if thin turf develops, sun or shade. Moss can survive weather extremes in a dormant state or by living symbiotically with blue-green algae. Algae, therefore, can be a precursor to moss encroachment and should be discouraged to prevent moss colonization.

Turf areas in partially shaded, damp locations become weak and begin to thin. Moss begins to predominate in these areas. Moss forms tangled, thick, green mat patches over the soil surface (Plate 5.5). Moss will develop on turf areas where grass is less dense than normal and surface soil moisture is high. Acidic, infertile soils with excessive thatch also favor moss development. If left untreated, these areas will continue to thin out and expand in size until a large mat forms, preventing growth of the grass and penetration of irrigation water. Moss mats typically development in summer following periods of rainy, overcast, warm days.

Cultural control involves a long-term, persistent program combining cultural and chemical control methods, realizing healthy turf is the only means to cure and prevent moss occurrence. Control begins by correcting those conditions which predispose the turf to moss growth. This involves reducing surface moisture by improving air circulation and light exposure by removing adjacent underbrush and selectively removing trees. Improve surface and subsurface drainage and reduce irrigation frequency and amount. Reduce freely available nitrogen at the site. Reduce irrigation and improve growth of the turfgrass where the moss is present so the turf can form a dense area. If the area occupied by moss is large, spiking, verticutting, and topdressing will help to break up and dry the mat. Moss turning orange-brown or golden brown in color indicates positive desiccation is occurring.

Several trends in fertility and moss development have been noted. For example, calcium-rich soil may encourage certain moss species, while moss tends to be discouraged in potassium adequate soils. Ammonium sulfate at 1/10 to 1/8 lb N/1,000 sq ft (4.9 to 6 kg/ha) applied weekly is thought to help desiccate moss and encourage competitive turf growth. Applying ground limestone (75 to 100 lb/1,000 sq ft, 3662 to 4883 kg/ha) or hydrated lime (2 to 3 lb/1,000 sq ft, 98 to 146 kg/ha, in 3 gallons, 11 L, of water) will help desiccate the moss and raise the soil pH level, which favors competitive turf growth. Diluted bleach and dishwashing detergent, chloride, ferrous sulfate at 4 to 7 oz/1,000 sq ft (12.7 to 22 L/ha), granular iron sulfate at up to 3 lb/1,000 sq ft (146 kg/ha), or ferrous ammonium sulfate at 10 oz/1,000 sq ft (31 kg/ha) also may help reduce moss growth. However, these should not be used on greens during hot temperatures, as they may cause varying levels of turf discoloration. Increase the mowing height because low mowing aggravates the problem. Spike or rake the dehydrated moss layer to remove any remaining impervious layer.

Chemical control is erratic and often unsuccessful, especially if agronomic practices are not corrected which favor moss growth and development. Products containing potassium salts of fatty acids (e.g., DeMoss) applied weekly at 2 to 3 oz/1,000 sq ft (6.4 to 9.5 L/ha) or formaldehyde may be used to control moss in turfgrasses. They control moss through a contact mode-of-action but should be carefully used and all label information followed closely. Chlorothalonil, a fungicide, provides good moss control if several conditions are followed. Application rate is 16 lb ai/acre (17.9 kg/ha) (e.g., Daconil Weather Stik at 4 oz/1,000 ft^2, 12.7 L/ha). Three consecutive weekly applications are needed with each applied in 5 gal water per 1,000 ft^2, 20 L/100 m^2). Best results occur when treatments are made above 80°F (26.6°C). The herbicide oxadiazon provides some preemergence control of some moss species.

LOCALIZED DRY SPOTS AND FAIRY RINGS

Fairy rings and localized dry spots (LDS) are caused by a number of basidiomycete fungi, probably *Lycoperdon* spp. There may be other reasons for development of localized dry spots that are not due to fungi such as coating of sand particles by humic substances, initial poor mixing of the greens mix, buried rocks and other debris, and tree roots near the soil surface.

Localized dry spots are most noticeable on close-cut areas such as tees and putting greens, usually during the warmer months of the year. Localized dry spots caused by fungi have been observed primarily on greens less than three to four years old, especially those aggressively topdressed with sand.

Dry spots are several inches to several feet across and often irregularly shaped (Plate 5.6). An affected area will appear drought stressed, despite daily irrigations or rainfall. "Puffball" mushrooms may be present throughout the dry area, but these signs are not always apparent. The fungus has colonized (covered) the sand particles in the root-zone mix. Due to this fungal covering, the sand is now hydrophobic and repels water, despite heavy rainfall or watering. It is believed that as fungi mycelium decomposes, organic substances are released which coat and bind the coarse sand particles so tightly together as to prevent water penetration. A test for hydrophobic soil is simply placing droplets of water along the length of a soil core (Figure 5.8). Hydrophobic soils will not readily allow water penetrations while hydrophilic soils will.

Cultural control begins when the hydrophobic sand is broken up and wetted. This can be accomplished by spiking the dry patch every five to seven days. For a small area, a pitchfork or similar tool will accomplish this task. Irrigate the dry patch by hand several times a day, in addition to any normal irrigation or rainfall. The addition of a wetting agent to the water is also useful. Some programs of prevention by utilizing several applications of certain wetting agents have been successful. The water repelling action of the fungal colonized sand must be eliminated before the grass will recover from the drought stress. Using high pressure water injection cultivation in combination with a wetting agent helps to alleviate symptoms.

No chemical control options currently are registered, although several types of commercial wetting agents are available. Providing consistent and widespread LDS control with commercial wetting agents has been difficult to achieve. This may be related to the various fungi thought to be responsible for LDS. Superintendents should experiment with commercial materials on a nursery or practice green to ensure no turfgrass phyto-

Figure 5.8. Water droplet test to determine if soil underneath a golf green is hydrophobic, causing localized dry spots.

Figure 5.9. Hydraulic fluid damage to a golf green.

toxicity will occur under normal use and that positive control is achieved. Flutolanil as listed for fairy ring control may reduce the severity of localized dry spot.

HYDRAULIC FLUID SPILLS/LEAKS

An inherent problem with most hydraulically driven reel or rotary mowers is eventual leaks from hoses and deteriorating seals (Figure 5.9). These leaks are almost always fatal to the grass. Some recovery may occur if spills are on the first green mowed, since the heat and pressure in the mower has yet to reach lethal status and the area is then immediately flushed with a soap-containing water solution. However, turf damage usually results from later leaks from the physical burn caused by the extremely hot hydraulic fluid and soil residue of the petroleum-based fluid. In such instances, managers strip the damaged sod and underlying soil, replace, regrade, and resod.

Section IV

Pest Management and Control

6 Weed Control and Plant Growth Regulator Use

Weed management is an integrated process where good cultural practices are employed to encourage desirable turfgrass ground cover as well as the intelligent selection and use of herbicides. A successful weed management approach involves the following:

1. Proper weed identification
2. Prevention of weed introduction
3. Proper turfgrass management or cultural practices
4. If necessary, the proper selection, use, and application of a herbicide.

Properly identifying turfgrass weeds in the past has been difficult because many weeds were not included in traditional identification manuals. Weeds included in these manuals were largely targeted for row crop agriculture, hence their pictures were made in nonmowed situations, making it difficult for turf managers to identify these in mowed conditions. The most current and extensive turfgrass weed identification guide is, *Color Atlas of Turfgrass Weeds*. It contains 225 weeds, almost 600 color photographs, and complete descriptions of each weed including its biology, specific identification characteristics, geographical distribution, reproductive means, and control recommendations. This is available through Ann Arbor Press at 1-800-487-2323 or www.sleepingbear press.com. Its ISBN number is 1-57504-142-1.

WEED LIFE CYCLES

1. Annuals. Complete life cycles in one growing season, with reproduction primarily by seeds,
   a. Summer annuals. Annuals that complete their life cycles from spring to fall. Summer annual grasses, as a class, are generally the most troublesome in turf.
   b. Winter annuals. Plants that complete their life cycles from fall to spring.
2. Biennials. Plants that complete their life cycles in two growing seasons.
3. Perennials. Plants that complete their life cycles in three or more years and tend to be the most difficult class of plants to control due to multiple reproductive means they often possess such as seeds, rhizomes, stolons, tubers, nutlets, and bulbs.

Timing of Herbicide Application

Herbicides also are classified as to the time the chemical is applied in respect to turfgrass and/or weed seed germination. Although the majority of herbicides may be classified into one category, atrazine (AAtrex), simazine (Princep), dithiopyr (Dimension), and pronamide (Kerb) are notable exceptions. They are used as both preemergence and postemergence herbicides.

Preplant Herbicides

These are applied before turfgrass is established, usually to provide nonselective, complete control of all present weeds. Soil fumigants, such as metam-sodium (Vapam), methyl bromide (Terrogas, Dowfume, Bromogas, others), and dazomet (Basamid), and nonselective herbicides such as glyphosate (Roundup) may be used as nonselective preplant herbicides.

Preemergence Herbicides

Preemergence (PRE) herbicides are applied to the turfgrass site prior to weed seed germination and form a barrier at, or right below, the soil surface. Most preemergence herbicides prevent cell division during weed-seed germination as the emerging seedling comes into contact with the herbicide. Weeds that already have emerged (visible) at the time of application are not controlled consistently by preemergence herbicides since their primary growing points escape treatment.

Postemergence Herbicides

Postemergence (POST) herbicides are applied directly to emerged weeds. In contrast to preemergence herbicides, this group of herbicides provides little, if any, soil residual control of weeds. A complete chemical weed control program can be accomplished with postemergence herbicides, provided multiple applications are used throughout the year. However, due to the necessity of repeat applications and temporary turfgrass injury, most turfgrass managers use postemergence herbicides in conjunction with a preemergence weed control program. Postemergence herbicides are useful to control perennial grasses and broadleaf weeds that are not controlled by preemergence herbicides. Certain postemergence herbicides also may be used on newly established turfgrasses. Table 6.8 at the end of the chapter cross lists common and trade names of turfgrass herbicides.

Preemergence Herbicides for Bermudagrass Golf Greens

Fewer preemergence herbicides are labeled for golf greens than other turf areas due to the liability associated with these valuable areas. However, several are available for bermudagrass greens (Table 6.1). The user should check the latest herbicide label to ensure these are still available for green use.

Effectiveness of Preemergence Herbicides

The effectiveness of preemergence herbicides varies because of many factors. Included are application timing in relation to weed seed germination, soil types, environ-

Table 6.1. Preemergence herbicides for bermudagrass putting greens (refer to herbicide label for specific turf species and use listing).

Trade Names	Ingredients
Weedgrass Preventer; Betasan	bensulide
Goosegrass/Crabgrass Control	bensulide + oxadiazon
Southern Weedgrass Control	pendimethalin
Dimension	dithiopyr
Devrinol	napronamide
Kerb	pronamide
Rubigan	fenarimol

mental conditions (e.g., rainfall and temperature), target weed species and biotype, and cultural factors (e.g., aerification) that follow application. Preemergence herbicides generally are most effective for annual grass control although some annual small seeded broadleaf weeds also are suppressed. Table 6.2 lists the expected control of common annual grass and several broadleaf weeds for various preemergence herbicides.

Timing of Preemergence Herbicides

An important consideration in using preemergence herbicides is application timing. Most preemergence herbicides act as mitotic inhibitors, meaning they prevent cell division. Since the germinating shoot and root tips are the two major sites of cell division, preemergence herbicides must contact these plant structures in the soil. Application should therefore be timed just prior to weed seed germination since most preemergence herbicides become ineffective on emerged (visible) weeds. If applied too soon prior to weed seed germination, natural herbicide degradation processes may reduce the herbicide concentration in the soil to a level resulting in ineffective or reduced control. If applied too late (e.g., weed seedlings are visible) the weeds may have grown above or its roots grown below the thin layer of preemergence herbicide located at the soil surface, resulting in less effectiveness.

Crabgrass germinates from February through May when soil temperatures at a 4-inch (10 cm) depth reach 53° to 58°F (11.7° to 14.4°C) for a continuous 24-hour period. Alternating dry and wet conditions at the soil surface, as well as light, greatly encourages crabgrass germination. Crabgrass germination often coincides with flowering of early spring plants such as redbuds, pears, and cherry trees, but these may not always be reliable indicators.

Goosegrass germinates when soil temperatures at the 4-inch (10 cm) level reach 60° to 65°F (15.6° to 18.3°C). It also requires light for optimum seed germination and is very competitive in compacted soils. Normally, because of higher temperature requirements for germination, goosegrass germinates two to four weeks later in spring than crabgrass. This often coincides with flowering of later blooming plants such as dogwoods and azaleas. If herbicides are applied at the time for crabgrass control, the material will begin to break down in the soil and goosegrass control will be reduced. Therefore, when developing a goosegrass weed control program delay preemergence spring herbicide applica-

121

Table 6.2. Preemergence herbicide efficacy ratings (refer to herbicide label for specific species and use listing).

Herbicide	Crabgrass	Goosegrass	Annual Bluegrass	Common Chickweed	Henbit	Lawn Burweed	Speedwell spp.	Spurges	Woodsorrel (Oxalis)	FL Pusley	Phyllanthus sp.	Purslane
benefin (Balan)	G-E[1]	F	G-E	G	G	P	P	P	—	—	—	—
benefin+oryzalin (XL)	E	G	G	G	G	—	P	F	F-G	—	—	G
benefin+trifluralin (Team Pro)	F-G	F	G	G	G	—	—	F	F	G	—	—
bensulide (Betasan, PreSan)	G-E	P-F	F	P	P	P	P	—	—	—	—	F
bensulide + oxadiazon	E	G-E	G-E	G	—	—	G	G	—	—	—	—
dithiopyr (Dimension)	E	G-E	G-E	G	G	—	G	P	G	—	—	F
fenarimol (Rubigan)	P	P	G-E	P	P	P	P	G	P	P	—	—
isoxaben (Gallery)	P-F	P	P-F	E	G	E	G-E	F	G	F-G	—	G
metolachlor (Pennant)	F-G	P-F	G	F	—	—	—	F	P	G	P	F
napropamide (Devrinol)	G-E	G	G	E	P	E	E	F-G	G	P	P	G
oryzalin (Surflan)	E	G	G-E	G	G	F	P	F-G	G	P	—	G
oxadiazon + prodiamine	E	G-E	G-E	G	G	G	G	G	G	G	F-G	G
oxadiazon (Ronstar)	G-E	E	G-E	P	P	P	G	G	G	G	F-G	G
pendimethalin (Pre-M)	E	G-E	G-E	E	G	G	G-E	G	G	G	F-G	G
prodiamine (Barricade)	E	G-E	G-E	G	F-G	F-G	F-G	P	G	G	F-G	G
pronamide (Kerb)	P-F	P	G-E	E	E	P	E	P	P	P	—	G
simazine (Princep T&O)	P-F	P	E	E	E	G-E	E	F-G	F	G	—	G

[1] E = Excellent, >89% control; G = Good, 80 to 89% control; F = Fair, 70 to 79% control; P = Poor, <70% control; — = Data not available. These are relative ratings and depend on many factors such as environmental conditions, turfgrass vigor or health, application timing, etc., and are intended only as a guide.

tion three to four weeks before the application date targeted for crabgrass control unless preemergence crabgrass control is also desired. In areas lacking frosts, crabgrass and goosegrass often behave as short-term perennials, germinating year-round and expanding in size over several years.

Annual bluegrass (*Poa annua*) begins to germinate in late summer through early fall when daytime temperatures consistently drop into the mid-70°s F (21°C). Typically, a second major flush of annual bluegrass germination occurs in early winter (December 15–January 15) when days are bright, air temperatures are in the 60°s F (15.6°C), and night temperatures are cold (<35°F, 1.7°C). Thin turf areas and excessively wet areas generally have earliest Poa germination.

Sequential or Repeat Applications

Repeat applications of preemergence herbicides are generally necessary for full season control for crabgrass, goosegrass, and annual bluegrass. Most herbicides begin to degrade soon after application when exposed to the environment. Usually, the level of degradation that occurs from six to 16 weeks after application reduces the herbicide concentration to the point that poor control of later germinating weed seeds, such as goosegrass, occurs. Repeat applications, therefore, are necessary between 60 to 75 days after the initial use for season-long preemergence weed control. Note: On those areas to be established with turf, most preemergence herbicides should not be used two to four months prior to seeding or overseeding. Severe root damage and reduced turfgrass seed germination may result.

Core Aerification and Preemergence Herbicides

Core aeration has not traditionally been practiced following a preemergence herbicide application. This procedure was believed to disrupt the herbicide barrier in the soil and thus allow weed germination. Research, however, indicates that core aerification immediately prior to or one, two, three, or four months after applications of many preemergence herbicides does not stimulate large crabgrass emergence. Heavy verticutting, however, especially following aerification, may disrupt the herbicide barrier, allowing weed seed germination.

POSTEMERGENCE WEED CONTROL

Postemergence herbicides are generally effective only on those weeds which have germinated and are visible. Timing of application should be when weeds are young (two to four leaf stage) (Figure 6.1) and actively growing. At this stage, herbicide uptake and translocation is favored, and turfgrasses are better able to fill in voids left by the dying weeds. Turfgrass species' tolerance to postemergence herbicides are listed in Tables 6.3 and 6.4.

Figure 6.1. Young weeds (one to five leaf stage) are easiest and cheapest to control. Waiting until weeds are more mature requires multiple applications for control, increasing costs and the potential of turf injury. Shown are young goosegrass plants in a bermudagrass golf green

Broadleaf Weed Control

Broadleaf weeds in turf have traditionally been controlled with members of the phenoxy herbicide family (e.g., 2,4-D, dichlorprop, MCPA, and mecoprop) and benzoic acid herbicide family (e.g., dicamba) (Table 6.8). All are selective, systemic foliar-applied herbicides. Only a very few broadleaf weeds, especially perennials, are controlled with just one of these materials. Usually, two- or three-way combinations of these herbicides and possible repeat applications are necessary for satisfactory weed control. Various MCPP formulations also are available. Sequential applications should be spaced 10 to 14 days apart and only healthy-growing, nonstress turf should be treated.

Until recently, these various herbicide combinations were the main chemicals for broadleaf weed control. Clopyralid (Lontrel), triclopyr (Turflon), and various combinations with other herbicides have been introduced as alternatives to phenoxy herbicides for broadleaf weed control.

Triclopyr belongs to the Picolinic Acid herbicide family. Compounds in this family are noted for their high degree of activity. These herbicides are up to ten times more potent than 2,4-D on certain broadleaf weed species. They are rapidly absorbed by the roots and foliage of broadleaf plants, and are readily translocated throughout the plants via both xylem and phloem tissues. Problems with this herbicide family include its soil mobility and the extreme sensitivity to it by many ornamentals and most warm-season turfgrasses. Turflon also helps suppress kikuyugrass in bermudagrass. Clopyralid (Lontrel) also is one of the newer members of this herbicide family. It is currently marketed in a mixture with triclopyr (Confront) for use on labeled cool- and warm-season turfgrasses. Lontrel is noted for its high activity on leguminous (nitrogen fixing) plants such as clover, vetch, kudzu, and lespedeza (Table 6.5).

Table 6.3. Established turfgrass tolerance to postemergence broadleaf herbicides (refer to herbicide label for specific species listing).

Herbicides	Bentgrass Greens	Bentgrass Fairways	Ryegrass	Tall Fescue	Fine Fescue	Kentucky Bluegrass	Buffalograss	Seashore Paspalum
Broadleaf Weed Control								
atrazine (Aatrex)	NR	NR	NR	NR	NR	NR	NR	NR
bentazon (Basagran T&O)	NR-I	I	S	S	S	S	S	S-NR
bromoxynil (Buctril)	NR	NR	S	S	S	S	NR	NR
carfentrazone+2,4-D+MCPP+dicamba (Speed Zone North)	NR	S	S	S	S	S	NR	NR
carfentrazone+MCPA+MCPP+dicamba (Power Zone)	NR	NR	S	S	S	S	NR	NR
carfentrazone+2,4-D+MCPP+dicamba (Speed Zone St. Augustinegrass)	NR	S	S	S	S	S	S	S
chlorsulfuron (Corsair, TFC)	NR	–	NR	NR	I-S	S	NR	S
clopyralid (Lontrel)	NR	–	S	S	S	S	S	NR
2,4-D	I^a	NR	S	S	S	S	–	S
MCPP (mecoprop)	S	–	S	S	S	S	–	S
dicamba (Vanquish)	–	–	S	S	S	S	I-NR	NR
2,4-D + dicamba	–	–	S	S	S	S	NR	S
2,4-D + dichlorprop (2,4-DP)	–	–	S	S	S	S	S	S
2,4-D + MCPP	–	–	S	S	S	S	NR	NR
2,4-D + triclopyr (Turflon)	NR-I	NR	S	S	–	S	NR	NR
2,4-D + MCPP + dicamba	–	–	S	S	S	S	I-NR	NR
2,4-D + MCPP + 2,4-DP	–	–	S	S	S	S	NR	NR
MCPA + MCPP + 2,4-DP	–	–	S	S	S	S	NR	NR
MCPA + triclopyr + clopyralid	S	S	S	S	S	S	S	NR
halosulfuron (Manage)	NR	–	NR	NR	S	S	NR	S
imazaquin (Image)	NR	NR	NR	NR	NR	NR	S-NR	NR
metsulfuron (Manor)	NR	NR	NR	NR	–	–	S	NR
simazine (Princep T&O)	NR	NR	NR	NR	NR	NR	S	NR
triclopyr (Turflon)	NR	NR	S	S	S	S	NR	NR
triclopyr + clopyralid (Confront)	NR	–	S	S	–	S	S	NR

Table 6.3. (Continued)

Herbicides	Bahia-grass	Bermuda-grass	Carpet-grass	Centipede-grass	St. Augustine-grass	Zoysia-grass	Overseeded Ryegrass/Blends
Broadleaf Weed Control							
atrazine (Aatrex)	NR[a]	S-I(D)	I[b]	S	S	I	NR
bentazon (Basagran T&O)	S	S	S	S	S	S	S-I
bromoxynil (Buctril)	S	S	S	S	S	S	S
carfentrazone+2,4-D+MCPP+dicamba (Speed Zone North)	NR	S	NR	NR	NR	S	S
carfentrazone+MCPA+MCPP+dicamba (Power Zone)	NR	S	NR	NR	NR	S	S
carfentrazone+2,4-D+MCPP+dicamba (Speed Zone St. Augustinegrass)	S	S	NR	S	S	S	S
chlorsulfuron (Corsair, TFC)	I	S	I	I	I	I	NR
clopyralid (Lontrel)	S	S	S	S	S	S	S
2,4-D	S	S	—	S-I	—	S	S-I
MCPP (mecoprop)	S	S	—	—	—	S	—
dicamba (Vanquish)	S	S	—	—	—	S	—
2,4-D + dicamba	S	S	—	—	—	S	S-I

2,4-D + dichlorprop (2,4-DP)	S	—	—	—	S	S
2,4-D + MCPP	S	—	—	—	S	S
2,4-D + triclopyr (Turflon)	NR	NR	NR	NR	NR	NR
2,4-D + MCPP + dicamba	S	—	—	—	S	S
2,4-D + MCPP + 2,4-DP	S	—	—	—	S	S
MCPA + MCPP + 2,4-DP	S	—	—	—	—	S
MCPA + triclopyr + clopyralid	S	S	S	S	S	S
halosulfuron (Manage)	S	—	S	S	S	S
imazaquin (Image)	NR	—	S	S	S-I	NR
metsulfuron (Manor)	NR	—	S	S	S	NR
simazine (Princep T&O)	NR	—	S-I	S-I	S-I(D)	NR
triclopyr (Turflon)	NR	NR	NR	NR	NR	NR
triclopyr + clopyralid (Confront)	—	NR	S	S	—	S

[a] S=Safe at labeled rates; I=Intermediate safety, use at reduced rates; NR=Not Registered for use on and/or damages this turfgrass; D=Dormant turf only.

[b] Carpetgrass tolerance to herbicides listed has not fully been explored.

These are relative rankings and depend on factors such as environmental conditions, turfgrass vigor or health, application timing, etc., and are intended only as a guide.

Table 6.4. Established turfgrass tolerance to postemergence grass herbicides (refer to herbicide label for specific species listing).

Herbicides	Bentgrass Greens	Bentgrass Fairways	Ryegrass	Tall Fescue	Fine Fescue	Kentucky Bluegrass	Buffalograss	Seashore Paspalum
Grass Weed Control								
asulam (Asulox)[a]	NR[b]	NR	NR	NR	NR	NR	I-NR	NR
clethodim (Envoy)	NR	NR	NR	NR	NR	NR	NR	NR
diclofop (Illoxan)	NR	NR	NR	NR	NR	NR	S-NR	NR
DSMA, MSMA, CMA	NR-I	I	S-I	I	I	I	I	NR
ethofumesate (Prograss)[c]	NR-I	I	S	S	I	S	NR	S-NR
fenoxaprop (Acclaim Extra)	NR-I	I	S	S	S	S	NR	NR
fluazifop (Fusilade II)	NR	NR	NR	S-I	NR	NR	NR	NR
metribuzin (Sencor Turf)	NR	NR	NR	NR	NR	NR	NR	NR
pronamide (Kerb)	NR	NR	NR	NR	NR	NR	NR	S-NR
sethoxydim (Vantage)	NR	NR	NR	NR	S	NR	NR	NR
quinclorac (Drive)	NR	I	S	S	I	S	S	S-NR

Herbicides	Bahia-grass	Bermuda-grass	Carpet-grass	Centipede-grass	St. Augustine-grass	Zoysia-grass	Overseeded Ryegrass/Blends
Grass Weed Control							
asulam (Asulox)	NR	S-I	NR	NR	S-I	I-NR	NR
clethodim (Envoy)	NR	NR	NR	S	NR	NR	NR
diclofop (Illoxan)	NR	S	NR	NR	NR	NR	NR
DSMA, MSMA, CMA	NR	S-I	NR	NR	NR	S-I	NR
ethofumesate (Prograss)c	NR	D	NR	NR	NR	NR	I
fenoxaprop (Acclaim Extra)	I-NR	I-NR	NR	NR	NR	I	I
fluazifop (Fusilade II)	NR	NR	NR	NR	NR	I	NR
metribuzin (Sencor Turf)	NR	S-I	NR	NR	NR	NR	NR
pronamide (Kerb)	S	S	NR	S	S	S	NR
sethoxydim (Vantage)	NR	NR	NR	S	NR	NR	NR
quinclorac (Drive)	NR	S-I	NR	NR	NR	S	S

a Asulam is labeled for 'Tifway' (419) Bermudagrass and St. Augustinegrass.

b S=Safe at labeled rates; I=Intermediate safety, use at reduced rates; NR=Not Registered for use on and/or damages this turfgrass; D=Dormant turf only.

c Ethofumesate is labeled for use on dormant bermudagrass overseeded with perennial ryegrass.

These are relative rankings and depend on factors such as environmental conditions, turfgrass vigor or health, application timing, etc., and are intended only as a guide.

Table 6.5. Expected control of broadleaf weeds with turf herbicides (consult specific herbicide label for weed species listing).

Weed	Life cycle	Atrazine/Simazine	2,4-D	MCPP	Dicamba	2,4-D + MCPP	2,4-D + 2,4-DP	2,4-D + MCPP + dicamba	Bentazon	Bromoxynil	Chlorsulfuron	Clopyralid	Imazaquin	Metsulfuron	Triclopyr	2,4-D + triclopyr	Triclopyr + clopyralid	MCPA + triclopyr + clopyralid	Quinclorac
Aster	P[a]	—	G	—	—	F	G	F	P	P	—	G	—	G	—	F	G	G	—
Bedstraw, smooth	P	G[b]	P	P-F	G	F	F	G	—	—	G	—	—	P	F-G	G	G	G	—
Beggar-ticks	A	F-G	G	F	G	—	F	G	G	—	—	—	—	—	—	G	G	G	—
Betony, Florida	P	—	E	F	F	—	F	F-G	P	—	—	—	—	G	G	G	G	—	—
Bittercress, hairy	WA	—	E	G	E	E	E	E	—	P	—	—	G	E	G	—	—	G	—
Bindweed, field	P	—	F-P	E	G	E-F	G	E	P-F	—	F	—	—	G	G	G	—	—	E
Burclover	A	F	G	F	F-G	E-F	E	E-F	—	P	G	G	G	G	F	—	E	G	—
Buttercups	WA,B&P	—	F	P-F	F	E	E	E	P	P	F	G	—	E	—	G	G	G	—
Buttonweed, Virginia	P	E	G	F	E	F	E-F	E	P	P	—	F	—	P	G	F-P	—	G	—
Carpetweed	SA	E	G	—	E	G	E	E	—	—	G	—	—	E	—	G	G	G	—
Carrot, wild	A,B	—	E-F	G	—	E	P-F	E	—	—	—	—	—	—	G	F	E	E	—
Catsear	P	E	—	E	G	—	E	E	—	—	G	—	—	E	—	G	—	E	—
Chamberbitter	SA,P	E	G	E-F	G	—	—	—	F-G	P	—	P	—	—	—	—	—	—	—
Chickweed, common	WA	E	G	G	G	E	E	E	P	P	G	—	G	E	P-F	E	E	E	—
Chickweed, mouse-ear	WA,P	F	G	G	G	E	E	E	—	—	G	—	G	E	G	E-F	E	E	—
Chicory	P	—	E-F	G	E-F	E-F	E	E	—	—	F	G	—	E	—	G	E	G	—
Chiquefoil, common	P	—	G	—	G	E-F	E-F	E-F	—	—	G	G	—	—	—	—	—	—	E
Clover, crimson	SA	—	G	G	G	E	E	E	—	G	G	G	—	F	F-G	—	E	E	E
Clover, hop	WA	E	F-G	F	G	E	E	E	P	P	G	F	G	E	—	E	E	E	E
Clover, white	P	G-E	G-E	G	E	E	E	E	—	—	—	—	G	F	—	E-F	E	E	E
Cudweed	WA	—	G-E	F	G	G-E	G-E	E-F	G	G	—	F	—	E	F-G	G-E	G-E	G	—
Daisy, English	P	E-F	F	F	F	G	G-E	F-G	P	—	—	—	—	—	—	G	G-E	G	—
Daisy, oxeye	P,B	G-E	G	G	G	F	F	F-G	—	P	G	F	—	—	—	—	G	—	—
Dandelion	P	G-E	F	—	F	F-G	E	F-G	G	—	—	—	F	E	G	F-E	E	G	F-G
Dayflower, spreading	SA	E-F	G	F-G	G	F-G	F-G	F-G	—	—	—	—	P-F	P-F	—	F-E	—	G	P
Deadnettle, purple	WA	G-E	F	F	F	F	E	F-G	G	—	—	—	G	—	G	F-G	F	—	G
Dichondra	P	E-F	E	F	E-F	E	E	F-G	—	P	G	—	—	—	—	—	E	—	E

Weed	Life cycle
Dock, broadleaf & curly	P
Dog fennel	P
Doveweed	SA
Evening primrose, cutleaf	WA
Falsedandelion, Carolina	WA,B
Filaree, redstem	WA
Garlic, wild	P
Geranium, Carolina	WA
Groundsel	WA
Hawkweed	P
Healall	P
Henbit	WA
Horseweed	WA,SA
Ivy, ground	P
Knawel	WA
Knotweed, prostrate	SA
Kochia	SA
Lambsquarters	SA
Lespedeza	SA
Mallow	P
Medic, black	A
Moneywort	P
Mugwort	P
Mustard, wild	WA
Nettle, stinging	P
Onion, wild	P
Parsely-piert	WA
Pearlwort	WA
Pennywort (dollarweed)	P
Pepperweed, Virginia	WA
Pigweed	SA
Pineapple-weed	WA,SA
Plantains	P
Purslane, common	SA
Pusley, Florida	SA
Ragweed, common	SA
Rocket, yellow	WA,B
Shepherd's purse	WA

Table 6.5. (Continued)

Weed	Life cycle[a]	Atrazine/Simazine	2,4-D	MCPP	Dicamba	2,4-D + MCPP	2,4-D + 2,4-DP	2,4-D + MCPP + dicamba	Bentazon	Bromoxynil	Chlorsulfuron	Clopyralid	Imazaquin	Metsulfuron	Triclopyr	2,4-D + triclopyr	Triclopyr + clopyralid	MCPA + triclopyr + clopyralid	Quinclorac
Sida	A	—	—	—	—	—	—	F-G	G	—	—	—	—	G	—	—	—	G	—
Smartweed	SA	G	G	—	G	—	G	G	G	G	G	G	G	G	G	G	F-G	G	—
Sorrel, red	P	—	G	E	G	G	F	G	G	G	—	G	G	G	F-G	—	E	G	—
Speedwell, common	WA	F	F	F	F-P	G	G	G	P	—	G	G	F	G-E	F-G	G	F-G	G	E
Speedwell, corn	P	E	F-P	F	F-P	G	G	G	P	G	—	G	—	—	F-G	G	F-G	G	—
Speedwell, germander	WA	F	P	F	P	G	G	G	P	—	—	G	—	—	F-G	G	F-G	G	—
Speedwell, purslane	WA	F	—	F	—	G	G	G	P	—	—	G	—	—	F-G	G	F-G	G	E
Speedwell, thymeleaf	P	F	P-F	F	P	F	F	G	P	P	—	G	—	—	F-G	E-F	E-F	G	G
Spurge, prostrate	SA	E-F	F	G	G	G	F	G	P	—	—	—	—	E	F-G	F	E-F	G	G
Spurge, spotted	SA	E	F-P	G	G	G	F	G	P	P	—	—	—	E	F-G	F	E-F	G	G
Spurry, corn	P	F	F	G	F-G	F	F	G	P	—	—	—	—	—	F-G	E-F	F	G	—
Spurweed (lawn burweed)	WA	F-G	P	E-F	E	E-F	F	E	E	F-G	—	—	—	G-E	F-G	E	E	G	—
Strawberry, Indian mock	P	—	F	F	E-F	F	P	E-F	—	F-G	—	—	—	—	—	—	—	—	G
Thistles	B,P	P	G	G	G	E-F	E-F	E	G	G	F	G	G	G	G	G	G	G	G
Vetch, common	WA,SA	E	G	G	G	G	F	G	—	—	—	G	G	E	F	F	E	G	G
Violet, Johnny-jumpup	WA	—	F-P	F-P	E-F	F-P	F-P	F-P	P	P	—	—	P-F	—	F	F	F-G	F-G	F-G
Violet, wild	WA	—	F-P	F-P	E-F	F-P	F-P	F-P	P	P	F	—	P-F	—	F	F	F-G	F-G	F-G
Woodsorrel, creeping	P	F	P	P	G	P-F	P-F	P-F	P	P-F	—	P	—	F-G	F-G	F-G	E-F	—	—
Woodsorrel, yellow	P	F	P	P	G	P-F	F-P	E-F	P	P-F	G	P	—	E-F	F-G	—	E-F	—	—
Yarrow	P	—	F	F	E	G	G	E-F	G	G	G	—	—	E-F	F-G	G	—	G	—

[a] A = annual; B = biennial; P = perennial; SA = summer annual; WA = winter annual.

[b] E = excellent (>89%) control; F = fair to good (70 to 89%), good control sometimes with high rates, however, a repeat treatment 1 to 3 weeks later, each at the standard or reduced rate is usually more effective, especially on perennial weeds; P = poor (<70%) control in most cases. Not all weeds have been tested for susceptibility to each herbicide listed.

Chlorsulfuron (Corsair, TFC 75DF), a sulfonylurea herbicide, is labeled for selective broadleaf weeds and tall fescue control in certain cool-season turfgrasses. Bermudagrass is a warm-season grass tolerant to this material. Rates range from 1 to 5 oz product per acre (3 to 15 kg/ha), depending on the weed species present. Table 6.5 lists the effectiveness of commonly used postemergence herbicides for broadleaf weed control.

Grass Weed Control

Traditionally, for bermudagrass, postemergence grass weed control was achieved with single and repeat applications of the organic arsenicals (e.g., MSMA, DSMA, CMA). Two to four applications spaced seven days apart generally are required for complete control, especially with perennial grassy weed species. The rate and number of applications necessary for weed control usually increases as weeds mature (Plate 6.1). On cool-season turfgrasses and zoysiagrass, organic arsenicals can be very phytotoxic, especially when used during high temperatures (>90°F, 32°C). Control also is reduced if rainfall occurs within 24 hours of treatment. Recently, new herbicide releases have provided alternatives to the arsenicals for postemergence grass weed control (Table 6.6). Decreased phytotoxicity as well as reduced number of applications are often associated with these herbicides.

Postemergence control of crabgrass species and goosegrass has traditionally been with organic arsenicals (e.g., MSMA/DSMA). As previously mentioned, repeat applications with a short time interval between applications (five to seven days) are required especially for goosegrass, dallisgrass, or bahiagrass control. Increasing phytotoxicity usually results for bermudagrass and zoysiagrass with repeat applications at higher temperatures.

In order to increase herbicidal activity on goosegrass, various combinations with other herbicides are used with the organic arsenicals. High rates of metribuzin (Sencor Turf), an asymmetrical triazine, gives excellent control of goosegrass, but bermudagrass has marginal tolerance. Lower rates of metribuzin combined with arsenical herbicides provide good to excellent goosegrass control. However, this combination should only be used on well-established bermudagrass that is actively growing and also is maintained at mowing heights greater than 1/2-inch (1.3 cm). The use of metribuzin with MSMA or DSMA increases activity on goosegrass but a certain degree of phytotoxicity and a number of escaped weeds may still occur.

Diclofop-methyl (Illoxan), a member of the aryl-oxy-phenoxy herbicide family, controls goosegrass with good turf tolerance. Little damage to bermudagrass, including putting greens, occurs and repeat applications are not usually necessary. This herbicide is most active on younger, lower mowed goosegrass. Weed control is relatively slow, often requiring two to three weeks to occur. The weed control spectrum also appears to be limited, with goosegrass and ryegrass being the most susceptible grass species. Treated areas should not be overseeded with perennial ryegrass for at least six weeks after herbicide application. Diclofop also should not be mixed with any other postemergence herbicides, especially 2,4-D or MSMA as reduced goosegrass control and increased turfgrass phytotoxicity may result. An exception involves controlling mature, clump-forming plants. Mature (clumping) goosegrass plants are poorly controlled with Illoxan. In these instances, scalp (close mow) mature plants, allow several days regrowth, and then use the

Table 6.6. Guide to grass weed control with postemergence turfgrass herbicides (refer to herbicide label for specific species listing).

Herbicide[a]	Crabgrass	Goosegrass	Annual Bluegrass	Sandspur	Dallisgrass	Thin (Bull) Paspalum	Ryegrass	Smutgrass	Bahiagrass	Carpetgrass	Tall Fescue	Bermudagrass	Quackgrass
atrazine (Aatrex)	P-F[b]	P	G-E	F	P	P	G-E	F-G	F	P	F	P-F	—[c]
asulam (Asulox)	G	F	P	F	P	P-F	—	F	P	G	G	P	—
chlorsulfuron (Corsair, TFC)	P	P	P	P	P	P	G	F	P	P	G	P	G
clethodim (Envoy)	E	G-E	G	G	—	—	G-E	—	—	—	P	G	G
diclofop (Illoxan)	P	G-E	P	P	—	P	G	—	P	G	P	G	—
DSMA, MSMA	G	F	P	G	F	F-G	P	P	F	G	P	P	—
ethofumesate (Prograss)	P	P	F-G[d]	P	P	P	P	P	P	—	P	P-G	—
fenoxaprop (Acclaim Extra)	G-E	G-E	P	G	P	P	P	P	G	—	P	F-G	—
fluazifop (Fusilade II)	G-E	G	F	G	P	P	G-E	P	G	—	P	G	G
metribuzin (Sencor)	F-G	G-E	G	—	F	P	F	P	P	—	F	P	—
metsulfuron (Manor)	P	P	P	P	P	P	G	P	G	P	F	P	F
pronamide (Kerb)	P	P	G-E	P	P	P	G-E	P	P	P	G	P	F
sethoxydim (Vantage)	G-E	G	P	G	P-F	P	P	P	G	—	P	F-G	G
simazine (Princep T&O)	P-F	P	G-E	P-F	P	P	G-E	F	F	P	F	P-F	—
quinclorac (Drive)	E	P	P	—	F	P	P	P	P	P	F	P	—

[a] Repeat applications usually 5 to 14 days apart are needed for most herbicides and weeds. This is especially true as weeds mature, producing flowers and seedheads.

[b] E = excellent (>90%) control with one application; G = good (80 to 90%) control with one application; F = Fair to good (70 to 89%) control sometimes with high rates, however a repeat treatment 1 to 3 weeks later each at the standard or reduced rate is usually more effective; P = poor (<70%) control in most cases.

[c] — = Control unknown as all weeds have not been tested for susceptibility to each herbicide listed.

[d] Ethofumesate provides good to excellent control of most true annual biotypes of annual bluegrass but only poor to fair control of perennial biotypes.

herbicide. The other option involves tank mixing diclofop with metribuzin (Sencor 75DF) at 1/4 to 1/2 lb/a (0.28 to 0.56 kg/ha). Again, use on smaller plants when possible. Expect turf phytotoxicity for 7 to 21 days following this combination treatment. Turf managers often spot-treat goosegrass in an effort to save money. Although effective, a certain level of turf discoloration can be expected from this (Plate 6.2).

Quinclorac (Drive), a quinolinecarboxylic acid herbicide family member, provides postemergence crabgrass, signalgrass, barnyardgrass and foxtail control in bermudagrass and zoysiagrass. Drive also controls some broadleaf weeds such as pennywort, speed-wells, dandelion, and black medic. With repeat applications about three weeks apart, Drive suppresses torpedograss and kikuyugrass. Drive, however, has little goosegrass and dallisgrass activity, or activity on other *Paspalum* species. Avoid drift onto ornamentals.

SPECIAL WEED MANAGEMENT SITUATIONS

Poa annua Control

Annual bluegrass (*Poa annua* L.) is the most troublesome winter annual grass weed on bermudagrass golf courses (Plate 4.6). Its low growth habit and unique ability to thrive in moist, compacted areas makes it difficult to control with management practices alone. Annual bluegrass has a lighter green color than most grass species used to overseed golf greens, and produces numerous seedheads that disrupt the playing surface. Also, due to low heat tolerance, annual bluegrass quickly dies in warm weather, leaving areas bare until the bermudagrass has time to fill in.

Chemical control of annual bluegrass is difficult to achieve due to: (1) inability of most preemergence herbicides to prevent annual bluegrass germination selectively while allowing desirable overseeded grass to become established, and (2) most postemergence herbicides effective on annual bluegrass also damage the desirable overseeded grass species.

In recent years, annual bluegrass has quickly reached epidemic proportions for many golf courses. Reasons for this are numerous: (a) a variety of true annual and various perennial biotypes are present; (b) the switch of many golf courses to the similar *Poa trivialis* for overseeding greens reduces selective herbicide options; (c) increased overseeding of fairways generally increases golf course *Poa annua* populations; and (d) the occurrence of herbicide resistant plants have increased the incidence of Poa and continues to mount frustration for members and superintendents alike. Current resistance involves members of the dinitroaniline (DNA) and triazine (atrazine, simazine) herbicide families.

Control Options

The following discusses various Poa control options on golf courses. These include using selective and nonselective herbicides and plant growth retardants.

Ten Step Plan to Control *Poa annua* in Golf Greens

1. Fumigate all soil mix before planting.
2. Begin with and retain good drainage to prevent soil compaction and excessive soil moisture which favors Poa.
3. Use certified seed, sprigs, or sod free of Poa when planting.
4. Obtain and maintain good turf density to reduce Poa invasion.
5. Aerify consistently to relieve soil compaction. Soil compaction favors Poa.
6. Use fumigated sand/soil when topdressing or repairing damaged turf.
7. Use preemergence herbicides in spring and early winter.
8. Use PGRs in spring and fall to reduce Poa competition and seedhead development.
9. Hand pick or wick nonselective herbicide (e.g., glyphosate) on small (e.g., 1-inch, 2.5 cm, diameter) Poa plants.
10. Plug larger spots with Poa-free turf.

Preemergence Control

Preemergence annual bluegrass control is currently achieved with several herbicides. Each has its own precautions before use, and if these are not followed, unsatisfactory results may occur.

Pronamide (Kerb 50WP). Pronamide must be applied before annual bluegrass germination and planting of overseeding grass (Figure 4.6). Sixty days is the minimum recommended period between application and overseeding. A 1 to 2 lb/a (1.1 to 2.2 kg/ha) application rate of actual product is used.

Superintendents who have to apply pronamide closer than 60 days before overseeding can offset the problems of reduced ryegrass seed germination by applying a thin layer of charcoal. The charcoal will bind the pronamide and reduce the chances of it damaging the overseeded ryegrass. However, the mess and dark color associated with charcoal applications and the risk of it not working must be considered before use. Activated charcoal should be applied at two to four pounds per 1,000 sq ft (98 to 195 kg/ha) and reseeding should be no sooner than seven days following charcoal use.

Fenarimol (Rubigan 1AS). Fenarimol is currently the standard product for preemergence Poa control in overseeded bermudagrass greens. Rubigan is actually a systemic fungicide used to control several turfgrass diseases, that also gradually reduces annual bluegrass populations without adverse effects to overseeded grasses or to bermudagrass. Application should occur before overseeding and germination of annual bluegrass. A treatment scheme consists of two (6 oz/1,000 ft^2 each, 19 kg/ha) or three (4 oz/1,000 ft^2 each, 12.7 kg/ha) sequential treatments, with the final application being two weeks before overseeding with perennial ryegrass or four weeks prior to overseeding with *Poa trivialis* or bentgrass. A follow-up application of 2 oz/1,000 ft^2 (6.4 kg/ha) in early January may be necessary for heavy *Poa annua* populated greens. For the 50 WSP Rubigan formulation, two 1.5 oz or three 1 oz applications should be made per 1,000 sq ft (4.6 or 3.1 kg/ha) and spaced as discussed for the 1 AS formulation. The total should not exceed 3 oz/1,000 sq ft (9.2 kg/ha). Unlike Kerb, Rubigan does not appear to affect either overseeded perennial ryegrass or bermudagrass, but the necessity of properly timed repeat application can be a drawback for those with limited budgets and labor. Also, if *Poa trivialis* or creeping bentgrass is used for overseeding, the last fenarimol application should be at least 30 days before overseeding or a delay in seed germination can occur. Poa control should not be expected to exceed 95%.

Bensulide (Betasan, Pre-San). Bensulide also provides varying preemergence annual bluegrass control and an acceptable stand of ryegrasses is obtainable when seeding is delayed four months after herbicide application. This could, however, be influenced by environment and management practices. The ryegrass tolerance range is narrow. Current label directions indicate that 100 lb per acre (112 kg/ha) of the 12.5G formulation or 2.5 gallons of the 4L formulation should be applied (12 lb ai/A, 14 kg/ha) per acre (23.4 L/ha). This four-month waiting period allows enough bensulide to be in the soil to control the Poa but also be low enough to not interfere with germination of the overseeded grass. If the treated area needs to be seeded sooner than four months after application, powdered, activated charcoal can be used to deactivate the bensulide as discussed previously. The turf should be irrigated immediately after application to wash the charcoal into the soil. Reseeding should occur no sooner than seven days after applying the charcoal.

Benefin (Balan 2.5G). Benefin also may be used at 115 to 120 lb/a (129 to 134 kg/ha) in areas to be overseeded with ryegrass for preemergence annual bluegrass control. A minimum waiting period of 45 days must be observed between the 115 lb/a (129 kg/ha) benefin application and ryegrass overseeding while 12 to 16 weeks are necessary for the 120 lb/a rate (134 kg/ha). This use of benefin is recommended only on larger areas such as golf course fairways and athletic fields and not on golf greens. Neither benefin nor bensulide remain for long periods when applied to wet soils. Poa control with these materials under wet conditions generally is unsatisfactory.

Dithiopyr (Dimension 1L, G). Dimension also may be applied to actively growing golf greens for preemergence control of annual bluegrass as well as crabgrass and goosegrass. Do not use within three months of seeding or sprigging. A total of 1 lb ai/A (1.7 kg/ha) is allowed yearly but not to exceed 1/2 lb ai/A (0.56 kg/ha) per application. Provides early (one to three leaf stage) postemergence crabgrass (some species) control. For preemergence *Poa annua* control, an eight week interval is needed before ryegrass overseeding. A repeat application should be made in early winter. Granular formulations work best.

Postemergence Control

Ethofumesate (Progress 1.5EC) provides early postemergence annual bluegrass control in bermudagrass. However, to prevent undesirable turfgrass injury, the application rate, timing, and frequency are important (Figure 6.2). If applied in fall before bermudagrass dormancy, an immediate cessation of bermudagrass growth occurs. A delay in spring transition from ryegrass to bermudagrass also occurs with early fall application. Spring greenup of bermudagrass can be severely retarded with February applications (Plate 6.3). Therefore, ethofumesate should only be used where sufficient cold weather occurs for complete bermudagrass dormancy and applied during late fall (e.g., late November) through early winter (e.g., no later than January 15). Progress, therefore, should not be used in tropical regions. Ethofumesate is not labeled for golf greens, zoysiagrass, or fine fescues. Application rate is 2 qt/a (4.8 L/ha) (or 1 lb ai/a, 1.1 kg/ha) applied 30 to 45 days after overseeding with a repeat application 21 to 28 days later.

Figure 6.2. Selective *Poa annua* control in ryegrass overseeded with two applications of ethofumesate (trade name: Prograss).

Prograss should only be used on areas overseeded with ryegrass and not *Poa trivialis,* bentgrass, or fine fescue.

Plant Growth Retardants

Certain plant growth retardants (PGRs) such as Embark and paclobutrazol also help suppress the seedheads of *Poa annua* in overseeded bermudagrass fairways. Timing is critical and the club must be willing to accept some degree of short-term turfgrass discoloration (or phytotoxicity). PGRs, however, should not be used on overseeded golf greens for *Poa annua* seedhead suppression.

Mefluidide (Embark 2S, Embark Lite 0.2S). Apply at 0.05 to 0.125 lb ai/acre (Embark 2S – 0.5 pt/A, 0.6 L/ha; Embark Lite – 2 to 5 pt/A, 2.3 to 5.9 L/ha) to suppress annual bluegrass seedhead development (Plate 4.16). Mefluidide must be applied before seedheads emerge. Application timing varies between geographical locations, but is generally during January through early March (actual timing of application depends upon location and climatic conditions). Mefluidide is foliar absorbed. Do not apply to turf within four growing months after seeding, and do not reseed within three days after application. Treated turf often appears less dense and temporarily discolored. Adding 1 to 2 qt (0.9 to 1.8 L) of a nonionic surfactant per 100 gal (379 L) of spray solution may enhance suppression; however, discoloration may also be increased. Iron applications may lessen discoloration. Mefluidide formulations are not recommended for use on golf course putting greens. Read and follow label recommendations before use.

Paclobutrazol (Trimmit/TGR Turf Enhancer 2SC). Apply at 6.4 to 48 fl oz/a (0.1 to 0.75 lb ai/acre, 0.11 to 0.84 kg/ha) in late winter to early spring after growth of desired grasses has resumed and one to two mowings has occurred. Do not apply after March 15 to avoid delaying greenup of bermudagrass. Paclobutrazol is root absorbed and 1/4-inch

(0.64 cm) rainfall or irrigation water should be applied within 24 hours of application. Repeat applications may be made three to four weeks apart. Not recommended for use on 'Tifdwarf' bermudagrass. Do not use if *Poa annua* populations exceed 70%.

Ethephon (Proxy 2L). Proxy is applied at 1.7 gal/acre (16 L/ha) or 5 fl oz/1,000 ft^2 (16 L/ha) and only to actively growing turfgrass that is not suffering heat, moisture, disease, or insect stress. Seven to 10 days are necessary for activity. Repeat applications can be made four weeks following the first for bentgrass and fescues and seven weeks for Kentucky bluegrass and perennial ryegrass. Do not apply to golf greens. It is not necessary to add a spreader/sticker.

Other Problematic Weeds

Annual Blueeyed-grass *(Sisyrinchium rosulatum)*

Blueeyed-grass is a winter annual, and a member of the Iris family. It appears similar to goosegrass except it is a cool-season annual; its leaves flat, light green, all clustered at the base; has zigzag shaped stems; flowers pale purple to white with a rose-purple eye ring; and reproduces by seed. Other *Sisyrinchium* species also occur. Control: Products containing atrazine or simazine applied twice 30 days apart. Prompt (a premix of atrazine and Basagran) also works well. Sencor also provides excellent control in tolerant turfgrasses. Products containing two- or three-way broadleaf herbicide mixtures applied at least twice seven days apart also work. The key to control is to apply products in fall when the weed is immature.

Bahiagrass *(Paspalum notatum)*

A perennial that often escapes from roadside planting of seed (Figure 6.3). Control: Postemergence control in bermudagrass and zoysiagrass is with Manor (metsulfuron) 60DF at 1 oz/a (3.1 kg/ha) applied twice three to four weeks apart. Repeat MSMA/DSMA applications at 1 to 2 lb ai/a (1.1 to 2.2 kg/ha) every five to seven days starting in spring will also eventually control bahiagrass. Normally, at least three applications are needed with MSMA or DSMA.

Crabgrass *(Digitaria spp.)*

Includes Southern, Smooth, Large, Blanket, India, and Tropical crabgrasses (Figure 6.4). A group of mostly summer annual grasses but will perennate in subtropical and tropical locations. Reproduces predominately by seed, secondarily by stolons. Control: Preemergence control includes members of the dinitroaniline herbicide family and other preemergence products (e.g., benefin, bensulide, dithiopyr, napropamide, oryzalin, oxadiazon, pendimethalin, and prodiamine). Apply when soil temperatures at the 4-inch (10 cm) level remain above 50°F (10°C) for 24 consecutive hours. Postemergence control includes repeat applications of MSMA or DSMA, asulam, atrazine, quinclorac, or metribuzin.

Figure 6.3. Bahiagrass is a perennial weed in fine bermudagrass due to its clumping growth habit (top) and prolific production of Y-shaped seedheads (bottom).

Figure 6.4. Crabgrass in bermudagrass.

Dallisgrass *(Paspalum dilatatum)*

A perennial grass escaping from forage/hay production. Control: Postemergence control in bermudagrass is with repeat MSMA/DSMA applications at 1 to 2 lb ai/a (1.1 to 2.2 kg/ha) every five to seven days starting in spring. Must stay on schedule. Adding Sencor 75DF at 0.19 to 0.25 lb/a (0.2 to 0.3 kg/ha) to MSMA or DSMA increases control but also increases turf injury. Water before treatment if turf is drought-stressed. In other grasses, spot treat or rope wick with Roundup Pro (4S) using 2 fl oz/gal (15.5 mL/L) water. Begin in spring, repeat in two to three weeks. Avoid desirable plants.

Goosegrass *(Eleusine indica)*

Goosegrass is a summer annual grass. It thrives in wet, compacted soils. Control: Preemergence control: split applications 60 days apart of PRE herbicides such as Barricade, Dimension, Pendimethalin, Ronstar, or Surflan. First application is in early spring when soil temperatures at 4-inches (10 cm) reach 63°F (17.2°C) for 24 consecutive hours. POST control is with Illoxan 3EC at 1 to 1.4 qt/a, 2.3 to 3.3 L/ha (Figure 6.5) or, Sencor 75DF (0.19 lb/a, 0.2 kg/ha) + MSMA (1 lb ai/a, 1.1 kg/ha). Sencor should not be used on golf greens. Avoid drought- and heat-stressed turf.

Kyllinga spp.

These are several troublesome Kyllinga species occurring in turf (Plate 6.4). Perennial species include: (a) *K. brevifolia;* "Perennial" or "Green" kyllinga; (b) *K. gracillima* = *K. brevifolioides;* no common name; (c) *K. nemoralis;* "White" kyllinga. Annual species include: (a) *K. pumila;* no common name; (b) *K. squamulata;* no common name; and

Figure 6.5. Diclofop (trade name: Illoxan)-treated goosegrass (right) versus nontreated (left). The goosegrass population was so intense that it effectively outcompeted the bermudagrass.

(c) *K. odorata* = *C. sesquiflorus;* "Annual" kyllinga (Note: *K. odorata* acts as an annual in the U.S. but is a short-lived perennial in the tropics).

These appear similar to nutsedges except kyllinga species do not form underground nutlets (or tubers). Perennial kyllinga species form patches from rhizomes. Currently, *K. nemoralis* (or "White" kyllinga) is thought to be restricted in the U.S. to Hawaii. However, it probably can survive in portions of the mainland including Southern California and South Florida. Control: Annual kyllinga species can be controlled with Basagran, Image, Manage, or repeat applications of MSMA or DSMA. Perennial species require repeat applications of Image, Image + MSMA, or Manage spaced three to four weeks apart.

Lawn Burweed or Spurweed *(Soliva pterosperma)*

Burweed is a low-growing, freely branched winter annual broadleaf weed. Its leaves are opposite, twice divided into narrow segments or lobes; flowers small and inconspicuous; fruits have sharp spines; and it reproduces by seed. Control: Preemergence or postemergence applications of simazine or atrazine in midfall provide excellent control. Prompt and Sencor also work well in tolerant turfgrasses. Repeat applications of two- or three-way broadleaf herbicide mixtures also provide control. Key to control is applications in fall when weeds are small. Once the weed is mature enough where spurs form in late winter, control is reduced.

Sandbur (Sandspur) *(Cenchrus spp.)*

This is a summer annual. Control: Preemergence control is in early spring with split applications 60 days apart of PRE herbicides such as Barricade, Dimension, Pendimethalin,

Ronstar, or Surflan. Postemergence control in bermuda/zoysia is with MSMA at 1 lb ai/a (1.1 kg/ha). Repeat in five to ten days.

Smutgrass *(Sporobolus indicus)*

A clumping perennial grass; leaf blades flat, very thin; seed often infected with black fungus (or smut); reproduces by seed (Figure 6.6). Control: Selective control has been very elusive. Summer atrazine or simazine applications provide approximately 50% control. However, expect temporary turfgrass damage with this. TFC and Corsair 75DF (chlorsulfuron) have smutgrass listed on its label, but control can be erratic. Nonselective control is spot spraying or rope wicking glyphosate (Roundup Pro). If rope wicking, treat in two directions. Hand removal is often necessary, followed by preemergence herbicide use.

Spreading Dayflower *(Commelina diffusa)*

An escape from the ornamental industry; summer annual; fleshy, smooth stems; flowers with three blue petals; reproduces by seed and stem fragments; prefers moist habitats. Control: Products containing atrazine or simazine applied twice 30 days apart. Prompt (a premix of atrazine and Basagran) also works well as does metsulfuron (Manor). Tank mixes of MSMA or DSMA with Sencor or multiple application of two- or three-way broadleaf herbicide mixtures also provide good control but can cause phytotoxicity to certain turfgrass species.

Tall Fescue Clumps *(Festuca arundinacea)*

A perennial grass. Control: Postemergence control in Kentucky bluegrass, fine fescue, zoysiagrass, or bermudagrass with TFC 75 DF or Corsair at 4 to 5 oz/a (12 to 15 kg/ha) or as a spot treatment at 2 grams/2 gal water. Repeat in 60 days. In dormant bermudagrass, spot treat with Roundup Pro 4L at 2 oz/gal (15.6 mL/L) water; avoid desirable green plants.

Thin or Bull Paspalum *(Paspalum setaceum)*

Clump-forming perennial grass; leaf blades flat, hairy to almost smooth with a fringe of stiff hairs along the leaf margins; common in sandy soils; reproduces by seed and clump fragments. Control: Repeat applications of MSMA or DSMA are required every seven days until complete control is achieved.

Torpedograss *(Panicum repens)*

A perennial grass that is normally an aquatic weed with robust, sharply pointed, creeping rhizomes; reproduces primarily by rhizomes. Control: Nonselective control is with at least three applications of glyphosate (Roundup Pro), each spaced three weeks

Figure 6.6. Smutgrass is a perennial grass weed that is difficult to cleanly mow and due to its thin, wiry leaves, difficult to control with foliar-absorbed herbicides.

apart. Other nonselective control involves fumigating with methyl bromide and replanting. Selective control (or suppression) has recently become available with quinclorac (Drive). Drive should be applied two or three times spaced three to four weeks apart. Expect some minor temporary turfgrass discoloration.

Kikuyugrass (Pennisetum clandestinum)

Tough perennial grass with vigorous, thick, aggressively growing rhizomes and stolons. Control: Avoid movement of contaminated soil. Fumigate contaminated soil before using or planting. Selective postemergence control with repeat applications of quinclorac (Drive), triclopyr (Turflon), or triclopyr plus MSMA. Repeat application every three to four weeks or when weed regrowth is evident.

Spurges (Chamaesyce spp.)

Summer annual broadleaf weeds that include spotted, prostrate, garden, and roundleaf spurges. These often act as indicator plants for high nematode-containing soils, thus a nematode assay is suggested. Control Strategies: Manor 60DF at 1/4 oz/a (0.018 kg/ha) provides best control. Two- and three-way mixes of 2,4-D, dicamba, and MCPP also work. Repeat applications of the mixes may be necessary as plants mature.

Virginia Buttonweed (Diodia virginiana)

A perennial that reproduces from fleshy roots, cut plant pieces, and above- and belowground-produced seed. Physically dig if only a few plants are present. Remove all plant parts and soil. Refill with fresh soil and weed-free sod. Control: Postemergence suppression is with two-way or three-way herbicides with 2,4-D, dicamba, + MCPP. 2,4-D is most effective, therefore, use combination products with a high concentration of it. Repeat in three to four weeks. Corsair 75 DF at 5 oz/acre (15 kg/ha) + 0.5 lb ai/a 2,4-D applied twice 60 days apart is an effective combination.

Wild Garlic/Onion (Allium spp.)

These are cool-season perennials. Wild Onion has offset bulblets and a fibrous coat on the central bulb. Control: Postemergence control is with Image 1.5L at 2 pt/a (2.3 L/ha) in December. Repeat with 1 pt/a (1.2 L/ha) in early March. Add 0.25% nonionic surfactant (1 qt/100 gal water, 2.5 mL/L). Also, 2,4-D LV ester alone or two- or three-way combination products. Treat in November, March, and again the following November. Manor 60DF at 1 oz per acre (0.07 kg/ha) also provides good control. In completely dormant turf (no green stolons or shoots), Roundup Pro 4L can be used at 1 pt/a (1.2 L/ha), repeat in 3 to 4 weeks.

Nutsedge Control

The predominant sedge weed species in turfgrasses are yellow and purple nutsedge. Other, problem members of the *Cyperus* and *Kyllinga* genus include annual or water sedge, perennial and annual kyllinga, globe sedge, Texas sedge, flathead sedge, and cylindrical sedge. Path or slender rush, a member of the rush (Juncus) family, also can occur in some turf situations.

Sedges generally thrive in soils that remain wet for extended periods of time due to poor drainage or excessive irrigation. The first step in sedge weed control is, therefore, to correct the cause of continuously wet soils. Do not overirrigate an area and, if necessary, provide surface and subsurface drainage.

Yellow and purple nutsedge are low-growing perennials resembling grasses. Sedges, in general, are yellow-green to dark-green in color, with triangular stems bearing three-ranked leaves unlike the two-ranked leaves of the grass family. Yellow and purple nutsedge have fibrous root systems with deep-rooted tubers or nutlets for reproduction. Seedhead color is often used to distinguish between these two major nutsedges. Leaf tip shape is another distinguishing method. Leaf tips of purple nutsedge are generally thicker and more rounded than yellow nutsedge leaf tips which are very narrow, ultimately forming a needle-like end. Yellow and purple nutsedge have a great capacity to reproduce and spread due in part to their massive underground tuber and rhizome systems.

Historically, chemical control of most sedges was with repeat applications of 2,4-D or the organic arsenicals (MSMA, DSMA). Although effective, these treatments are slow to kill the weeds and repeat applications are generally necessary, resulting in extensive damage in certain turf species (Table 6.7).

Selective yellow nutsedge control is available with bentazon (Basagran T&O) with minimum turf damage. Control of most other sedges, except purple nutsedge, also will result from bentazon treatments. Bentazon is a contact material, meaning it will control only those portions of the weeds contacted by the spray. Complete coverage of the weeds

Table 6.7. Relative sedge control to various herbicides (refer to herbicide label for specific species listing).

	Sedges				
Herbicide(s)[a]	Annual Sedge	Purple Nutsedge	Yellow Nutsedge	Annual Kyllinga Species	Perennial Kyllinga Species
Preemergence Control					
Pennant (metolachlor)	G[b]	P	G	F-G	P
Ronstar 2G (Oxadiazon)	G	P	P	F	P
Postemergence Control					
Basagran T&O (bentazon)	G	P	G	F-G	F-G
Image (imazaquin)	G	F-G	F	G	G
Manage (halosulfuron)	G	G-E	G-E	G	F-G
MSMA/DSMA/CMA	G	P-F	F	G	G
Image + MSMA/DSMA	G	F-G	G	G	G

[a]Repeat applications are necessary for complete control from all herbicides. This interval is from 5 days for MSMA/DSMA up to 3 to 8 weeks for Manage or Image.

[b]E = excellent (>89%) control; F = Fair to Good (70 to 89%), good control sometimes with high rates, however a repeat treatment 1 to 3 weeks later each at the standard or reduced rate is usually more effective; P = poor (<70%) control in most cases. These are relative rankings and depend on many factors such as environmental conditions, turfgrass vigor or health, application timing, etc., and are intended only as a guide.

is therefore necessary for greatest bentazon activity. Even with good herbicide coverage, regrowth will normally occur from the roots and tubers, and repeat applications will be necessary.

Purple and yellow nutsedge, as well as several other sedges, can be suppressed with imazaquin (Image). Selective broadleaf weeds, such as pennywort, are also controlled with imazaquin. As with bentazon, repeat applications possibly over several years will be required to control all the underground reproductive parts with imazaquin. The addition of MSMA increases the activity of either bentazon or imazaquin and broadens the range of weeds controlled. However, this tank-mix should be used only on actively-growing bermudagrass or zoysiagrass. Image should not be used on desirable cool-season turf species.

Halosulfuron (Manage) also has good control on most sedges and also has good turf tolerance. Halosulfuron is somewhat slow, requiring two to three weeks for control and as with other sedge control materials, repeat applications three to four weeks after the initial treatment are necessary, especially when trying to control perennial sedges or kyllinga species (Table 6.7). Sedges, like most weeds, are most susceptible if treated prior to seedhead production.

PLANT GROWTH REGULATORS

Plant growth regulators (PGRs) or inhibitors are increasingly being used on golf courses to suppress seedheads and vegetative growth of desirable turfgrasses, enhance turfgrass quality, and manage annual bluegrass (*Poa annua*) growth and development.

Figure 6.7. Plant growth regulator (PGR) use in bermudagrass turf has increased due to their ability to reduce vertical growth, thus clippings encourage tighter turf stand density and provide the illusion that different bermudagrass off-types appear as the same.

Depending upon the turfgrass and situation, PGRs may reduce mowing costs, prevent scalping, increase turf density, and decrease the need to mow steep slopes (Figure 6.7). Traditionally, PGRs were used in the United States to suppress bahiagrass (*Paspalum notatum*), Kentucky bluegrass (*Poa pratensis*), and tall fescue (*Festuca arundinacea*) seedhead production in low maintenance areas such as highway roadsides, airports, and golf course roughs. However, in recent years new products have been registered for use on most high maintenance turfgrasses.

Bermudagrass Growth Suppression

Trinexapac-ethyl (Primo 1EC, Primo 25WSB)

Primo 1EC at 3.0 to 6.0 fl oz/A (0.22 to 0.4 L/ha) and Primo 25WSB at 1.35 to 2.7 oz/A (0.09 to 0.2 kg/ha) may be used on hybrid bermudagrass putting greens (Plate 6.5). A one hour rain-free period is needed after application. Trinexapac-ethyl is foliar absorbed. Mowing one to seven days after application improves appearance. Repeat applications are three to five weeks apart to maintain growth suppression but do not exceed 21 pt/A (25 L/ha) of Primo 1EC or 174 oz/A (12 kg/ha) of Primo 25WSB per year. Trinexapac-ethyl will suppress seedheads on hybrid bermudagrass, but only partial seedhead suppression is observed on other turfgrass species. Temporary turf discoloration may follow treatment. It is not necessary to add a surfactant to trinexapac-ethyl. Primo formulations may also be used to enhance the establishment of cool-season turfgrasses in bermudagrass (overseeding). Apply Primo before verticutting, spiking, scalping, etc., and one to five days before overseeding. Primo does not adequately suppress *Poa annua* seedheads.

Plant Growth Promoters

An available plant growth promoter is RyzUp (formerly known as ProGibb) from Abbott Laboratories. RyzUp is gibberellic acid which encourages cell division and elongation. When used, RyzUp helps initiate or maintain growth and prevent color changes (e.g., purpling) during periods of cold stress and light frosts on bermudagrass such as Tifdwarf and Tifgreen. Oftentimes, fall golf tournaments may experience an early light frost before the overseeding has become established. RyzUp helps the turf recover from this discoloration. RyzUp, however, will negate the effects of GA-inhibiting PGRs, thus should not be used in conjunction with them if the PGR effects are desired.

Precautionary Statements

When using any postemergence herbicide, certain precautions should be followed to minimize any problems. Treat the weeds when they are young (e.g., two to four leaf stage). Larger weeds require repeat applications. This will increase the chance of phytotoxicity and increase labor costs with added wear and tear on equipment. Treat when the weeds, and preferably the turf, is actively growing and good soil moisture is present (Plate 6.6). Treating when the weed is actively growing results in better herbicide uptake and translocation, thus better efficacy. If weeds are treated after they begin to flower or produce seedheads, herbicide activity will be reduced and repeat applications will be necessary. If seedheads or flowers are present, mow the weeds as low as possible, wait several days until new regrowth is evident, and then make the herbicide application. Allowing weeds to produce seedheads may add to the soil's weed seed reserve, therefore mowing or herbicide treatments should be in advance of seedhead development.

An adjuvant (surfactant, wetting agent, or crop oil concentrate) is generally needed by most postemergence herbicides. The label should be consulted, however, as many postemergence herbicides already contain them. If other pesticides are to be tank-mixed with herbicides, always conduct a compatibility test unless the specific tank-mix is recommended on the herbicide label. Indiscriminate tank-mixing can lead to chemical compatibility problems (e.g., flakes, gels, precipitates) in the spray tank and may result in excessive turfgrass injury. As application volumes and pre- or posttreatment irrigation recommendations dramatically vary between herbicides, fungicides, and insecticides, it usually is not advisable to tank-mix the various types of pesticides. Compatibility tests should also be conducted when mixing herbicides with liquid fertilizers. The herbicide label will usually contain information on how to conduct a compatibility test. Table 6.8 cross lists current common herbicide names with trade names and their manufacturers and/or distributors.

Table 6.8. Common and trade names of turfgrass herbicides.

Common Name	Trade Name(s)
Ammoniated soap of fatty acids	Quick-fire
Asulam	Asulox 3.34L, Asulam 3.3
Atrazine	AAtrex, Atrazine Plus, Purge II, Aatrex 90, Atrazine 4L, Bonus S, St. Augustine Weedgrass Control + others
Benefin	Balan 2.5G. 1.5EC, Crabgrass Preventer, + others
Benefin + oryzalin	XL 2G
Benefin + trifluralin	Team 2G, Crabgrass Preventer 0.92%, Team Pro
Bensulide	Betasan, Pre-San 12.5 & 7 G, Bensumec 4L, Lescosan, Weedgrass Preventer, Betamec, Squelch, + others
Bentazon	Basagran T/O 4L, Lescogran 4L
Bentazon + atrazine	Prompt 5L
Bromoxynil	Buctril 2L, Brominal 4L, Bromox 2E, Moxy 2E
Cacodylic Acid	Montar, Weed Ender
Chlorsulfuron	TFC 75DG, Corsair 75DF
Clethodim	Envoy 0.94 EC
Clopyralid	Lontrel T&O 3L
CMA (CAMA)	Calar, Ortho Crabgrass Killer - Formula II, Selectrol
Corn gluten	Dynaweed, WeedzSTOP 100G
Dazomet	Basamid
Dichlobenil	Casoron 4G, Dyclomec 4G, Norosac 4G
2,4-D	2,4-D Amine & Ester, Weedone LV4, Dacamine, Weedar 64, AM-40, 2,4-D LV4, Dymec, Lesco A-4D, + others
2,4-D + clopyralid + dicamba	Millennium Ultra 3.75 lb/gal
2,4-D + clopyralid + triclopyr	Momentum
2,4-D + dicamba	81 Selective Weedkiller, Four Power Plus, Triple D Lawn Weed Killer, Banvel 2,4-D
2,4-D + dichlorprop (2,4-DP)	2D + 2DP Amine, Turf D + DP, Fluid Broadleaf Weed Control, Weedone DPC Ester & Amine + others
2,4-D + dichlorprop (2,4-DP) + dicamba	Super Trimec, Brushmaster
2,4-D + mecoprop (MCPP)	2D Amine + 2MCPP, 2 Plus 2, MCPP-2,4-D, Phenomec, Ortho Weed-B-Gon Lawn Weed Killer + others
2,4-D + MCPP + 2,4-DP	Broadleaf Granular Herbicide, Dissolve, Triamine, Tri-Ester, Jet-Spray 3-Way Weed Control, Turf Weeder + others
2,4-D + MCPP + dicamba + MCPA and/or 2,4-DP	Trimec Southern, Three-Way Selective, Eliminate DG, 33-Plus, Dissolve, Triamine 3.9 lb/gal, TriEster, Triplet, Trex-San, Weed-B-Gon, 2 Plus 2, Bentgrass Selective Weed Killer, Trimec Bentgrass Formula, Strike 3, Broadleaf Trimec, MECAmine-D, Trimec 992, Weed-B-Gon for Southern Lawns, Formula II, + others
Dicamba	Vanquish 4 L, K-O-G Weed Control, Bentgrass Selective, Banvel 4S + others
Dicamba + MCPA + MCPP	Encore DSC, Tri-Power Dry, Trimec Encore
Diclofop	Illoxan 3EC
Dithiopyr	Dimension 1L
Diquat	Reward LS, Watrol, Vegetrol, Aquatate
DSMA	Ansar, DSMA Liquid, Methar 30, Namate, DSMA 4
DSMA + 2,4-D	Weed Beater Plus

Table 6.8. (Continued)

Common Name	Trade Name(s)
Ethofumesate	Prograss 1.5L
Ethephon	Proxy 2L
Fenarimol	Rubigan 1AS, Patchwork 0.78G
Fenoxaprop	Acclaim Extra 0.57EC
Fluazifop	Fusilade II T&O, Ornamec
Flurprimidol	Cutless 50WP
Glufosinate	Finale 1L
Glyphosate	Roundup Pro, Roundup ProDry, Gly-Flo, AquaNeat, Razor, Rodeo, Ortho Kleenup, Weed Wrangler, Touchdown Pro + others
Halosulfuron	Manage 75WP
Hexazinone	Velpar 2L
Imazameth	Plateau 70DG
Imazaquin	Image 1.5L, 70DF
Isoxaben	Gallery 75DF
Isoxaben + trifluralin	Preen 1.9G, Snapshot TG
MCPA	Weedar MCPA 4 lb/gal, MCPA-4 Amine + others
MCPA + clopyralid + dichlorprop	Chaser Ultra
MCPA + clopyralid + triclopyr	Battleship
MCPA + MCPP + 2,4-DP	Triamine II, Tri-Ester II
MCPA + dicamba + triclopyr	Eliminate, Three-Way Ester II
MCPP	Mecomec 4, Chickweed & Clover Control, Lescopex, MCPP-4 Amine, MCPP-4K + others
MSMA	Daconate 6, Dal-E-Rad, Crab-E-Rad, MSMA 6.6L, Drexar 530, Buano 6L, 120 Herbicide, Daconate Super, 912 Herbicide, MSMA Turf, Summer Crabicide, Target MSMA, + others
MSMA + 2,4-D +MCPP + dicamba	Trimec Plus (Quadmec)
Mefluidide	Embark
Metribuzin	Sencor 75DF
Metolachlor	Pennant 7.8 lb/gal
Metsulfuron	Manor 60 DF, Escort 60 DF
Methyl Bromide	Brom-O-Gas, Terr-O-Gas, MB 98, MBC
Napropamide	Devrinol 50 DF, 2G, 10G, Ornamental Herbicide 5G
Napropamide + oxadiazon	PrePair 6G
Norflurazon	Predict
Oryzalin	Surflan AS 4 lb/gal
Oxadiazon	Ronstar 2G, 50WP
Oxadiazon + bensulide	Goosegrass/Crabgrass Control
Oxadiazon + dithiopyr	SuperStar
Oxadiazon + prodiamine	Regalstar 1.2G
Oxyfluorfen	Goal 2XL
Oxyfluorfen + oxadiazon	OO-Herbicide 3G
Oxyfluorfen + pendimethalin	OH2
Oxyfluorfen + oryzalin	Rout

Paclobutrazol	Turf Enhancer 50WP, 2SC, Trimmit 2SC
Pelargonic Acid	Scythe
Pendimethalin	Pre-M & Pendulum (60 DG, WP, 3.3EC, 2G), Turf Weedgrass Control, Halts, Corral 2.68G
Prodiamine	Barricade 65WDG, Endurance 65 WDG, Factor 65 WDG, RegalKade 0.5G
Pronamide	Kerb 50WP
Quinclorac	Drive 75 DF
Rimsulfuron	TranXit GTA
Sethoxydim	Vantage 1.0 lb/gal
Siduron	Tupersan 50WP, 4.6%
Simazine	Princep 4 lb/gal, T&O, 80WP, Simazine, Wynstar, + others
Sulfometuron-methyl	Oust 75DG
Triclopyr	Turflon Ester 4L
Triclopyr + 2,4-D	Turflon II Amine, Chaser 3L, Chaser 2 Amine
Triclopyr + clopyralid	Confront 3L
Triclopyr + MCPP + dicamba	Cool Power 3.6 lb/gal, Horsepower 4.56 lb/gal, 3-Way Ester II
Trifluralin	Treflan 5G, Trifluralin 4EC, Trilin 4ED, 5EC
Trinexapac-ethyl	Primo 1EC
Xanthomonas campentris	X-Po

7 Insects

Insects on bermudagrass are generally a local or regional problem in occurrence and also are often very seasonal (Figure 7.1). In subtropical and tropical growing regions, mole crickets are the most destructive turf insects. Armyworms, grass scales, and bermudagrass mites are periodic problems. Various white grubs and cutworms are troublesome, especially in the northern transition climatic zone.

An insect management program involves:

1. Correctly identifying the insect and its damage pattern.
2. Understanding the insect's life cycle, biology, and aesthetic thresholds.
3. When justified, selecting and properly applying the appropriate control method. Current control options are listed at the end of the chapter in Tables 7.2, 7.3, and 7.4.

LEAF FEEDERS

Sod Webworms

Sod webworms (order Lepidoptera, family Acrolophidae, Pyralidae) comprise a large number of grass feeding larvae (caterpillars) and adult moths. Most sod webworms are native to North America and found throughout the country, especially the eastern half. Over 30 species occur in North America but only about 15 species of webworms attack turfgrasses, with Tropical sod webworms, *Herpetogramma phaeopteralis* Guerne, being the one most often in bermudagrass growing areas.

Description and Biology

Larvae of the tropical sod webworm have a dark yellowish-brown head and the body is greenish and hairy with numerous black spots scattered over their bodies resembling rows of shield-like spots (Figure 7.2). Larvae are 1/25 inch (1 mm) long when first hatched and grow to 3/4 inch (1.9 cm) long. Most sod webworm larvae curl into a ball when disturbed. Adult moths are small, dingy brown to almost white-colored with a wing span of 3/4 inch (1.9 cm) and delicate fringes along the wing borders. Resting adult sod webworm moths have a very long, distinct, snoutlike labial palpi extending in front of their heads, giving a tube-like appearance. However, unlike other webworms, adult tropical sod webworms do not fold their wings against their bodies but hold them out in a triangular pattern like most other moths. Adults often hide in grass or shrubbery and are attracted to lights at night. When disturbed, adult moths fly short distances in a

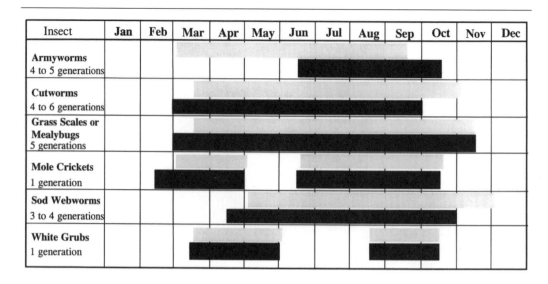

Insect	Jan	Feb	Mar	Apr	May	Jun	Jul	Aug	Sep	Oct	Nov	Dec
Armyworms 4 to 5 generations												
Cutworms 4 to 6 generations												
Grass Scales or Mealybugs 5 generations												
Mole Crickets 1 generation												
Sod Webworms 3 to 4 generations												
White Grubs 1 generation												

☐ Typical insect damage periods   ■ Typical control timings

Figure 7.1. Typical damage periods, control timings, and generations per year for insects on bermudagrass in the United States.

Figure 7.2. Sod webworm larva (right) and adult (left) (Courtesy of Don Short).

zigzag pattern. Sod webworm adults are identified by varying wing color patterns and male genitalia, while larvae are extremely difficult to separate.

Most sod webworms overwinter as larvae tightly coiled in silk-lined tunnels or cases. In spring, the larvae pupate within these and the adults emerge, mate, and lay eggs.

During the day, moths rest in shrubbery adjacent to turf areas. At dusk they fly in a zigzag pattern over the turf, depositing clusters of 6 to 15 eggs on grass leaves. Eggs hatch in approximately seven days when temperatures are at least 78°F (25.6°C) and larvae progress through seven instars, requiring 25 days. When temperatures are lower (72°F, 22.2°C), eight larval instars occur requiring 45 to 50 days to complete their development. They pupate on the soil surface and emerge as adult moths in seven days. Life cycle from egg to adult requires 5 to 6 weeks at 78°F (25.5°C) and 12 weeks at 72°F (22.2°C).

During most years there are two generations in north and central Florida and up to four generations yearly in south Florida. The tropical sod webworm does not overwinter further north than central Florida during most years. In south Florida, economic damage to grass usually begins in May or June. Further north, it is usually August before larval populations develop in sufficient numbers to cause damage.

Feeding Symptoms/Signs

Adult sod webworms do not feed but larvae damage grass by chewing the blades or severing the blades above the thatch and pull this into their silk-lined tunnels. When first hatched, they only rasp the surface or skeletonize the blades. Outbreaks seem to appear almost overnight. Damaged areas appear grayish and usually are only two to three feet in diameter. Often damage is first noticed adjacent to shrubbery and flower beds since moths rest in the foliage and lay more eggs in nearby turf. Moths are attracted to dark green, healthy turf, therefore golf greens provide a choice site for them.

When larvae become larger they notch the blades and the grass becomes ragged in appearance. Injury initially appears as small closely cropped grass patches as grass blades are clipped just above the crowns. Green frass (fecal) pellets are often below eaten turf tissue. Damaged areas then become larger and fuse. Continued feeding gives the turf a close-cropped yellowish and then a brown appearance from the exposed thatch underneath. Removing dead stems by brushing or raking exposes the shortened green stems remaining from grazing larvae. Webworms normally do not kill turf crowns, only feed on their leaves and stems. Turfgrasses therefore normally can recover from insect feeding if the webworm is controlled and proper fertilization and watering practices are used. Bermudagrass and bluegrass are most often attacked.

Sod webworms (except Tropical sod webworm) live in small tunnels of silk and grass in the thatch or soil and overwinter as larvae in these silk-lined tunnels. When feeding, birds often pull out the paper-like white sacs, leaving them laying on the grass. Sod webworms are mostly night feeders and retreat to these tunnels during the day after feeding on individual grass blades. During the day they rest in a curled position on the soil surface.

Detection and Control Strategies

Approximately 5 to 12 larvae per square foot (0.9 m²) are required to cause economic damage. Irregular brown spots resembling dollarspot disease are early signs of damage (Figure 7.3). The presence of larvae can be confirmed by parting the grass and

Figure 7.3. Sod webworm damage on golf greens often resembles dollar spot disease except with a tunnel in the center.

observing the soil surface in suspect areas for frass or pellets or for curled-up resting larvae. Larvae also leave trails of silk as they move about, which are easily seen in the morning. They also can be flushed to the grass surface by using a soap mixture of two tablespoons of liquid dishwashing detergent in two gallons of water or a similar pyrethrin solution. Early morning is the best time to sample since larvae are close to the surface. Flocks of birds that frequently return to a turf area, especially in early morning, or the presence of large numbers of moths flying over the turf area at dusk, usually are an indication that sod webworms or other caterpillars are present. Numerous moths flying at dusk, collecting on doors, windows, and around lights often indicate egg-laying periods. The birds often produce pencil-sized holes in the turf as they dig in the silken tunnels for the webworms. The turf area should be monitored for webworms once a week during the season they are most active in your area. Damage is most evident in late summer when populations have increased and grass growth slowed.

Long residual control of the tropical sod webworm is difficult (Table 7.2). There are many overlapping generations and the moths are continually flying into the turf area and depositing eggs. Insecticide sprayed on the grass may be removed within a few days by mowing, leaving the new grass without defense. Also, insecticides exposed to the weather, especially the sun, break down more rapidly than when irrigated into the soil. Applications should be made as late in the afternoon as possible. Treat areas beyond infected greens and/or tees to control migrating larvae from other areas.

Control of early instar larvae is possible with various microbial insecticides derived from *Bacillus thuringiensis* var *kurstaki* or Bt spodoptera active strains (often indicated as Bt). These microbial insecticides are stomach poisons, therefore the insect must ingest them to be effective. Preirrigating the turf and allowing the grass to grow several days after Bt application increases its effectiveness and should be repeated every four to

Figure 7.4. Young fall armyworm larva. Notice the dorsal stripes.

five weeks during summer. Control is best on young larvae. Several insect pathogenic nematodes also are being screened as possible control measures, as are some fungal endophytes.

Fall Armyworm

Spodoptera frugiperda (Smith) is the fall armyworm. The 'common' or 'true' armyworm is *Pseudaletia unipuncta* (Haworth), (order Lepidoptera, family Noctuidae), also listed previously as *Leucania extranea* and *Cirphis unipuncta*. Fall armyworm larvae are the injurious stage and are 1-1/2 inches (3.8 cm) long when mature. They are greenish when small and dark brown when fully grown (Figure 7.4). They have a light dorsal stripe with darker bands on each side of it running the length of each side of the body. Larvae also have a distinct inverted yellow-shaped 'Y' on their heads. If touched, larvae coil tightly. Adult moths are brownish with light and dark markings and a distinct white blotch near the tip of each front wing. They have a wing span of about 1-1/2 inches (3.8 cm).

Distribution and Biology

Life cycle of the fall armyworm varies considerably according to the region and is very similar to the sod webworm, however armyworms pupate in the soil. Armyworms continuously reside in Central and tropical South America and the West Indies. They also survive mild winters in the Gulf Coast region of the United States but are not able to withstand freezing temperatures further north. They spread each spring from these areas into the eastern United States and into southern New Mexico, Arizona, and California, reaching the northern states in fall, thus their name. In the Gulf Coast region during mild winters, larval and pupal stages overwinter and emerge as new adults in early spring. Typically, only one generation occurs per year in northern areas and they die each fall with freezing temperatures. Several generations occur yearly in the southeastern United States. The first generation cause turf damage in May to mid-June. A second generation may occur from June and July and a third from August til frost. The second or third generation typically causes the most damage. Eggs are laid on the grass blades or almost any object near the turf area. They are laid in clusters and are covered with grayish, fuzzy scales from the body of the female moth. Egg hatch is seven to ten days during cool periods and only two to three days in summer. Maturity requires 12 to 30 days, with the shorter times during summer. A generation takes five to six weeks.

Feeding Symptoms/Signs

Despite its name the fall armyworm is capable of causing damage to turfgrass in the spring, especially following cool, wet springs, which may reduce populations of natural parasites. However, most damage occurs during late summer and early fall after populations have increased during the season and often migrate northward with weather fronts. Damage is often most severe during dry seasons. Larval feeding is similar to webworm feeding except it usually does not occur in patches, but in more uniform and larger areas. Larvae feed day or night, but are most active early in the morning or late in the evening. Younger larvae feed on leaf margins, giving them a ragged look. Larger larvae eat all aboveground leaves and stems, resembling a mowing. Bentgrass, bermudagrass, fescue, bluegrass, ryegrass, and grain crops are most often attacked.

Detection and Control Strategies

Soap flushing can bring the larvae to the soil surface. Birds feeding and the presence of green fecal pellets also indicate armyworm presence. Adult moths are often attracted to lights at night during flight periods. Threshold levels vary on lower maintenance turf, but control may be justified if one armyworm is found per square foot (0.9 m^2) on a green (Table 7.2). Treatments should be made as late in the afternoon as possible to take advantage of early evening feeding. Current strains of *Bacillus thuringiensis* are not very effective for control unless early-stage larvae are treated and repeated every four to five weeks. Stoloniferous grasses, such as bermudagrass, generally recover from armyworm feeding since they do not destroy plant crowns. Nonstoloniferous grasses, such as fescue, may not fully recover.

Bermudagrass Mites

The bermudagrass mite, *Eriophyes cynodoniensis* Sayed (order Acarina, family Eriophyidae), is sometimes a pest in all bermudagrass growing states. It is also commonly referred to as the 'bermudagrass stunt mite.' Bermudagrass mites are not true insects but are more closely related to spiders.

Description and Biology

The mites are extremely small, only about l/130 of an inch (0.2 mm) long, yellowish-white and somewhat worm- or pear-like in shape with only two pairs of short legs. A microscope with at least 30X magnification is needed to detect them. Only female mites are known.

The bermudagrass mite is probably native to Australia but has spread to New Zealand, Africa, and America. It is found in all bermudagrass growing regions in the United States. They multiply very rapidly, requiring only about seven days to complete their life cycle. This short life cycle allows for rapid buildup during late spring and summer. Eggs are deposited under the leaf sheath, and after hatching, mites molt two times before reaching adulthood. All stages are found under the leaf sheaths. Mites appear well adapted to hot temperatures and become relatively inactive during cold temperatures. They spread through infected plants, clippings, machinery, mobile insects, and even by the wind, but not on bermudagrass seed.

Feeding Symptoms/Signs

Since the bermudagrass mite is so small it remains hidden beneath the leaf sheath. It can be identified more easily by symptoms of grass damage. The mite sucks plant juices with their needle-like mouth parts which causes a characteristic type of damage. Damage is first noticed in spring when bermudagrass lacks its normal vigorous growth at this time. Grass blades turn light green and abnormally curl and typical vigorous spring growth is noticeably absent. Internodes shorten, tissues swell, and the grass becomes tufted so that small clumps, often bushy in appearance, are noticed. This rosette growth form is often called 'witches brooming' (Figure 7.5). This characteristic growth is believed to be caused by a toxin injected into the developing grass node. The grass loses its vigor, thins out, and may die. Injury is more pronounced during dry weather and especially when grass is stressed due to poor maintenance. Since damage is often associated with drought stress, providing adequate moisture and nutrients helps the grass outgrow mite damage.

Detection and Control Strategies

Infestations usually develop in taller mowed grass, such as rough areas, around sand traps, and along canals and fence rows. To aid in reducing populations, mow as close as practical and collect and destroy grass clippings from infested areas. In general, as the mowing height is decreased, mite numbers are decreased. A wetting agent in the spray mixture will improve pesticide results. Spread appears most common by moving infested turf. Threshold for control is suggested when four to eight witches broomed tufts are seen per square foot (0.09 m^2).

Use resistant varieties such as Tifgreen (328), Tifdwarf, FloraTeX, and Midiron bermudagrasses. Coarser varieties such as Common and Ormond appear more susceptible. A preventive control approach consists of maintaining good soil moisture as dry conditions tend to favor mite damage and increasing fertility to encourage new turf

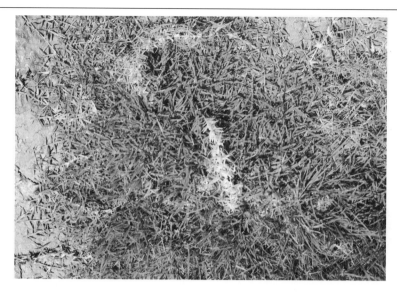

Figure 7.5. Turf symptoms (often referred to as 'witches brooming') from bermudagrass mite feeding.

growth. Commercial insecticides are available but may require frequent application (e.g., every three weeks) since mites have such a short life cycle.

Grass Scales or Mealybugs

Over 37 species of mealybugs have been associated with grasses. Two major grass scales occur: (1) the rhodesgrass mealybug, also called rhodesgrass scale, *Antonia graminis* (Maskell); and (2) the bermudagrass scale, *Odonaspis ruthae* Kotinsky (order Homoptera, family Pseudococcidae and Diaspididae). These are not common pests but do occasionally occur from South Carolina to California, most often on bermudagrass and St. Augustinegrass, especially that growing in shade. Rhodesgrass scale derives its name from feeding on its favorite host, rhodesgrass (*Chloris gayana* Kunth), a coarse-textured pasture grass. The buffalograss mealybug, *Tridiscus sporoboli* (Cockerell) and *Trionymus* sp., is often found on buffalograss but appears to cause little economic damage.

Description and Biology

The rhodesgrass mealybug body is round and dark brown but is covered with a white cottony secretion that appears like tufts of cotton on the grass. Male mealybugs resemble tiny gnats with a single pair of wings and three pairs of red eyes. Adult males are not considered harmful to turfgrasses. The bermudagrass scale is oval shaped, white, wingless, and approximately 1/15 of an inch (1.7 mm) in diameter (Figure 7.6). They prefer the taller grass in rough areas, especially in heavily thatched and shaded areas. They also are found around sand traps, along fence rows and other similar areas. When the scales hatch into the crawler stage, they migrate beneath the leaf sheath, usually at the nodes. Only the youngest, immature stages are mobile. Adults settle on the leaf or

Figure 7.6. Rhodesgrass mealybug (scale) feeding on bermudagrass stems.

stem, insert their needle-like mouthparts, become immobile and eventually start excreting a white, cottony, waxy covering (shell).

Life cycles of both insects range from 60 to 70 days, and there are up to five generations per year in the southern United States. Continuous generations occur from Orlando, Florida south.

Feeding Symptoms/Signs

As mentioned, bermudagrass and St. Augustinegrass are their favorite hosts. They infest the crown, nodes, or under leaf sheaths, not the leaves and withdraw plant sap with their piercing/sucking mouthparts. Infested grass slowly loses vitality, discolors, and later appears to be suffering from drought. Stunting and thinning of the grass stand occurs under high infestation levels. Under heavy infestations, plants are often covered with tiny masses of white, waxy secretions. Injury is most severe during extended hot, dry (stressful) periods and is often confused with dry spots or disease. The rhodesgrass mealybug produces considerable honeydew, and other insects such as ants or bees may be present on heavily infested turfgrass.

Detection and Control Strategies

Plant leaves should be pulled away from the stems, sheaths, and nodes and examined for tiny, white cottony masses. Ants feeding on the honeydew also can indicate mealybugs. Since these insects produce more damage during dry weather, keep the turf well irrigated and fertilized. Cultural control includes collecting grass clippings, which will contain some scales, and destroying these. Several insecticides provide control but are rarely needed. If needed, thorough spray coverage is necessary and a surfactant should be added.

Figure 7.7. Mole cricket. Turf damage occurs from the extensive tunneling which disrupts the turf surface and leads to soil desiccation.

ROOT FEEDERS

Mole Crickets

Mole crickets (order Orthoptera, family Gryllotalpidae) are considered the most serious turfgrass pest in sandy, coastal plain areas from North Carolina to Texas. Bermudagrass, bahiagrass, and centipedegrass are severely damaged by them. Seven species exist in North America but only the following four are serious pests:

- The Tawny mole cricket, *Scapteriscus vicinus* Scudder (previously called the Changa or Puerto Rican mole cricket), is the most damaging.
- The Southern mole cricket, *Scapteriscus borelli* Giglio-Tos, is second most damaging.
- The Short-winged mole cricket, *Scapteriscus abbreviatus* Scudder, is found in isolated areas.
- The Northern mole cricket, *Gryllotalpa hexadactyla* Perty, is the only species native to the United States, and is least damaging.

Description, Distribution, and Biology

Mole crickets are 1 to 1-1/2 inches (2.5 to 3.8 cm) long when mature and possess spade-like front legs that are well adapted for tunneling through the soil like their mammal counterpart (Figure 7.7). Nymphs resemble adults but are smaller and wingless. Two species of mole crickets are widespread in the southern United States, the Southern mole cricket and the Tawny mole cricket. The color patterns of the two species usually are distinct; the tawny mole cricket is a lighter creamy (or tawny) brown, while the Southern mole cricket is grayish to dark brown and usually has four distinct light spots on its prothorax (top shell behind the head). The two species also can be distinguished by their dactyls (digging claws). The Southern mole cricket has a "U" shaped space between

Typical Mole Cricket Activity Periods

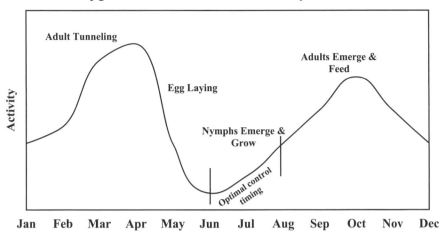

Figure 7.8. Typical life cycle or activity periods of mole crickets. Generally, small nymphs from early June to early August are easiest and cheapest to control while adults in October through May are the most difficult.

the dactyls (claws) while the Tawny has a "V" shaped space. A third species, the Short-winged mole cricket is abundant locally, especially along the southeast and southwest coasts in Florida. It is similar in appearance to the Tawny mole cricket, but has short wings and cannot fly. The Southern, Tawny, and Short-winged species were introduced into the southeastern United States around 1900 as stowaways in sand used as the ballast material of South American ships. They are found throughout the coastal plain region of the Southeast, and northern Argentina, Uruguay, and Brazil. A fourth species, the Northern mole cricket, is native to the United States, but is not considered to be a major pest. It is found east of the Rocky Mountains including Michigan, Ohio, and southern Ontario, Canada. It primarily inhabits moist soil adjacent to water.

Two major flights occur each year. In the spring, starting in February in Florida and peaking in March, Tawny mole cricket adults are attracted to lights with major flights during a full moon (Figure 7.8). Southern mole cricket flights begin in March in Florida and peak in early May. As a rule of thumb, biological events of mole crickets are delayed by one week as one moves south to north by 100 miles (161 km), thus flight periods of each cricket species are delayed about a month in more northern areas such as North Carolina. Flights also may be delayed during cool, wet, windy weather conditions. The spring flight is the larger of the two flights. The second flight (the dispersal flight) is made in fall between August and December. This dispersal flight enables new generation adults to reach previously uninfested areas, locations previously protected from crickets, and areas already populated by these insects. The flights may be up to six miles (9.7 km) per night.

Mole crickets mate and disperse via flying in the spring. Adult males attract females by using a harp-shaped area located on its wing between the two forelegs. This 'harp' resonates to produce a mating call. Males construct trumpet-shaped chambers at the soil surface during the mating period to increase the intensity of the mating calls. Hollow tops of these chambers are often visible in early spring.

Flushing should be performed throughout this period and females constantly inspected for egg development. This is performed by dissecting the abdomens of several females and looking for BB-like rounded eggs that are hard and dark yellow to brown in color. These will be laid within 10 days. If eggs are flat, soft, and yellow-green in color, the female is not ready to lay eggs. Most of the eggs are laid within the first 12 inches (0.3 m) of soil, but cool and/or dry weather may cause these chambers to be constructed at a greater depth. Females usually lay about four clutches of eggs per year, and average 35 eggs per clutch. Adult males die after mating while adult females die after depositing their eggs.

In most southern areas, oviposition (egg laying) begins in late March with a peak in May. Eggs hatch in 20 to 25 days. Their emergence is complete by mid-June. A soap flush will be needed to detect the first instar nymphs. Nymphs resemble adults but are smaller and wingless. Nymphs undergo incomplete (or gradual) metamorphosis. Nymphs feed and mature throughout the summer, molting five to eight times, although their wing buds do not appear until the last two instars. Adults begin to appear in the fall. Tawny mole crickets overwinter mostly as adults, Southern mole crickets overwinter primarily as large nymphs. In most of the Southeast, the Southern and Tawny mole crickets have only one distinct generation per year.

Tawny mole crickets tend to tunnel deeper into the soil than the Southern, which tend to dig and feed near the soil surface. This is important as the Tawny mole cricket may escape the lethal effects of some surface-applied insecticides. The Tawny mole cricket also tends to dig two V- or Y-shaped tunnels, presumably to provide an alternative route of escaping enemies.

The life cycle of the Tawny mole cricket is similar in south Florida, although oviposition and egg hatch occur a few weeks earlier. The Southern species has two generations per year in south Florida. Its egg-laying occurs in early spring and again in summer, through September. Generations of short-winged mole crickets are not discrete. Egg laying occurs year-round and peaks in late spring or summer and then again, to a lesser degree, in winter.

Feeding Symptoms/Signs

Mole crickets damage turf in several ways. Tawny and Short-winged mole crickets are herbivorous and consume all parts of the grass plant. The Southern mole cricket is a predator and a scavenger, feeding on earthworms and insects, and is believed not to prefer plant material as food. All three species tunnel through the surface layer of the soil, causing considerable mechanical damage to the grass roots (Figure 7.9). The tunneling also loosens the soil so that the grass often is uprooted, resulting in desiccation and can disrupt and break preemergence herbicide barriers, enabling weeds to germinate. As one walks across infested turf, the ground often feels spongy because of burrowing and displacement of soil near the surface.

Most mole cricket tunneling occurs at night, with the highest activity occurring a few hours after dusk and again just before dawn. They are especially active after rain showers or after irrigation in warm weather. Most activity within the top two inches (5 cm) of soil occurs when night temperatures are above 60°F (15.6°C) and a full moon occurs. Both nymphs and adults tunnel in the top inch of soil and come to the surface to feed

Figure 7.9. Severe mole cricket damage to bermudagrass. Damage occurs from extensive insect tunneling and subsequent drying of the soil.

when soil is moist and may tunnel up to 20 feet (6 m) per night in moist soils. Their feeding and tunneling are greatly reduced during cold weather or when soil is dry.

Detection and Control Strategies

In order to control mole crickets, a clear understanding of their life cycle and behavioral patterns is essential (Figure 7.8). Without this understanding, successful control is unrealistic. Maps of each golf hole are useful in scouting and should be made in October or November indicating heavily infested areas (Figure 7.10). Additional mapping should be made in late winter through spring when overwintering mole crickets become active. Tawny mole crickets typically infest the same sites yearly. Mapping can pinpoint these preferred sites, enabling spot treatment of heaviest infested areas. Spring mapping during periods of adult activity provides knowledge on where the majority of nymphs reside and where to apply your insecticide during early summer. If these areas are not mapped, by the time one sees activity in mid- to late summer, insecticides become less effective.

To determine which species is prevalent in your particular area and the relative population level, use the following soap flush. Mix three tablespoons (44 mL) of lemon-scented liquid dishwashing detergent in 2 gallons (7.6 L) of water. Apply the soap mixture over a 2 X 2 foot (0.3 m²) area of infested turf using a two-gallon (7.6 L) sprinkling can. Mole crickets present will surface in a few minutes. Flushing late in the afternoon or early in the morning, especially in moist soil, is best. This technique also may be used to verify the presence and developmental stage of nymphs.

The majority of turf damage occurs in the late summer and fall when the nymphs are reaching maturity and are at the most difficult time to control. Tunneling damage also occurs in late winter and spring from overwintering adult crickets. Damage subsides in May after eggs are deposited and most adults have died. It usually is mid-July before

Figure 7.10. Mole cricket management should follow traditional IPM strategies by mapping out high population sites in spring and fall so spot treatment can be used when possible. Shown is a high population area next to a bunker.

nymphs reach sufficient size to again cause noticeable turf damage. Most eggs are laid during late April and May and hatch in early June. It is during this period, after peak egg hatch and while the nymphs are small, that a pesticide should be applied (Figure 7.8). Timing of the pesticide application is one of the most important aspects of successful mole cricket management. Mid- to late June usually is the optimum time to obtain maximum control with an insecticide application.

In south Florida, peak hatch time for the Tawny mole cricket is early May, therefore an insecticide should be applied during late May. The Southern species peak hatch time occurs in June and July. Proper timing for an insecticide to control this species would be mid- to late July. If approximately equal populations of the two species are present, apply a pesticide in late June.

As mentioned, mid- to late June is generally the best time to control mole crickets with insecticides (Figure 7.8). This is when nymphs are large enough to feed on or near the soil surface when insecticides are applied. Materials with longest soil residual (three to six weeks) should be used to control the various hatching nymphs at this time (Table 7.1). Other shorter-lived materials such as acephate, chlorpyrifos, or pyrethroids are effective but must be reapplied with new nymph hatching. Turf should be moist before insecticide treatments are made, and it is important to apply the pesticide as late in the day as possible, dusk being the optimum time. Follow label directions explicitly regarding safety, dosage, application and irrigation information. Later-hatching nymphs should also be treated with another long residual material in mid-July. Commercial baits are especially effective for this mid-July application. Moist soil and dry turf foliage at the time of application provide best control with baits. Irrigation after bait application should not occur for several days as this may degrade the material.

By August, nymphs have grown considerably and become more difficult to control. Baits generally are still effective at this time. Most commercial insecticides also are effec-

Table 7.1. Comparison of insecticides registered for mole cricket control in turf.

Material	Common Name	Formulation	Residual	Comment
Chipco Choice; TopChoice	fipronil	0.1%G	very long	Caution use label.
Turcam	bendiocarb	2.5G	long	Several formulations for various sites.
Merit	imidacloprid	75WP, 0.5G	intermediate	Best for nymphs, apply at egg hatch.
Scimitar	lambda-cyhalothrin	0.88 EC	intermediate	Low odor; controls nymphs and adults.
Advanced Lawn 24 Hour Grub Control	trichlorfon	6.2G	intermediate	—
Meridian	thiamethoxam	—	intermediate	Best for nymphs, apply at egg hatch.
Orthene, Pinpoint, Velocity	acephate	75, 15G	short	Standard for nymphs in summer.
Baits				
Sevin	carbaryl	5%	short	Baits are best for mid- and late season nymphs.
Mole Cricket Bait (Dursban Pro)	chlorpyrifos	—	short	

tive at this time. These should be applied when soils are moist to encourage cricket activity nearer the surface. Most insecticides (baits and Orthene are exceptions) need irrigation following application to move the material into the soil.

By fall, numerous adults are present. At this time they cause extensive damage and are difficult to control. Feeding continues throughout the fall until cold temperatures drive the crickets further down in the soil. Since adults can burrow deep in the soil profile, they can often escape the target zone of many surface-applied insecticides. Spot treatment generally is the best method of controlling adults. Timing for control is at dusk as feeding is optimum at this time.

In spring, feeding by adults declines as they prepare tunnels to lay eggs. Cutting open several fertilized females in spring helps better pinpoint when they will begin to lay eggs. Young eggs are white to almost clear in color and turn tannish brown just before being laid. When approximately 50% of the developing eggs inside the females become hard and BB-like, eggs will be laid in about one week and should begin to hatch in approximately one month. No registered insecticide provides outstanding control of adults in a single application at this time. Spot treating the most damaged areas is the most economical means of control at this time. Parasitic nematodes also work best on adult crickets, thus may be considered at this time. Table 7.1 lists control options for mole crickets. Many products are subsurface applied, either through liquid injection or granular-slit application (Figure 7.11). Subsurface application bypasses much of the thatch that can tie up and reduce insecticide efficacy. This also reduces potential exposure and degradation by sunlight and rainfall and reaches deep burrowing insects.

The parasitic nematodes, *Steinernema scapterisci* and *S. riobravis,* and the red-eyed Brazilian fly, *Ormia depleta,* are being utilized as biological control agents against mole crickets. These natural enemies were imported from South America and are specific mole cricket parasites and harmless to nontarget organisms. The nematodes enter the crickets through the mouth or spiracles. They penetrate the gut and enter the hemocoel where bacteria is released in the hemolymph. The mole cricket then dies from bacterial poisoning. The nematodes pass through several generations inside the dead mole cricket. About 100,000 nematodes emerge from a single insect. The red-eyed fly, a tachinid, locates mole crickets by their singing and deposits live maggots on or near their host.

As with most biological control agents, the beneficial nematodes and the red-eyed fly are slower to control the mole cricket host and control will never be 100%. However, as the populations of these beneficial organisms increase, control effectiveness also increases. The parasitic nematodes are most effective on adult crickets which are prevalent during early spring (e.g., February in Florida, March in North Carolina) and early fall (October to November before frost). Providing good soil moisture also is necessary for survival of these parasitic nematodes. Although somewhat effective, current biological control means do not produce the level of control desired for most golf courses. They may prove beneficial in roughs and other lower maintenance areas as well as wetlands and other environmentally sensitive areas.

White Grubs

White grubs, (order Coleoptera, family Scarabaeidae), are the larvae of scarab beetles and are among the most serious insect pests in the northern United States. In the south-

Figure 7.11. Many mole cricket control products are subsurface-applied to reduce exposure and enhance biodegradation from rainfall and/or sunlight.

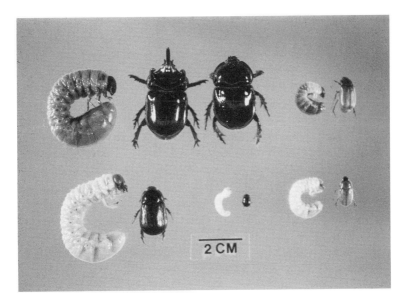

Figure 7.12. Various white grubs can be found as pests in turf.

ern United States they typically are more of a problem in localized areas. Although over 1,500 different scarab beetles occur in North America (Figure 7.12), the most common in turf include:

- Japanese beetle, *Popillia japonica* Newman, is the most commonly found grub.
- May beetle, *Phyllophaga* sp.

- Black turfgrass ataenius, *Ataenius spretulus* Haldeman
- Green June beetle, *Cotinis nitida* (Linnaeus)
- Masked chafer, *Cyclocephala* sp.
- European chafer, *Rhizotrogus majalis* (Razoumowsky)

Native species to the United States include masked chafers, black ataenius, and various May or June beetles. Introduced species include Japanese beetle, European chafer, Asiatic garden beetle, and Oriental beetles.

Description and Biology

The grub larvae are similar in appearance. They have white to cream-colored robust bodies with brown heads, have three pairs of small legs and a dark area at the rear of their 10-segmented abdomen. Depending on the species, they range from 3/8 to 2 inches (1 to 5 cm) long when mature and rest in a C-shaped position, especially when disturbed.

Black Ataenius grubs are quite small, 1/4-inch (0.6 cm), compared to May and June beetles. The black ataenius grubs tend to be a more serious problem in northern states, especially on bluegrass and bentgrass roots. Specific identification of larvae is difficult and is based on the form, shape, and arrangement of coarse hair, bristles, or spines (the raster) on the end abdominal segments.

Scarabs have a complete life cycle involving eggs, larvae, pupae, and adults. Depending on the species, less than one year up to four years is required to complete their life cycle. May beetles (also called Junebugs) require multiple years. The most common is a one-year life cycle and includes masked chafers, oriental beetles, Asiatic garden beetles, European chafer, and green June beetles.

For most white grub species such as *Cyclocephala,* females burrow through the thatch into the soil where their eggs are deposited. Their eggs are usually laid during May or June one to two inches below the soil surface. During July through August eggs hatch and the young larvae begin feeding on turfgrass roots. The grubs continue feeding on the grass roots, molt twice and grow larger until winter and then work their way deeper into the soil just below the frost line to overwinter. The following spring they return to the root zone and continue to feed on grass roots until April to June. They then pupate a few inches below the soil surface and adult beetles emerge during May and June to mate and lay eggs to start the cycle again. Turf damage from grubs with annual life cycles usually is most evident in late summer (late August and September), with less damage apparent during the spring feeding season.

Bothynis have a one- to four-year life cycle depending on the species. *Popillia* have a one-year life cycle in most of the United States but require two years in the more northern latitudes, and their larvae are peculiar in that they crawl on their backs. *Phyllophaga* have a three-year life cycle. Species with more than one-year life cycles spend the extra year or two in the grub stage, feeding throughout the growing season and moving deeper into the soil each winter.

Ataenius have different life cycles than other white grubs and involve two generations per year in most areas. The adults overwinter in protective areas such as ground covers or tall fescue clumps, emerge in late March through April, and lay eggs during May through mid-June. Larvae emerge from late May through mid-July, feed and grow

Figure 7.13. Typical white grub damage to bermudagrass where the turf appears moisture- and/or nutrient-deficient. White grubs typically sever turf roots, reducing the soil area from which it can extract moisture and nutrients.

through two molts. In late June and July, mature larvae cease feeding and burrow deep into the soil to pupate. Adults emerge in late July and August. These first generation adults begin laying eggs in July and produce a second generation. The second generation beetles emerge, feed on grass roots during July and August, mate, and fly to overwintering wooded sites at the perimeter of the turf facility in September and October. Turf damage from *Ataenius* is most obvious in July, especially if the weather is hot, and again in August.

Feeding Symptoms/Signs

Grubs feed on all species of grass. They feed on the roots at, or just below the soil-thatch interface and cause large patches of turf to die. Damage is most pronounced from mature grubs in late summer and early fall (August through October) and less so during spring (April and May). During heavy infestations, the soil surface may become very loose and spongy to walk on. In severe cases, roots are pruned so extensively that the turf mat can be rolled back like a carpet. Symptoms of grub infestation include a gradual decline forming a yellow mosaic pattern, or grass consistently wilts in an area even though adequate water is available (Figure 7.13). Continued feeding causes larger patches of turf to die. Additional turf damage may occur from predatory animals such as armadillos, birds, skunks, raccoons, moles, or opossums. Unlike the other white grubs, Green June beetles grubs do not feed primarily on plant roots but uproot the grass and push up small mounds of soil. Adult scarab beetles do not feed on turfgrasses, however some adult scarab beetles (e.g., Japanese beetle) aggressively feed on ornamental plants and trees during June and July.

Figure 7.14. Typical ant hill mound found in turf.

Figure 7.15. Tunneling from a ground mole.

Detection and Control and Strategies

Good turf management such as adequate moisture and fertilization help the turf withstand moderate grub infestations. Adult beetles are often found in swimming pools, in areas under lights, or slowly crawling across turf areas. To check for grubs, use a spade to cut three sides of a one-foot square piece of sod. The cuts should be two inches deep at the edge of one of the off-color areas. Force the spade under the sod and lay it back. See if the grass roots are chewed off and sift through the soil looking for the larvae.

Figure 7.16. Soil casts from extensive earthworm activity.

Check several places in the turf area. As a rule of thumb, if an average of three to seven grubs are found per square foot (0.09 m²), an insecticide should be applied.

Biological control has been provided by strains of the bacterium, *Bacillus popilliae* and *B. thuringiensis* (Bt), and parasitic nematodes, *Steinernema* sp. The milky disease from these bacteria is most active on Japanese beetle grubs. Grubs ingest this while feeding and the bacterium causes the body fluids to turn a milky white color (hence the name) prior to grub death. Bt produces crystalline proteins that destroy the insect's gut lining. Bacteria population buildup and control require an extended time period, typically three to five years. The parasitic nematodes show promise but must be applied yearly and the soil kept moist.

Commercial insecticides are partially (75 to 90%) effective. This is due in part to the insect's subterranean habit of the larvae which reduces the effectiveness of most surface-applied insecticides. Timing is critical and should be when grubs are small and actively feeding. Larger grubs in fall are much more difficult to control and tend to go deeper in the soil when temperatures cool. These grubs emerge in spring and are also very difficult to control. July through early fall (more specifically: early to mid-August) is probably the optimum time to apply an insecticide for grub control. Control will be more effective if the soil is kept moist for several days before treatment to encourage grubs to come closer to the soil surface. Apply as late in the afternoon as practical and irrigate immediately with 1/2 inch (1.3 cm) of water for maximum effectiveness. Thatch control also is extremely important as excessive thatch tends to bind or tie up most insecticides. Enhanced soil degradation of certain insecticides used for grub control also is currently suspected.

Ataenius control is best timed in spring when adults are laying eggs. If control methods are delayed until damage is evident, control becomes less effective since the grubs have finished feeding and are less affected by the insecticide. Insecticides should be lightly watered-in to move them into the thatch layer where the insects are located. Alternative

173

Table 7.2. Cross reference of insecticides for major bermudagrass turf pests.

Insecticide	Armyworm	Bermudagrass Mites	Billbugs	Cutworms	Fire Ants	Leafhoppers	Mole Crickets	Sod Webworm	White Grubs
Advanced Lawn 24 Hour Grub Control				✓			✓	✓	✓
Advanced Lawn Season-Long Grub Control							✓		✓
Amdro Bait/Amdro Granular Insecticide					✓	✓		✓	✓
Astro	✓				✓			✓	
Award Fire Ant Bait					✓				
Bacillus thuringiensis (Dipel, Javelin, XenTari)	✓			✓					
Chipco Choice; TopChoice					✓		✓		
Conserve SC	✓	✓	✓	✓	✓	✓		✓	
DeltaGard	✓	✓	✓	✓	✓	✓	✓	✓	✓
Diazinon AG600, 50W, 5G	✓			✓	✓			✓	
Distance Fire Ant Bait		✓	✓		✓				
Dursban PRO	✓			✓		✓	✓	✓	✓
Dylox				✓				✓	
Kelthane		✓							
Mach 2	✓		✓	✓				✓	✓
Meridian	✓		✓	✓			✓	✓	✓
Merit 75WP, 0.5G			✓	✓			✓		✓
Orthene TT&O	✓			✓	✓	✓	✓	✓	

Pinpoint 15G

Scimitar GC or CS

Seige Fire Ant Bait

Sevin 10G

Sevin 80 WSP

Sevin SL

Suspend SC

Talstar Flowable & Granular Formulations

Tempo 2, 20WP, and 20WP GC

Turcam 2.5G

Turplex Bioinsecticide

Varsity Fire Ant Bait

Velocity 15G

White Grub & Sod Webworm Insecticide

Table 7.3. Cross reference table of insecticides for nuisance turfgrass pests.

Insecticide	Ants	Chiggers (Red Bugs) Ticks	Imported Fire Ants	Fleas	Centipedes Millipedes Pillbugs Sowbugs	Snails Slugs	Wasps Bees
Advanced Lawn Fire Ant Killer			✓				
Amdro Bait			✓				
Amdro Granular Insecticide	✓		✓				
Astro	✓		✓	✓	✓		✓
Award Fire Ant Bait	✓	✓	✓	✓			
Chipco Choice; TopChoice			✓	✓			
Deadline Granules							✓
Diazinon AG600	✓	✓	✓		✓	✓	
Diazinon 50W	✓	✓	✓		✓		
Diazinon 5G	✓	✓	✓		✓		
Dursban PRO	✓	✓	✓	✓			
Metaldehyde 7.5G						✓	
Orthene TT&O	✓	✓	✓	✓	✓	✓	
Pinpoint 15G	✓	✓	✓	✓	✓	✓	
Scimitar GC	✓	✓	✓	✓	✓	✓	
Sevin SL	✓	✓	✓	✓	✓	✓	
Talstar	✓	✓	✓	✓	✓	✓	
Tempo 2, 20WP, and 20WP GC	✓		✓	✓			
Turcam 2.5G	✓		✓	✓			
Velocity 15G	✓		✓				

control timing is when larvae begin to hatch from late May on. These applications should be thoroughly watered-in to move the materials through the thatch to the soil layer.

Imidacloprid (Merit) is a relatively new insecticide with longer (three to four month) residual activity than many of the faster-acting organophosphates and carbamates. This allows a broad treatment window. It is very effective for recently hatched grubs but is less effective against older second or third instars. Optimum use is four to six weeks before egg hatch with application timing from early June (best) through early August (least) in most areas. Imidachloprid also has activity on mole crickets, armyworms, cutworms, hunting billbugs, and tropical sod webworms.

Halofenozide (Mach II) is also a new insecticide which accelerates premature molting of larvae. It provides two to three month residual control and is normally applied from mid-June until egg hatch. Halofenozide also has activity against older (second and third instar) grubs, thus can be used for early curative control into mid- to late summer. It is most effective on black turfgrass ataenius, Japanese beetles, and masked chafer grubs. Halofenozide also helps control leaf-feeding caterpillars such as armyworms, cutworms, and sod webworms.

Thiamethoxam (Meridian) is the latest insecticide for grub control. Like imidacloprid and halofenozide, thiamethoxam has longer residual activity. It is most effective when applied in May or early June. It also controls other insects such as mole crickets, armyworms, cutworms, hunting billbugs, and tropical sod webworms.

Table 7.4. Insecticides (chemical, common, and trade names) for control of turfgrass insect pests.[a]

Chemical Family	Common Name	Trade Name Examples
Amidinohydrazone	Hydramethylnon	Amdro, Siege
Bioinsecticides Bacteria and their various strains (gut disrupters)	*Bacillus thuringiensis* var. or subsp. kurstaki	Bactur, Bactospeine, Caterpillar Attack, Dipel, Javelin, SOK-Bt, Thuricide, Topside, MVP, Steward, Worm-Ender, + others
	(strain EG7826)	Lepinox
	tenebrionis or *san diego*	M-One, M-Trak, Trident II
	israelensis	VectoBac, Mosquito Attack, Bactimos, Skeetal, Teknar, + others
	japonensis	TBA
	aizawai	XenTari, Certan, Mattch
	buibui	M-Press
	Bacillus popilliae and *B. lentimorbus*	Doom, Japidemic, Milky Spore Disease, Grub Attack, + others
Bacterial-derived products: Spinosad (believed nervous system disrupter)	*Spinosyn* sp. (strain A & D) or *Saccharopolyspora spinosa*	Conserve SC
Fungi (cuticle disrupter)	*Beauveria bassiana* (strain JW-1)	Naturalis-T&O, etc.
Beneficial nematodes	*Steinernema* sp.	Vector TL & MC, Cruiser, Proactant, Biosafe, Exhibit, Scanmask
	Heterorhabditis sp.	Bioquest
	Heterorhabditis bacteriophora	Cruiser
Carbamate	Bendiocarb	Turcam
	Carbaryl	Sevin, Sevimol, Carbaryl, Carbait 5, Carbamec, + others
	Fenoxycarb	Award
Chlorinated hydrocarbon	Dicofol	Kelthane
	Lindane	Gamma-Mean 400, Lindane
Chloronicotinyl (neonicotinoid)	Imidacloprid	Merit, Marathon
Neonicotinoid	Thiamethoxam	Meridian

Category	Common name	Trade names
Insect growth regulators & feeding deterrents (botanical)	Azadirachtin (Neem)	BioNeem, Turplex BioInsecticide, Azatin
Diacylhydrazine	Halofenozide (molt accelerator)	Mach 2
Organophosphate	Acephate	Orthene Turf, Tree & Ornamental Spray, Pinpoint, Velocity
	Chlorpyrifos	Dursban, Mole Cricket Bait
	Diazinon	Diazinon
	Ethoprop	Mocap
	Fonofos	Crusade, Mainstay
	Isazophos	Triumph
	Isofenphos	Oftanol, Insecticide IV
	Malathion	Malathion
	Trichlorfon	Dylox, Proxol, Grub Control, Trichlorfon
Phenyl pyrazoles	Fipronil	Chipco Choice; TopChoice
Pyrethroid (synthetic)	Bifenthrin	Talstar
	Cyfluthrin	Tempo, Decathlon
	Cypermethrin	Cynoff, Demon TC
	Deltamethrin	DeltaGard GC, Suspend
	Fluvalinate	Mavrick Aquaflow
	Lambda-cyhalothrin	Scimitar, Battle
	Permethrin	Pounce, Astro, Perm-X, Prelude, Torpedo, Permethrin

[a] In the United States, the Food Quality Protection Act (FQPA) will affect the registration of many traditional pesticides, most notably the organophosphate insecticides. The future of these is uncertain.

8 Nematodes

Nematodes are microscopic, nonsegmented roundworms, generally transparent and colorless. They cause damage to plants as they feed by puncturing the cells of the root system with their stylet (a hollow, oral spear), injecting digestive juices into cells, and drawing liquid contents from cells as a food source. They feed only on living plant tissue.

Since nematodes damage turfgrass root growth and development, injury symptoms often go unnoticed until soil water becomes limiting. These symptoms are many times confused with environmental stress symptoms, thus may be difficult to diagnose. Nematode populations are also distributed very erratically in soil (great variation in numbers within a few feet is common), so aboveground symptoms also appear in areas of irregular size and shape, with boundaries between healthy and damaged turf not sharply defined (Figure 8.1). Nematode damage rarely is uniform or ends abruptly; a problem that has distinct, sharp boundaries between good and poor turf is probably not caused by nematodes (Plate 8.1).

Nematodes most often associated with bermudagrass include (Table 8.1): sting (*Belonolaimus longicaudatus*), lance (*Hoplolaimus* species), and stubby-root (*Paratrichodorus* species). Activity is generally greatest in mid- to late spring (e.g., May), and again in fall (e.g., September through October) just prior to and after midsummer heat. These times follow active growth of turfgrass roots and during mild weather. The result of nematode feeding becomes most apparent when conditions become unfavorable (e.g., hot and dry) for the turfgrass.

Control of nematodes should begin before the green is planted. Only nematode-free soil should ever be introduced into or on a golf green. Soils should be fumigated prior to planting and if sprigs or sod is used to plant a green these should be nematode-free.

Plant nematodes are aquatic animals that live in the soil water film or in plant fluids. They are very well adapted parasites of plants. Females produce a few dozen to over 500 eggs each. When a host plant is unavailable, eggs of some species survive for years but hatch quickly when stimulated by exudates from plants. Their activity, growth, and reproduction increase as soil temperatures rise from about 50°F to about 90°F. Generation time is between three and six weeks for many nematodes.

DIAGNOSIS OF NEMATODE PROBLEMS

Although diagnosing nematode problems is often difficult, there are several clues that are used during the investigative process. These include the type of symptoms, pattern and timing of damage, previous history, nematode species present, and the results of

181

Figure 8.1. Nematode damage to bermudagrass golf green.

nematode counts. Precise diagnosis, however, can only be made by a soil sample assay from affected sites.

Root Symptoms

These include lesions, galls, stubby swollen root tips, lateral root proliferation, and/or stunted shallow root systems with few feeder roots (Figure 8.2). Common symptoms associated with certain nematodes are described above. The penetration and movement of endoparasitic nematodes within roots leave openings that allow root invasion by secondary microorganisms in the soil such as fungi. The result is accelerated rotting (blackening) of roots, less feeder (or secondary) roots, and proneness of plants to wilting (Plate 8.2). The physiological and biochemical responses of the turfgrass to the invasion by the nematodes and microorganisms weaken the host further and may even break overall host resistance. Heavily affected root systems have much less soil clinging to them when a plug is pulled from the turf compared to unaffected turfgrass stands. The root symptoms, however, are not unique to nematodes and should always be considered in conjunction with other observations when diagnosing nematode problems.

Aboveground Symptoms

These appear as wilting, thinning or gradual decline, yellowing of leaves but without lesions or deformities. Again, these symptoms are not unique to nematodes and can be caused by heat or drought stresses, nutrient deficiency, fungal diseases, insect feeding, soil compaction, prolonged saturation of soil with water, or chemical contamination. The turfgrass is weakened by the nematode damage and is unable to outcompete invad-

Table 8.1. Nematodes affecting bermudagrasses and damage threshold levels often used to justify nematicide application (Esnard et al., 2001).

Common Name (Scientific Name)	Threshold[a] (No./100 cc soil)
Endoparasitic	
Root-knot	80
Meloidogyne spp.	
Lesion	150
Pratylenchus spp.	
Ectoparasitic	
Sting	10–20
Belonolaimus longicaudatus	
Lance	80
Hoplolaimus spp.	
Stubby-root	100
Paratrichodorus spp.	
Sheath	80–200
Hemicycliophora spp.	
Spiral	200–600
Helicotylenchus spp.	
Awl (especially bermudagrass in wet locations)	80
Dolichodorus heterocephalus	
Dagger (rarely a turf pest)	150–300
Xiphinema spp.	
Stunt (rarely a turf pest)	100–400
Tylenchorhynchus spp.	

[a] Threshold level ranges commonly used in research by universities.

Figure 8.2. Severe nematode damage to primary turf roots (right) compared to healthy plants (left).

Figure 8.3. Certain plants appear able to withstand nematode pressure. Shown is spurge (*Chamaesyce* sp.), which is commonly found in high nematode-infested bermudagrass.

ing weeds such as sedges, knotweed, pusley, and spurges (Figure 8.3). Nematode-affected areas may appear more weedy than other turf areas.

Pattern of Damage

Nematodes do not cause uniform damage to an expanse of turfgrass (as occurs, for example, in rust diseases). Rust fungi produce millions of dry spores that are easily dispersed over long distances in open air by the wind. Nematodes, however, produce a mere 50–500 eggs (per female). These eggs are in the soil environment and are not immediately and easily dispersed from the source by an active agent (such as the wind). Nematodes do not migrate >1 meter in one growing season and must depend on movement in surface water runoff, irrigation water, soil clinging to equipment, sod or plugs for long-range movement. Nematodes, therefore, show an irregular (somewhat patchy) horizontal and vertical distribution in the soil. Symptoms aboveground also follow this irregular distribution, but nematode-affected areas usually do not show distinct sharp boundaries. However, these symptoms resemble early stages of many fungal diseases of turfgrasses and could be misdiagnosed as nematode-related.

Timing of Damage

Plant parasitic nematodes are obligate parasites and feed most when the turfgrass roots are actively growing. They are therefore most numerous during mild weather, in late spring (May–June) and early fall (October–November) on warm-season grasses, and mid- to late spring and again in fall on cool-season grasses. The turf usually shows no aboveground symptoms of nematode damage until unfavorable environmental conditions prevail (for example, during hot, dry periods when soils are dry).

Soil Sampling

Nematode counts are the surest way to determine whether a problem in the turf is indeed caused by parasitic nematodes. Being free-living obligate parasites, nematodes require a living host to feed on, thus areas sampled should be on the outside perimeter of turf showing damage. Sampling should not begin until soil temperatures at the 2-inch (5 cm) depth reaches 50°F (10°C). It is good practice to take soil and root samples monthly so that changes in the populations of plant parasitic nematodes in the turfgrass stand can be monitored and kept below acceptable damage threshold levels. Given the irregular distribution of nematodes in the soil, it is imperative that adequate soil/root sampling be conducted in order to confirm the nematode problem to some degree of certainty. A standard 1-inch (2.5 cm) diameter soil sampler can be used to put a pint (500 mL) composite of 15 to 30 cores together from a 1,000 sq ft (93 m^2) area. Samples should be 4 inches (10 cm) deep and placed in an airtight bag and delivered to a nematode assay laboratory within three days. Golf course superintendents could be wasting precious time and thousands of dollars on fungicide applications if a problem is not correctly diagnosed as nematode related. The same waste of resources would occur if the problem is misdiagnosed as nematodal and nematicides are being applied when the real cause is another stress.

Both private and university laboratories provide good nematode assay services and should be consulted about the services they offer and instructions for taking and submitting samples. It is usually best to stick to one lab since assay methods and results differ between laboratories. The decision to use a nematicide should be based on the quality of turfgrass required and budget allowances. It should not always be predicated on some fixed threshold level of nematodes set by a laboratory. The level of damage tolerated by one golf course may be completely unacceptable on another. The most important management principle to go by is the fact that the health and vigor of turfgrasses directly affect their relative susceptibility to a given level of parasitic nematodes. In fact, the majority of nematode-induced damage is managed culturally, without nematicides. Nematicides only become necessary if populations reach unmanageable levels and/or if particularly virulent species, such as *Belonolaimus* spp. (sting), are present.

NEMATODE MANAGEMENT

Although there are no turfgrass cultivars available that are resistant to all nematode species, there are significant differences among turfgrass varieties in terms of the numbers and species of nematodes that feed on them and their proneness to damage caused by the feeding activities. Visual symptoms and even adequate soil/root sampling may sometimes not be enough to confirm a nematode problem. A positive growth response to an effective nematicide may sometimes be required for confirmation.

Turfgrasses tolerate some feeding by most nematodes and so the most practical strategy for nematode control is often the promotion of vigorous root growth (using recommended cultural practices and timely nematicide applications). To facilitate deeper penetration of the soil by roots, irrigate deeply (but less frequently) instead of shallow, daily watering. To achieve proper infiltration and adequate oxygen levels in the soil, coring with narrow, hollow tines or spiking should be performed (in late spring and early summer). Cultivation should be performed at times of the year when best turf recovery occurs; e.g., in late spring for warm-season turfgrasses and in mid-spring or early fall for cool-season turfgrasses.

Excessive fertilization with water-soluble nitrogen must be avoided since nematode numbers increase rapidly on succulent roots and, during periods of environmental stress (for example, in summer), the roots are placed under an additional strain. Organic forms of nitrogen have been shown to be associated with lower nematode numbers than inorganic forms. However, judicious use of a balanced fertilizer is always advocated.

Plant diseases, nutrient deficiencies and soil compaction should be managed or minimized in order to decrease the impact of nematode diseases on turfgrass stands. Avoid mowing low to prevent additional stress to the nematode-infested turfgrass stand forced to survive with reduced shoot biomass.

Certain soil amendments added to turf grown in sandy soils are known to improve soil composition and reduce the impact of plant parasitic nematodes. Preplant incorporation of colloidal phosphate and/or composted municipal sludge, or long-term use of the latter as a topdressing have been shown to reduce nematode damage to turfgrass stands.

Soil Fumigation before Planting

Soil fumigants are chemicals applied as gases or liquids that readily vaporize. They are toxic to the turfgrass but may be used to treat soil prior to seeding or planting to reduce plant parasitic nematodes, weeds, fungal pathogens, and other soilborne microorganisms. Turfgrasses established in fumigated soil show more uniform and vigorous growth. The fumigants used in turf are the gas methyl bromide, and the liquids 1,3-Dichloropropene (Telone II, Curfew), 1,3-dichloropropene + chloropicrin (Telone C-17, InLine) and metam-sodium (labeled as Vapam, Sectagon or Busan 1020). All three fumigants are Restricted Use pesticides that usually require special equipment and application only by licensed professionals especially when large areas are to be treated.

When using fumigants, best results are usually obtained when the old sod is first stripped from the area to be treated, followed by thorough tilling of the soil at least two weeks prior to the application of the fumigant to allow adequate decomposition of old roots. Tilling loosens the soil and permits more rapid and uniform diffusion of the fumigant. At the time of application the soil should be moist (not water-saturated). Too much fumigant escapes in dry soil and too little diffuses when pores are filled with water. The temperature of the soil should be about 50° to 80°F (10° to 27°C) (at a depth of 4 inches, 10 cm). Too much fumigant evaporates from hot soil, whereas diffusion is too slow in cold soil. For maximum effectiveness the treated area should be sealed immediately with a plastic tarp for several days. It is extremely important that the fumigated area is not recontaminated by accidental introduction of nematodes in soil clinging to tools, equipment, footwear, in runoff water, or in infested soil. Pests introduced into partially sterilized soil usually reproduce rapidly because of the lack of competition from microorganisms.

Nematicides for Established Commercial Turf

Only a few chemical nematicides are currently available for use on established turf-grass stands. They are the nonfumigant organophosphates fenamiphos (Nemacur 10G or 3 EC) and ethoprop (Mocap 10G). They can only be used on commercial turf (including golf courses and sod farms) where the risks of exposure can be minimized. The active ingredient in the granules or emulsifiable concentrate must be carried into the soil by an adequate amount of irrigation or rainwater (enough to reach the root zones and give effective control of nematodes but without product loss through leaching).

Nematicide applications should be made in autumn or spring (before nematode populations peak) during periods when soil temperatures are above 60°F (15.5°C), according to the product label. For granular formulations, gravity or "drop-type" granule spreaders are preferred (or required) over centrifugal types for more accurate application and for ensuring the safety of animals, humans and nontarget plants. Other applicator types are still being tested. For example, the suitability of shallow injection of narrow bands of granules in the turf that is popular for application of granular insecticides for mole cricket control is being tested for nematode control. Experiments comparing the effectiveness of broadcast application of granules versus subsurface injection of granules have shown similar effectiveness. Subsurface injection in fairways is practical and should reduce the potential for off-site movement of material.

Prior to application, physical soil treatments that aid soil penetration by water (such as core cultivation, vertical mowing, and mechanical thatch removal) should be done. Applications should be followed by adequate overhead irrigation in order to wash the active ingredient into the soil and avoid exposure of people, pets, and wildlife to the chemical.

Fenamiphos (Nemacur) is a systemic penetrant nematicide (absorbed by the roots and distributed throughout the grass) which gives some control of nematodes feeding within the roots. It is therefore effective against a fairly broad range of ecto- and endoparasitic nematodes. Fenamiphos affects nematodes by blocking enzymes in their nervous system, thereby interfering with motor function and causing irregular movements such as twitching, tremors, and eventual paralysis. During the prelethal phase or exposure to sublethal nematicide levels, feeding by the nematode stops. Recent research suggests that population suppression of sting nematodes in the field by fenamiphos (at 10 lb ai/acre, 11 kg ai/ha) is probably due to temporary incapacitation or irreversible sublethal effects caused by contact action and/or the systemic action of the nematicide. Fenamiphos has an intermediate water solubility (400–700 ppm) and medium adsorption potential. High soil and/or water pH can rapidly inactivate fenamiphos, thus it should be applied immediately after mixing or a buffering solution added to the tank-mix to modify the pH.

The following guidelines apply only for fenamiphos use on golf courses in Florida. These measures are designed to reduce the risk of exposure to birds and aquatic organisms. No more than 10 acres (4 ha) per golf course per day may be treated with Nemacur (3 EC or 10G). There must be a three-day interval before an additional 10 acres (4 ha) can be treated. Do not apply Nemacur closer than 10 feet (3 m) from bodies of water and surface fairway drains. Nemacur should not be applied to golf course turf between noon and sunset from June 1 to September 30 to avoid movement of pesticide by sudden downpours. It must not be used to control mole crickets.

At this juncture, instructions for the use of Nemacur remain the same as stated on the most current product label for other states in the Southeast. The safest guidelines are always on the product label. The product must be distributed evenly over the area to be treated and it must be washed immediately into the soil with at least 0.5 inches (1.3 cm) of water (usually up to the point when 1 inch [2.5 cm] of the top soil has become wet). Total irrigation should not result in puddling and runoff. Do not apply Nemacur where water runoff is likely to occur. The purchase and use of all formulations of Nemacur are restricted to certified applicators for uses authorized by their certification, or to persons under their direct supervision.

Ethoprop (Mocap) is not absorbed and translocated in nematicidal amounts within the plant and is therefore not effective for control of endoparasites such as the lance, cyst, and root-knot nematodes. It is most effective against sting, spiral, and awl nematodes but only moderately effective against ring, stubby-root and other ectoparasitic nematodes. It is currently labeled for golf course use but should not be applied to bentgrass, *Poa trivialis,* or ryegrass mowed at or below 3/8 inch (1 cm). Ethoprop is slightly soluble in water (700–750 ppm), has a medium half-life in soil (14 to 63 days), and has a weak to moderate binding potential in bare soil (K_{oc} of 26 to 120). Immediately after application of ethoprop, irrigate with at least 0.1 inch (0.25 cm) of water. Application of the nematicide to wet foliage and newly seeded areas should be avoided to prevent turfgrass injury. Mocap is less (but still) toxic to humans and animals than fenamiphos. Mocap 10G is the only formulation not categorized as Restricted Use Pesticide and may be applied to turf in a wider range of circumstances. Quantities, however, should not exceed 400 lb of Mocap 10G per acre (450 kg/ha) per year. Both ethoprop and fenamiphos are used for the control of mole crickets in turf, although the use of the latter for such a purpose is not advised in the state of Florida. The efficacy of fenamiphos and ethoprop against turfgrass nematodes is indicated in Table 8.2. The manufacturer's label must be followed in all cases involving the use of these pesticides.

Work is also progressing on using the soil fumigant, 1,3-dichloropropene (trade name Curfew), as a selective nematicide in bermudagrass turf. Currently, this material shows potential on bermudagrass turf when applied six inches deep at 5 to 6 gal/acre (47 to 56 L/ha) through chisels spaced 10 to 12 inches (25 to 30 cm) apart (Plate 8.3). Approval from the U.S. Environmental Protection Agency is currently pending.

Maximizing the Effectiveness of Nematicides

Neither fumigant nor nonfumigant nematicides completely eradicate plant parasitic nematodes. Some nematodes in deeper layers of soil and root tissue may escape exposure to lethal concentrations of the nematicide. Others are only temporarily paralyzed or disorientated by sublethal levels of the nematicide and will resume feeding when the chemical dissipates through diffusion, dilution, degradation, or leaching. Avoid the introduction of nematodes from other sources (for example, contaminated soil or sod). It is important to monitor the population levels of nematodes to know when nematicide treatments are needed.

Just before the nematicide application, cultivate the soil by coring, spiking, and perhaps vertical mowing to improve water infiltration. Aggressive cultivation may not be practical if damage by sting nematodes is severe. The soil should be moist (not water-

Table 8.2. Relative effectiveness of nonfumigant nematicides used in turfgrass nematode control.

Nematode	Phenamiphos (Nemacur)	Ethoprop (Mocap)
Sting	Good	Good
Awl	Good	Good
Spiral	Good	Good
Ring	Good	Moderate
Stubby-root	Good	Moderate
Sheath, Sheathoid	Good	Moderate
Lance	Good	Poor
Root-knot	Moderate	Poor

saturated) and at temperatures of 60°F (16°C) or greater (at 4 inches [10 cm] deep). Irrigate adequately immediately after application of the nematicide. Do not irrigate excessively.

Nematicides mainly affect nematodes. They do not stimulate plant growth directly. Nematicide-treated turfgrass therefore needs time to grow new roots in order to support new foliage and recover from nematode-induced stresses. Factors that limit root growth must be taken care of immediately after nematicide applications in order to achieve complete recovery of turf affected by nematode parasites. Ensure good drainage, adequate irrigation and aerification, balanced soil fertility, control of other pests and diseases, and reduced pedestrian traffic if possible. Aboveground plant responses after a nematicide application are usually slow or delayed.

Timing of applications is important. In the southeastern United States, a very good response of bermudagrass to Nemacur application in sting- and ring-infested soil is obtained by a mid-April application. This is normally several weeks after spring greenup. Presumably nematode populations are suppressed and new stolon and root development is allowed at the time of year when growth is maximized. Fall applications of nematicides to suppress damaging nematodes in bermudagrass turf may also be made, but overseeding establishment of cool-season grasses can be affected adversely if seeding and nematicide application coincide or the interval is short. If a nematicide application is necessary in the fall it should be done two to three weeks prior to the overseeding date. Postemergence applications of fenamiphos or ethoprop may damage *Poa trivialis*. Ethoprop is likely to damage any of the cool-season grasses.

Related to timing of applications, the use of certain preemergence herbicides for crabgrass or goosegrass control that act as inhibitors of cell division may inhibit response of bermudagrass to nematode suppression by nematicides. Although nematodes are suppressed by the nematicide application, turf may not respond because residual herbicides inhibit new stolons. Managers may opt to skip the preemergence herbicide application and use postemergence strategies instead, or use a material (e.g., oxadiazon, or Ronstar) that does not inhibit "tacking" of new stolons into treated areas. This becomes a problem when damage to bermudagrass is substantial and managers rely on new stolon development for recovery (e.g., rhizomes are absent or weakened).

Avoid overuse of any nematicide because soil microorganisms that can degrade the nematicide will build up to high population levels, decrease the efficacy and longevity of the chemical in subsequent applications, and consequently shorten the period of nematode control. Prolonged frequent use of a given pesticide also allows the buildup of one or more parasitic nematode species against which the chemical is less effective.

BIOLOGICAL CONTROL

There are several products on the market for management of plant parasitic nematodes using various natural products. For instance, mixtures of chitin from shells and urea have been shown to suppress root knot nematodes when the material is incorporated into soil. Microbes increase to enzymatically break down chitin (chitinases) which may, concomitantly, degrade nematode eggs in soil. ClandoSan is one commercial formulation of this. Another product utilizes preparations of sesame, which has been shown to be toxic to nematodes under some circumstances. Nematrol and Neotrol are commercial formulations. A proprietary blend of secondary alcohols reacted with ethylene oxide marketed under the name SAFE-T Green has been effective at reducing some nematode populations. Also, various bacteria have been shown to suppress nematodes and various commercial preparations of bacteria or bacterial products have come on the market. Incorporation of effective quantities of these materials into existing turf is problematic, as is the relatively high amounts of nitrogen as urea used to break down chitin.

Biological nematode control is also receiving much attention. Two insect-parasitic nematodes (*Steinernema riobravis* and *S. carpocapsae,* trade name Vector MC and others) have been used for mole cricket control. Their effectiveness, however, for certain plant-parasitic nematodes has been somewhat erratic.

Although many of these materials may suppress nematodes for short time intervals, none have given results in the field to date that compares with the efficacy of chemical nematicides. However, the need for safe and effective control of nematodes for turfgrasses in the Southeast has never been greater.

9 Diseases

Diseases on most bermudagrass greens are the exception and not the rule. Dollar spot, and periodically, leaf spot are the two most persistent diseases of bermudagrass. Dollar spot is a constant disease, especially during periods of warm weather and cool nights which produce heavy morning dews and during times when bermudagrass is not aggressively growing. Leaf spot typically occurs in fall or early spring, again, when the bermudagrass is not actively growing and thus cannot outgrow the disease symptoms. Spring dead spot also can be problematic on bermudagrass but is unpredictable where and when it occurs but does require complete winter turf dormancy to be expressed. Root and crown rot from various species of Pythium and Rhizoctonia species are diseases that rarely affect bermudagrass but may cause problems on overseeding, especially in fall.

Fungicides are normally not needed to control dollar spot or leaf spot diseases on bermudagrass. Often, a mild increase in fertility will stimulate enough bermudagrass leaf growth to outgrow the disease symptoms. Fungicides, however, are routinely needed on overseeded grasses to prevent or minimize Pythium and Rhizoctonia problems. Using fungicide-treated seed, monitoring soil moisture, and monitoring turf nutrient levels are key management practices to minimize the occurrence of these diseases. Table 9.1 lists current fungicides for disease control in bermudagrass and Table 9.2 provides a cross reference of trade names with common names.

BERMUDAGRASS DECLINE

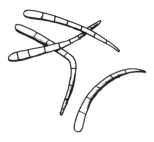

Bermudagrass decline, *Gaeumannomyces graminis* (Sacc.) Arx & D. Olivier var. graminis, is primarily observed during the summer and early fall months when temperatures are above 75–80°F (24 to 26.7°C) (including night) with high (>75%) humidity, cloudy skies, and frequent (almost daily) rainfall. This disease is mostly limited to putting greens due to the stress imposed by very low (<3/16 inch, 4.8 mm) cutting height

Table 9.1. Cross reference table of fungicides for major bermudagrass and overseeding grass diseases.

Fungicide	Algae	Anthracnose	Brown Patch	Curvularia Blight	Dollar Spot	Fairy Ring	Leaf Spot	Pink Snow Mold/Fusarium Patch
Aliette								
Banner Maxx		✓	✓		✓		✓	✓
Banol								
Bayleton		✓	✓					✓
Chipco 26019		✓	✓		✓		✓	✓
Cleary 3336		✓	✓	✓	✓		✓	✓
Compass			✓				✓	✓
Curalan			✓					✓
Daconil	✓	✓	✓		✓		✓	✓
Eagle		✓	✓		✓		✓	✓
Fore	✓				✓		✓	
Heritage		✓	✓			✓		✓
Koban/Terrazole								✓
PCNB			✓		✓		✓	
Prostar			✓			✓		
Rubigan		✓	✓		✓			✓
Spotrete 75			✓		✓			✓
Subdue Maxx								
Terraneb			✓					

Fungicide	Pythium Blight	Pythium Root Rot	Red Thread	Rhizoctonia Leaf & Sheath Spot	Rust	Spring Dead Spot	Strip Smut	Yellow Patch (Cool Weather Brown Patch)
Aliette	✓							
Banner Maxx		✓	✓		✓	✓	✓	✓
Banol	✓	✓						
Bayleton			✓		✓		✓	
Chipco 26019			✓					
Cleary 3336			✓				✓	
Compass			✓		✓			
Curalan			✓					
Daconil			✓	✓	✓		✓	✓
Eagle			✓		✓	✓	✓	
Fore	✓		✓		✓			
Heritage	✓	✓	✓			✓		✓
Koban/Terrazole	✓	✓						
PCNB								
Prostar			✓					
Rubigan			✓		✓	✓	✓	✓
Sentinel			✓				✓	
Spotrete								
Subdue Maxx	✓							
Terraneb	✓	✓						

Figure 9.1. Blackened, rotted roots of bermudagrass (right) typical of Bermudagrass Decline and Spring Dead Spot diseases.

(Plate 9.1). Tees and green approaches may also be affected if mowed excessively low. As a general rule the outer margins of a golf green exhibit the disease symptoms first, presumably due to added pressure from turning mowers, but can spread slowly across an entire green. It occurs on all types of putting greens—old, new, poorly-drained, well-drained. At this time it is assumed all plant material is infected and is ubiquitously found with all bermudagrass plants.

Damage Symptoms/Signs: This is a root rot disease, therefore the plant is easily stressed for water and nutrients. Foliar lesions are absent. By the time aboveground symptoms appear, the pathogens have been active on the roots for at least a few weeks and possibly months. Initial symptoms are irregular, yellow (chlorotic) patches ranging in diameter from a few inches to a few feet. Lower leaves will exhibit the aboveground symptoms first by becoming yellow and then brown (dead). Roots with initial symptoms will usually be thin and off-white in color with isolated black lesions. Eventually roots will turn black and rotted (Figure 9.1). Stolons and rhizomes may have black lesions also. Black strands of fungi (runner hyphae) will be present on the outside of roots (Figure 9.2), as well as hyphopodia (specialized hyphae visible microscopically on root surfaces). Entire plants may die resulting in an irregular thinning of the grass, and if not controlled, bare patches may develop (Plate 9.2). The outer perimeter (cleanup lap) of golf greens often show disease symptoms first, followed by symptoms across the entire green. This disease should not be confused with Pythium Root Rot, which causes a general decline across the entire green or limited portions of the green. Pythium Root Rot does not usually result in the death of the plant.

Cultural and Chemical Control Strategies: This disease is very difficult to control once it is established. Therefore, preventative measures which prevent or alleviate stress are the

Figure 9.2. Black, ectotrophically growing mycelium on bermudagrass stolons, which is typical of Bermudagrass Decline and Spring Dead Spot diseases.

best methods for completely controlling the disease or at least decreasing the potential damage.

1. Raise mowing height to 1/4 inch (6.4 mm), especially during stressful growth periods during the summer and early fall months. *This is the most important preventive measure.*
2. Aerify greens frequently to avoid compaction problems. Remove the cores.
3. Topdress after aerification with a topsoil mix containing at least 70% sand. More frequent top-dressing may be necessary on putting greens where the disease has been observed previously. It also covers up the lower leaves that are dying, leaving the "appearance" of a healthy, green playing surface.
4. Balance nitrogen applications with equal amounts of potassium. On new sand greens, monitor other nutrients as well—especially phosphorus and micronutrients. Fertilize to encourage rapid growth. Remember the roots are damaged and have to "work" for their nutrients in the top few inches of soil. Nitrogen should be applied with potassium in a 1:1 or 1:2 ratio. Acidifying nitrogen sources, such as ammonium sulfate, should be used. Apply micronutrients, especially iron and manganese, if they are in low supply or unavailable to the plant due to a high soil pH. A readily available source of phosphorus may be useful. Foliar feeding of nutrients may be useful if the root system is severely damaged.
5. Do not add dolomitic lime to greens. If it is necessary to add magnesium, use magnesium sulfate (Epsom salts). These pathogens prefer neutral to alkaline soil pH, so the addition of lime may increase their activity as the pH increases.

The fungicides fenarimol, propiconazole, thiophanate methyl, and triadimefon have been useful in controlling similar patch diseases (spring dead spot, summer patch, take-all patch) as indicated on their labels. However, best control is achieved when fungicides are used preventively, prior to symptom development. Do not use these excessively as they may have negative growth regulating effects on bermudagrass. Cultural control methods, especially raising the cutting height, should also be implemented at the same time. Control seems to be best when the fungicides are lightly watered into the root zone (but not below it) immediately after application. These fungicides penetrate the plant, but are xylem-limited (see fungicide section). The use of a contact fungicide on the leaf tissue may also be useful to prevent secondary leaf infections from occurring and to prevent algae formation in thin areas of the green (see algae section). Propiconazole should not be used during the warm summer months. If Rhizoctonia zeae is also present, do not use thiophanate methyl products since it is not sensitive to that chemistry.

BROWN PATCH (RHIZOCTONIA BLIGHT)

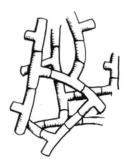

Brown patch, *Rhizoctonia solani* Kuhn, is the most widespread turfgrass disease. It affects all turfgrass species and is observed most often on creeping bentgrass, tall fescue, and annual bluegrass during warm (above 85°F, 29°C) weather when night temperatures are above 68°F (20°C) and foliage remains wet for extended periods. On warm-season grasses, including bermudagrass, zoysiagrass, St. Augustinegrass, and centipedegrass, AG-2-2, AG-2-2 LP of *R. solani* is most likely to occur in the spring or fall months when the temperatures are relatively cool and the turf surface stays continuously wet for several days due to heavy fog or extended rainfall (Plate 9.3). Disease incidence is usually greatest in low wet areas or on poorly drained soil. This disease in zoysia may be referred to as "large patch," and is caused by a particular strain (AG-2-2) of *R. solani* that is different from strains typically associated with brown patch in cool-season grasses (AG-1 or AG 2-2 IIIB). Strains from other warm-season grasses are similar to those collected from large patches in zoysiagrass.

In cool-season grasses, infection is triggered by a rapid rise in air temperature combined with either rainfall or extended periods of high humidity, resulting in the leaf canopy being continuously wet for 48 hours or more. Rhizoctonia species are found in all soils and survive unfavorable environments as dormant, thick-walled mycelia or as compact masses of thick-walled cells (bulbils) resembling sclerotia in plant debris. There is some evidence that infected but asymptomatic plants may become blighted when weather favors symptom expression and serve as primary inoculum for initiating new disease cycles.

Damage Symptoms/Signs: Symptoms of brown patch differ in cool-season grasses depending on the height of cut. On putting greens the disease begins as small circular light green to dark purplish patches that may turn yellow and then brown or straw-colored.

Patches may expand to several feet in diameter, and may or may not have green, relatively healthy appearing turf in the center of the patches. On lower heights of cut, a dark gray, purplish, or dark brown "smoke ring" may be visible, particularly under conditions of high relative humidity or when dew is on the green (Plate 9.4). This ring is composed of mycelium and freshly wilted, infected grass. These symptoms may change as the day progresses so that by late morning the patch appears more uniformly light brown, yellow-orange, or straw-colored.

Symptoms in warm-season grasses differ significantly from those observed in cool-season grasses. Discrete leaf lesions are not usually formed; rather, a soft, dark brown to purplish rot will occur on the lower portion of the leaf sheath. Whole leaf fascicles pull up easily due to this basal leaf sheath rot. Eventually, entire shoots will easily pull off the stolons. When the disease is active, the margins of patches exhibit yellowed shoots whose basal leaf sheaths are recently infected and rotted. So a yellow to light brown band of more recently affected shoots surround the more brown patch of affected turf. Roots are not normally affected by this pathogen or those causing disease in cool-season turfgrasses. Roots may decline, however, as foliage is destroyed. Patches up to 20 feet (6 m) in diameter may develop on hybrid bermudagrass, zoysiagrass, St. Augustinegrass, or centipedegrass during cool, wet weather and shoot greenup in the spring. Low, wet, poorly drained areas are most susceptible. As temperatures warm, turf vigor increases and it eventually grows over diseased areas, but cultivars or species with lower turf recuperative potential (like Meyer zoysia, or centipede) may still exhibit symptoms into the summertime, and weeds typically invade these weak areas of turf. These large patches are perennial in nature, and may reappear in the same location in following years, but expanded in size.

Cultural and Chemical Control Strategies: For cool-season grasses on overseeded greens, avoid excess nitrogen, especially readily available forms such as soluble liquids or quick-release nitrogen sources just prior to hot, humid weather. Complete elimination of nitrogen fertility is not advised because one still depends on new root and shoot growth to recover from disease and (hopefully) transient highly stressful high temperatures. Many superintendents have been successful with this approach year-round. Maintain adequate levels of phosphorus and potassium. Avoid excessive irrigation, and irrigate greens when dew is already present so leaves do not stay continuously wet. Dragging a hose across the turfgrass or whipping greens with a bamboo or fiberglass pole will also remove morning moisture. Increase air circulation by removing adjacent underbrush and consider tree removal to improve morning sunlight penetration to the green. Designers should take these factors into consideration before courses are constructed. Remove clippings on infected areas or when conditions favor disease development. Use sharp mower blades to reduce stress to the turf. Regularly core aerify to increase soil drainage, improve soil oxygen status, and to reduce thatch buildup. Increasing mowing height encourages turf recover, but this practice must be balanced with the available root system.

For brown patch management in warm-season grasses, avoid early fall applications of excess nitrogen. Fall fertilization can be beneficial, however, in improving turf quality and spring greenup if rates are not excessive. Improve drainage, as it has been observed that brown patch chronically appears in poorly drained areas. On golf course roughs where centipedegrass has been utilized, brown patch may become severe as superintendents water to establish fall overseedings of ryegrass in bermudagrass fairways. This may be an argument against centipedegrass for this purpose in areas that have chronic problems with this disease. Managing thatch accumulations will help to improve recuperative potential as well.

Preventive control (such as fall application for warm-season grasses) in chronic disease areas helps prevent spring disease symptoms. Azoxystrobin, chlorothalonil, cyproconazole, flutolanil, iprodione, PCNB (quintozene), propiconazole, triadimefon, and trifloxystrobin may be used for preventative control. Other times of the year, when favorable weather for epidemics is likely to be of short duration (spring, winter, and fall), curative approaches are successful. Apply on a 10 to 14 day schedule during hot humid weather when night temperatures exceed 68°F (20°C). Waiting for symptoms to develop before chemical control, however, may result in dead or thinned areas of turf that may not recover until favorable turf growing conditions resume in the fall. In summer, algae development becomes problematic under these conditions.

DOLLAR SPOT

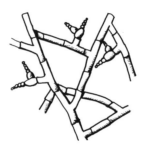

Dollar Spot, *Sclerotinia homoeocarpa* F. T. Bennett, is a disease observed most commonly on turfgrasses with very low nitrogen levels and dry soil during periods of warm, humid weather, especially in spring and fall when heavy dews occur. All turfgrasses are susceptible, with creeping bentgrass, ryegrass, annual bluegrass, and roughstalk bluegrass (*Poa trivialis*) being most susceptible for cool-season grasses, and bermudagrass and zoysiagrass for warm-season grasses. Activity begins at 60°F (16°C) and is optimum between 70° and 80°F (21° to 27°C), especially when free moisture is present. Although a very persistent disease, dollar spot does not normally cause quick, total kill of a turf area.

Damage Symptoms/Signs: Small (2 inches, 5 cm, diameter), bleached patches of dead grass on low-cut turf such as golf greens will develop first (Plate 9.5). Irregular, light tan lesions with distinct brown borders will be present on individual leaf tissue at the outside edge of the patch. Leaves may be girdled and collapse at the lesion even though the leaf tips remain green. In contrast, lesions caused by *Pythium* fungi generally are water-soaked in appearance, feel greasy to the touch, or do not have distinct borders around the bleached diseased leaf tissue. Lesions on taller mowed grass often die back from the tip and have straw-colored or bleached lesions shaped like a hourglass. On taller mowed turf, straw-colored blight areas 6 inches to 12 feet (15 cm to 3.5 m) in diameter develop which resemble fertilizer burn or skips, drought stress, dull mower injury, or dog injury.

White, cottony mycelium may be observed in early morning hours when dew is present and can easily be confused with early stages of Pythium blight or the web of spiders (Figure 9.3). Spider webs, however, are flat and do not cause leaf lesions while mycelium from dollar spot or Pythium blight is three-dimensional.

Dollar spot fungi do not form spores and disease spread is from mycelial growth and movement of infected plant parts, infested equipment, or traffic. The dollar spot fungi survive as winter dormant mycelium in plant parts and as thin flakes of fungal tissue on foliage or in soil. Damage is greatest on turfgrass growing under low moisture and nitrogen conditions. The disease often develops earlier in spring where it was not adequately controlled the previous fall. Spots in sod-forming grasses, such as bermudagrass and bentgrass, usually disappear once the disease is controlled; however, spots in bunch-type grasses, such as ryegrass, often remain due to their inability to fill-in the damaged areas. Severity usually peaks in late spring and again in late summer on cool-season grasses when night temperatures are cool enough to allow heavy early morning dew formation. On warm-season grasses, dollar spot occurs all season long.

Cultural and Chemical Control Strategies: When overseeding, plant resistant cultivars, blends, and mixtures of various grasses whenever possible. Recent released bentgrass cultivars Crenshaw and SR1020 are highly susceptible. Avoid extreme nitrogen deficiency. If the disease develops, provide a quick-release source of nitrogen such as ammonium sulfate; symptoms will subside, although control is not sustained as long as with some fungicides (Figure 9.4). Do not use this approach with creeping bentgrass in the Southeast. Maintain adequate phosphorus, potassium, and lime. Irrigate during early morning hours to limit periods of high humidity and remove leaf moisture by dragging a hose over the area or using a whipping pole to remove moisture. Avoid thatch buildup by aerifying, topdressing, and verticutting.

Prevent disease spread by removing clippings from infected areas, washing equipment before entering a noninfected area, and by encouraging golfers to clean their shoes between rounds. Raising the mowing height also reduces disease severity on golf greens.

Most fungicides labeled for control do a good job. These include chlorothalonil, fenarimol, iprodione, mancozeb, maneb, myclobutanil, propiconazole, thiophanate, thiram, triadimefon, and vinclozolin. Synergistic combinations of fungicides for dollar-spot control include propiconazole plus either triadimefon, iprodione, chlorothalonil, vinclozolin, or anilazine. A preventive spray program should be considered when daytime temperatures approach 70°F (21°C), with contact fungicides providing 10 to 14 day control while systemics provide 14 to 28 day control. Alternate between fungicide classes to minimize the occurrence of resistant strains. Resistance has been problematic for the benzimidazole class of fungicides (including thiophanate methyl) and the sterol biosynthesis inhibitors (fenarimol, propiconazole, triadimefon, cyproconazole, myclobutanil). Resistance to these fungicides appears to be long lasting, once induced. Resistance has also developed in response to overuse of iprodione or vinclozolin, but the pathogen populations become sensitive to these fungicides if they are not used for several years before being used once again. Strains of the fungus *Trichoderma* appears to be promising as biocontrol agents.

Figure 9.3. Mycelium associated with Dollar Spot disease.

Figure 9.4. Control of Dollar Spot disease (right) with fungicides.

FAIRY RING

Fairy Ring is caused by *Chlorophyllum, Marasmius, Lepiota, Agaricus, Amanita, Lycoperdon, Calvatia,* and other basidiomycetes (mushroom, toadstool, or puffball producing) fungi. The name fairy ring is from English folklore in which the rings were believed to be where fairies had danced. There are records of fairy rings in Europe over 100 years old and up to several hundred feet in diameter. Fairy rings are most common in soils with high organic matter, often where old tree stumps, lumber, and other organic debris were buried during construction or they may occur in soils of very poor fertility. Newly constructed putting greens, in which the root-zone mix consists of sand and an organic amendment (such as peat), may develop severe infestations after only a few years or even months. The fungi live by decomposing organic litter such as thatch and plant debris. Fairy rings caused by Lycoperdon (a common puffball) may develop on 100% sand-based greens as well. Fairy rings are most frequently observed during the summer months, presumably due to warm wet weather, which favors fungal growth.

Usually there is some form of stimulation of the turfgrass in the form of darker green rings or arcs in the turf (Plate 9.6). Grass stimulation associated with fairy rings is due to increased availability of nutrients, especially nitrogen, from decomposition of organic complexes in the soil by the fungi or from decomposition of the fungi themselves as the rings expand outward. Grass inside a fairy ring is usually in a state of decline and frequently infested with weeds or algae. This decline is thought to result from depletion of nutrients, lack of soil moisture due to an impervious mat of fungal tissue at or near the soil surface, a toxic agent, such as cyanide-containing compounds produced by the fungus or a combination of two or more of these.

Damage Symptoms/Signs: Fairy rings have been classified in several ways, depending on the symptoms and conditions induced. One classification describes them as belonging to two basic types: edaphic or lectophilic. Edaphic fairy rings are those induced by fungi that are soil inhabitants. Edaphic fairy rings occur as rings or arcs of green stimulated turf which may or may not be accompanied by adjacent areas of dead or declining grass. A mat of white- to cream-colored fungal mycelium may be present at or just below the soil line. This mat becomes very evident when a plug of grass is incubated in a sealed bag for two or three days. The soil beneath the rings may become very dry and difficult to wet during summer and autumn. There are three types of symptom expression described for edaphic fairy rings.

Type I rings—These have a zone of dead grass just inside a zone of dark green grass (Plate 9.7). These are more prevalent on new greens than on established ones. The dead grass may form from mushroom mycelia accumulating below the soil surface and causing the soil to become hydrophobic (water hating). Type I rings generally cause the most damage due to this soil drying which prevents water from getting to plant roots.

Type II rings—These have only a band of dark green turf, with or without mushrooms present in the band (Plate 9.8). On areas that are mowed frequently (greens and tees), mature mushrooms may never be observed but the "button" stage may be present at ground level. Turf is normally not killed.

Type III rings—These do not exhibit a dead zone or a stimulated dark green zone, but simply have a ring of mushrooms present (Plate 9.9). Mushrooms or puffballs often develop after rains or heavy irrigation during mild weather. Rings normally expand each year. The size and completeness (circular, semicircular, quarter circles) of the bands varies considerably (e.g., 1 to 100 feet, 0.3 to 30 m).

Lectophilic fairy rings (sometimes called "superficial" fairy rings) are those that are inhabitants of the thatch and upper soil surfaces. Lectophilic fairy rings occur in the thatch or mat of the turfgrass, and are less problematic although on putting greens they can be unsightly and may still induce hydrophobic conditions that require treatment. Rings may change to a scalloped damage pattern and infected soil often elicits a strong 'mushroom' odor.

Cultural and Chemical Control Strategies: Edaphic fairy rings are very difficult to control. If necessary for aesthetic purposes, mask the dark green ring symptoms with nitrogen fertilizers (especially for Type II rings). Remove mushrooms as some (e.g., *Chlorophyllum* spp.) are poisonous. Although it is possible to excavate and fumigate the fairy ring sites, it is quite likely the rings will return if the food source is still present underground. In some situations on putting greens, these rings are also associated with localized dry spots in which the fungi have colonized the sand particles. In those situations, it may be useful to spike the area, use wetting agents to increase water absorption. Also, aerify and remove soil cores to allow better nutrient and water penetration. Infected areas should be heavily hand-watered, being careful not to overwater adjacent, unaffected areas which could result in other diseases and problems. A hydrogun or tree root feeder provides good water soaking. Repeat as needed. Do not bury and plant over organic debris such as tree stumps, large roots and lumber, during the construction and establishment phases of turf areas.

Removing afflicted sod followed by soil fumigation, tilling, and replanting helps reduce fairy ring occurrence. Some success in temporarily suppressing fairy rings has recently been from using flutolanil. In the Southeast, flutolanil and azoxystrobin have worked for temporary suppression of rings caused by *Lycoperdon* puffballs. The flutolanil label indicates that best results occur when the material is applied following aerification and with the use of wetting agents. Prior to application, spike or aerify the area, apply the surfactant (wetting agent), and irrigate. The next day, apply the fungicide at 40 to 80 gallons per acre (375 to 750 L/ha). Immediately irrigate with 1/4 to 1/2 inch (10 to 20 cm) water. Keep the thatch moist for several weeks.

HELMINTHOSPORIUM DISEASES

Helminthosporium diseases are caused primarily by *Bipolaris* and *Drechslera* spp. (previously known as species of *Helminthosporium*). The fungi named above were previously considered to belong to the genus *Helminthosporium,* and sometimes the diseases they cause are still referred to as 'Helminthosporium' diseases. These fungi induce a variety of symptoms in many warm- and cool-season turfgrasses and attack all plant parts of the turfgrasses. Thus, leaf spots, crown rots, and root, crown, rhizome, and stolon rots may occur, depending on the specific disease. The two primary species occurring on bermudagrass include Zonate eyespot (*Drechslera gigantea* [Heald and Wolf] Ito) and Helminthosporium leafspot (*Bipolaris sorokiniana* [Sacc.] Shoemaker).

In general, leaf tissue as well as crowns, rhizomes, and roots may be affected. These diseases become severe under moderate temperatures in spring, fall, and summer under wet, humid conditions (Plate 9.10). Conidia (spores) of these fungi are abundantly produced in lesions and are dispersed by wind, water, and through dispersal of infested tissue removed by mowing.

Damage Symptoms/Signs: *Drechslera* species cause leaf spots during cool, humid conditions, with crown and root rot phases occurring during warm, dry weather or during wet periods following dry periods. *Drechslera* species occur mostly on cool-season grasses.

On bermudagrass, leaf spot is most pronounced in fall and early spring months when the grass is green but not actively growing due to cool temperatures. Leaf lesions are distinct and begin as tiny olive-green, water-soaked areas that become dark brown to purplish black (Plate 9.11). These lesions are usually surrounded by a yellow area of varying width that fades to the normal green of the leaf tissue. Older lesions may have a white or bleached area in the center of the lesion. Severely affected plants may become almost entirely yellow and gradually fade to a light tan in appearance. Affected areas are straw-colored ranging from two inches to several feet (5 cm to 2 to 3 m). Leaf spot rarely causes permanent damage to bermudagrass but can cause streaking, browning, and stand thinning under severe infestations (Plate 9.12). Turf normally fully recovers when good grass growing temperatures return.

Cultural and Chemical Control Strategies: Balance nitrogen levels with potassium. Avoid drought stress and reduce leaf surface moisture by watering deeply but infrequently. Avoid late afternoon and evening waterings and encourage good soil drainage. Encourage air movement and light penetration by removing shade sources and unneeded adjacent vegetation. Avoid thatch accumulation greater than ½ inch. Overuse of certain fungicides (benomyl) and phenoxy herbicides (MCPP, 2,4-D and dicamba) for broadleaf weed control may enhance disease development on cool-season grasses, or if used when bermudagrass is not actively growing. Avoid using these pesticides or treat preventatively for Helminthosporium disease control prior to their use.

Azoxystrobin, chlorothalonil, iprodione, mancozeb, trifloxystrobin, and vinclozolin provide control. Chronic problems with these diseases may be site-specific and preventive or curative control approaches should be used accordingly. Some disease enhancement has been noted with some of the sterol biosynthesis inhibitor fungicides. Preventive control is best. Begin applications in early spring after new growth is apparent and repeat at 7 to 21 day intervals until warm weather occurs. Curative control of the warm-weather group such as leaf blight and melting-out are often ineffective when symptoms are obvious since the fungus is well established and inaccessible in infected plant crowns, roots, rhizomes, and stolons.

PYTHIUM DISEASES

Pythium Blight (Cottony Blight, Greasy Spot, Damping-Off, Seedling Blight)

A number of Pythium species cause Pythium blight including: *Pythium aphanidermatum* (Edson) Fitzpatrick and other Pythium species such as *P. myriotylum* Drechs., *P. graminicola* Subrum., *P. arrhenomanes* Drechs., and *P. ultimum* Trow. All turfgrasses are susceptible, with the cool-season grasses, creeping bentgrass, annual bluegrass, and Kentucky bluegrass—being the most. Although this disease is rarely observed on bermudagrass, it is a disease of cool-season turfgrasses used for overseeding bermudagrass surfaces. It is most likely to occur when day and night temperatures exceed 85°F and 68°F (30° and 20°C), respectively, and when the relative humidity is high (~90%). Pythium blight can be a highly destructive disease (Plate 9.13).

Pythium species are water molds, thus require sufficient surface moisture for development. All soils contain Pythium species unless the soil has recently been fumigated. Pythium species that cause Pythium blight are facultative parasites; that is, they are saprophytes in the thatch or soil and quickly become pathogenic when favorable conditions develop. The fungi produce thick-walled sexual spores that survive for long periods in the soil. The germination and grow-in period of newly established bentgrass greens or overseeded cool-season grasses are ideal for disease development since fall temperatures can still be quite warm and the turf is being irrigated more frequently than normal. Extended periods of warm, foggy mornings also favor this disease, potentially destroying large areas in a short period of time. Greens that are situated in low, protected areas with poor sunlight penetration and air movement are most at risk. Bentgrass is more susceptible when saline soil conditions (and presumably high soluble salts from fertilizers) exist.

Damage Symptoms/Signs: Small, distinct reddish-brown patches of grass usually about one to six inches in diameter first appear as dark and water-soaked (slimy) but later shrivel and turn straw-colored as humidity and/or temperature decrease (Plate 9.14). Turf grown in shaded, low-lying areas adjacent to water where air circulation is poor and humidity highest is likely to become diseased first. The water-soaked, blackened leaves often feel greasy or slimy. If conditions become less humid during the day, bleached lesions can be observed on partially damaged leaves, but these lesions have no distinct border, which easily distinguishes them from dollar spot. Patches may spread quickly in a streaked pattern, usually following water drainage movement. White cottony mycelium may be observed in early morning when dew is present, but this sign of the disease is not always apparent (Plate 9.15).

Pythium fungi spread by direct mycelial growth as well as through a spore or spore-containing sack called sporangia and small swimming spores released from sporangia called zoospores. These fungi also produce thick-walled resting spores called oospores that may survive in soil and thatch for extended periods. Disease may spread rapidly when sporangia, zoospores, oospores, or infected plant parts are moved by water along drainage patterns, or by mowers or traffic. Often, two or more Pythium species may occur simultaneously, requiring growing the fungus on special laboratory media and microscopically examining the sporangia and oospores for specific identification. Being water molds, Pythium spores can survive in ponds used for irrigation, which makes control difficult as the turf is reinoculated with each watering.

Pythium Root Rot

Pythium Root Rot is caused by various *Pythium* spp. including *P. aristosporum* Vanterpool, *P. aphanidermatum* (Edson) Fitzpatrick, *P. arrhenomanes* Drechl., *P. graminicola* Subrum., *P. irregulare, P. myriotylum* Drechs., and *P. vanterpooli* Kouyeas & Kouyeas. These Pythium species are capable of infecting roots and crowns of overseeding grasses such as bentgrass, ryegrass, and roughstalk bluegrass, causing stunting and yellowing. Different levels of aggressiveness are associated with different species of Pythium. Pythium root rot is still poorly understood in the different turfgrasses. Symptoms may appear at any time of the year, but they will usually be associated with wet conditions either from too much precipitation or too much irrigation. Poor drainage and soil compaction conditions will compound this problem and encourage development of algae in areas where disease has weakened or killed the grass. Root damage from nematodes or *Gaeumannomyces* spp. also may contribute to this disease.

Damage Symptoms/Signs: Symptoms are typically a nonspecific decline in turf quality (Plate 9.16). However, circular patches in rings, arcs, or solid patches of a few inches up to about eight inches may occur in the spring or late summer. Small or large turf areas will become a general yellow or brown color and gradually begin to thin. Light green to yellow strips may develop, especially near the perimeter of greens. However, the areas do not normally thin to bare soil. Roots appear thin with few root hairs and have a general discoloration but are not black and rotted as they are with other root rotting diseases such as necrotic ring spot or Bermudagrass Decline. Foliar mycelium is absent, often causing confusion with melting-out disease or possibly anthracnose. Turf does not respond to fertilizer applications, especially nitrogen. This disease cannot be diagnosed from field symptoms alone. Microscopic examination of affected roots and crowns is required to determine if Pythium spp. are associated with the symptoms.

Cultural and Chemical Control Strategies:

Pythium Blight. Improve drainage, air circulation, and light penetration by removing shrubs, trees, and limbs and possibly adding fans in pockets of poor air movement. Reduce soil and leaf moisture because moisture control is a key to Pythium management;

therefore, early morning removal of dew and guttation water by poling or dragging a hose and utilization of early morning irrigation is beneficial. Plant fungicide-treated seed at the recommended amount, avoiding very high seeding rates. Avoid excessive use of nitrogen prior to warm weather. Minimize equipment or foot traffic across wet infected turf. Wash equipment before entering unaffected areas and encourage golfers to clean their shoes between rounds. Delay overseeding in late summer/early fall until the weather turns cool and dry. Alleviate soil compaction as this reduces turfgrass rooting, which then requires turf managers to irrigate lightly and frequently. Maintain a slightly acid soil pH, use properly balanced fertilization and avoid calcium deficiency.

Mancozeb, chloroneb, and ethazol provide quick short-term (e.g., five to ten days) contact control. Apply during hot (>80°F, 26.7°C), humid (≥85%) weather when night temperatures exceed 65°F (18°C). Be careful with the use of chloroneb and ethazole, as these are potentially phytotoxic to the turf. Azoxystrobin, fosetyl-Al, mefenoxam, metalaxyl, propamocarb, and trifloxystrobin provide longer residual (14 to 21 day) control if applied preventively. Whenever possible, plant seed treated with metalaxyl or ethazol. Otherwise, apply one of these fungicides immediately after the seed is planted. Reapply one of these fungicides approximately 7–14 days later (after the seed has germinated). Alternate between compounds to avoid development of fungicide-resistant strains of Pythium. A two-way combination of mancozeb and metalaxyl, mancozeb and propamocarb, propamocarb and metalaxyl, and propamocarb and fosetyl Al has been shown to be synergistic. Mancozeb plus chloroneb, however, are antagonistic and should not be used together. A combination of mancozeb and fosetyl Al, or azoxystrobin and chlorothalonil, or chlorothalonil and fosetyl Al have performed effectively for Pythium-induced diseases. Consult turf pathologists for specific rates and timing.

Due to the potential for rapid development of this disease and loss of large areas, turf managers growing cool-season grasses should consider a preventative fungicide program when hot, humid (e.g., foggy) weather is forecast. Alternating between contact and preventative fungicides should also help reduce the risk of resistance problems.

Pythium Root Rot. Chloroneb, ethazol, mancozeb, metalaxyl, fosetyl-Al, propamocarb, and azoxystrobin; to increase effectiveness, these fungicides, except for fosetyl-Al, should be either lightly watered into the root zone or applied in 5–10 gallons water per 1,000 square feet (20–40 L/100 m^2). At least two applications will probably be required. Several of these compounds do not have Pythium Root Rot listed on their labels for turfgrass. This is due to the inconsistent disease control that has been observed. Alternate between compounds to avoid development of fungicide-resistant strains of Pythium. Note that, except for mancozeb and azoxystrobin, these fungicides are specific for *Pythium* spp. only.

SPRING DEAD SPOT

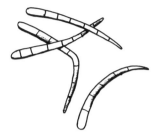

Spring dead spot is caused by several very closely related fungi including: *Gaeumannomyces graminis* (Sacc.) Arx & Olivier var. *graminis; Leptosphaeria korrae; L. narmari;* and/or *Ophiosphaerella herpotricha*. Spring dead spot is the most serious disease of bermudagrass in the United States where the bermudagrass undergoes complete dormancy in winter (Plate 9.17). The highest maintained turf is generally the most susceptible. Hybrid bermudagrasses which tend to produce excessive thatch are most prone to disease attack while cold hardy (nongreen) cultivars such as Midiron, Midfield, and Vamont are more resistant. The new ultra-dwarf' bermudagrasses with their excessive thatch/mat buildup potential appear highly susceptible to this disease (Plate 9.18). Late summer nitrogen applications, abundant fall moisture, and low temperatures in winter also predispose the grass for spring dead spot development. Spots generally begin to appear after the turf is at least three to five years old. Infected areas recover slowly and weeds frequently invade these areas during the summer. Presumably, fungi causing spring dead spot infect in the late summer and fall, and weaken the turf without visible symptoms. Factors that affect winter hardiness and spring greenup also affect spring dead spot symptom development and turf recovery. All of the four reported causal agents listed are slow-growing root ectotrophic fungi, similar to organisms causing take-all patch, necrotic ring spot, and summer patch. In fact. *Leptosphaeria korrae* has been reported to cause both necrotic ring spot and spring dead spot. The dark brown, black mycelium from the ectotrophic growing fungi directly penetrate roots, stolons, and rhizomes, filling the vascular tissue with a brown substrate and dark, spindle-shaped sclerotia (Figure 9.5).

Damage Symptoms/Signs: Dead, straw-colored spots two to three feet (0.3 to 0.9 m) in diameter appear in spring as affected bermudagrass begins to green up and are often confused with winterkill. Spring dead spot patches are sunken, generally well-defined and circular, in contrast to more diffuse dead areas caused by direct low-temperature injury. The roots and stolons of affected bermudagrass are severely rotted. Patches may enlarge over three to four years, often developing into rings, and then disappear. Affected spots may also remain greener in late fall going into winter. Patches in overseeded affected bermudagrass may resemble brown patch in spring (Plate 9.19). The patches are usually perennial in nature, recurring in the same location over several years. After a year or two from first occurrence, patches develop into doughnut or frogeye patterns with relatively nonsymptomatic bermudagrass in the centers. After several years, spring dead spot may entirely disappear from a site. Rhizomes and stolons from adjacent bermudagrass slowly fill in dead spots. This slow process allows summer annual weeds such as crab-

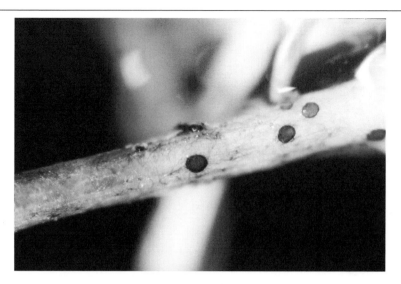

Figure 9.5. Sclerotia and mycelium (hyphae) associated with Spring Dead Spot on bermudagrass stolons.

grass to easily become established. Use of certain preemergence herbicides for summer annual grassy weed control may affect recovery from spring dead spot. Herbicides that work by inhibition of cell division (the dinitroanaline group, as well as dithiopyr) may inhibit new stolons from colonizing patches and slow recovery. Oxadiazon, on the other hand, does not inhibit rooting and might be a better choice of preemergence herbicide if one is needed. Managers may also opt to use postemergence techniques for weed control in areas prone to severe spring dead spot.

Cultural and Chemical Control Strategies: Spring dead spot is a disease of mature bermudagrass that is intensively managed. Use acidifying fertilizers such as ammonium nitrate/sulfate to help speed recovery and reduce disease severity. However, avoid excessive nitrogen fertilization and do not apply nitrogen in the fall. Raise mowing height and ensure adequate potassium levels in the fall. Reduce thatch by aerifying and pulverizing soil cores.

Some success (30% to 75% patch reduction) has been obtained following late summer (September) and early fall (October) application of azoxystrobin, fenarimol, myclobutanil, or propiconazole but should be used only after suggested cultural practices have been followed (Figure 9.6). These should be applied as drenches. Several years of consecutive use may be required from complete control as the patches are typically reduced in size following each yearly fungicide use.

Additional Bermudagrass Diseases

Anthracnose Leaf Blight

The causal agent for anthracnose is *Colletotrichum graminicola* (Ces.) Wils. There are several manifestations of anthracnose diseases in turfgrasses. Anthracnose diseases occur on many cool-season grasses as anthracnose leaf blight and occasionally as an-

Figure 9.6. Control of Spring Dead Spot of bermudagrass (background) with fall applied fungicides compared to untreated (front) (Courtesy Leon Lucas).

thracnose basal rot. Bermudagrass also may develop anthracnose leaf blight. On bermudagrass, the disease occurs in the fall as the growth of the grass slows (Plate 9.20). Although common on many cool-season grasses, anthracnose leaf blight usually is one of minor significance on bermudagrass greens except during late summer/early fall when the turf is not actively growing.

This pathogen attacks grass shoots and roots. Initial symptoms are small (size of a dime) yellowing of the turf that turns bronze in color if cool weather persists (Plate 9.21). Lower leaves of plants initially show symptoms as elongated reddish-brown lesions which may enlarge and eventually encompass the entire leaf blade. The disease occurs as irregular-shaped patches. A water-soaked black rot of crown tissue may be evident if sheath tissue is removed. The black fruiting bodies of the fungus (acervuli) can be seen growing in rows of infected plants during hot weather (Plate 9.22). These acervuli have black spines called setae protruding from leaf tissue. Affected turf areas may thin and have a yellow to orange or reddish-brown cast to the overall area. The fungus overwinters as a saprophyte in dead plant tissue in the thatch and on stems beneath the leaf sheath of live plants.

Adequate nitrogen fertility will help reduce the severity of anthracnose leaf blight in some areas during cool periods. Fungicides are rarely needed on bermudagrass if sufficient nitrogen is provided to continue turf growth. Azoxystrobin, fenarimol, chlorothalonil, propiconazole, thiophanate-methyl, triadimefon, and trifloxystrobin help reduce but not eradicate the disease. Apply systemics preventively at 21-day intervals. For best curative control, tank-mix a systemic fungicide with a contact and reapply in 14 to 21 days.

Curvularia Blight

Curvularia blight is caused by *Curvularia geniculata* (Tracy and Earle) Boedijn; *C. lunata* (Wakk.) Boedijn, and others. Bentgrasses and bluegrasses are most susceptible, especially during hot (≥85°F) temperatures but may attack bermudagrass during periods of slowed growth. Symptoms are similar to diseases caused by *Bipolaris* spp. and include tip dieback of infected plants, yellowish-colored turf and stands which thin in an irregular pattern (Plate 9.23). Brownish leaf lesions similar to leaf spot diseases may be present. Damaged plants from heat, drought, and/or herbicide stress are most susceptible. Curvularia blight is most common on newly established greens, and generally becomes apparent during spring on winter damaged plants and in mid- to late-summer on drought, fertility, or nematode stressed turf. The disease rarely kills the grass, but symptoms of yellow patches of a few inches in diameter are unsightly. *Curvularia* spp. survive periods of unfavorable growth as saprophytic mycelium on plant debris and tissue. Alleviating stress such as soil aeration, good irrigation practices, increasing mowing height, and proper fertility help plants resist infection. Fungicides which control leaf spot or anthracnose diseases also may be beneficial in controlling Curvularia.

Rust

Rust is caused by *Puccinia* spp. (such as *Puccinia graminis, P. striiformis, P. coronata, P. zoysiae*) or *Uromyces dactylidis*.

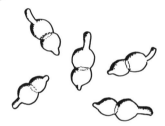

Rust traditionally has been a serious problem on Kentucky bluegrass, zoysiagrass, fescue, and less so on bermudagrass (Plate 9.24). The disease is most severe during cool weather in late summer and fall or early spring when conditions are less than adequate for good growth of the turfgrass. Especially affected are nitrogen-deficient grasses grown in shade.

Overall symptoms of severe rust infection are a thinned, clumpy turf. Heavily infected turf areas will appear yellow and produce a cloud of orange dust (urediospores) when the foliage is disturbed. The orange powdery material easily rubs off on hands, machinery, shoes, and clothing. Turf will appear thin, weak, and is more susceptible to drought and winter injury. Oval to elongated pustules, yellow to orange or reddish brown in color, are raised on the surface of leaves. These spores are dry and powdery and are spread easily by wind, machinery, shoes, and infected plants.

Management practices which provide steady grass growth during prolonged warm to hot periods when rust problems are most common should be followed. Maintain adequate nitrogen levels for sufficient growth to ensure weekly mowing will help reduce the severity of rust. Remove clippings and remove shade sources as low light intensity favors the disease. Wash equipment before entering an uninfected area. Water deeply but infrequently to encourage deep rooting and avoid drought stress.

Table 9.2. Trade names for common turf fungicides.

Common Name	Trade Name[a]
azoxystrobin	Heritage
chloroneb	Terraneb SP, Terremec SP
chlorothalonil	Daconil formulations, Manicure, Thalonil, Concorde, Echo
ethazole	Koban, Terrazole
fenarimol	Rubigan[b], Patchwork
fenarimol + chlorothalonil	Twosome Flowable Fungicide
flutolanil	Prostar
fosetyl Al	Aliette, Aliette Signature, Prodigy 80DG
iprodione	Chipco 26019, Chipco 26GT Flo
maneb	Manex, Maneb + zinc, Dithane M-22 Special, plus others
maneb (37%)+ zinc F	Pentathlon F
mancozeb	Fore, Dithane T&O, Tersan LSR, Manzate 200 Flowable, Protect T/O, Pentathlon DF, + others
mefenoxam	Subdue Maxx
metalaxyl	Subdue 2E, Pythium Control, Apron[d]
metalaxyl + mancozeb	Pace
myclobutanil	Eagle, Systhane WSP
PCNB (quintozene)	Terraclor, Turfcide, Engage, Penstar, Revere, Defend, PCNB, plus others
PMA + thiram	Proturf Broad Spectrum Fungicide
propiconazole[c]	Banner MAXX, Alamo
propamocarb	Banol
thiophanate methyl	Cleary 3336, Fungo, SysTec 1998, Cavalier, Scotts Systemic Fungicide
thiophanate + chloroneb	Scotts Fungicide IV
thiophanate + chlorothalonil	ConSyst, Spectro 90
thiophanate + iprodione	Scotts Fluid Fungicide
thiophanate + maneb (mancozeb)	Duosan
thiophanate + thiram	Bromosan
thiram	Spotrete 75, Spotrete-F, Thiramad, plus others
triadimefon	Bayleton, Scotts Proturf Fungicide 7, Accost 1G, Granular Turf Fungicide, Strike 25WP
triadimefon + flutolanil	ProStar Plus
triadimefon + metalaxyl	Scotts Fluid Fungicide II
triadimefon + thiram	Scotts Fluid Fungicide III
trifloxystrobin	Compass
vinclozolin	Curalan, Vorlan, Touche

[a] Presence of a fungicide in this list does not constitute a recommendation. Trade names are used with the understanding that no endorsement is intended nor is criticism implied of similar products which are not mentioned. All chemicals should be used in accordance with the manufacturer's instructions. Do not add adjuvants, surfactants, etc. to fungicides unless specified by the label. Check labels carefully to determine usage on residential, or commercial turf areas and other restrictions.

[b] Usage of this product may lead to decline of *Poa annua* in treated turf areas.

[c] Not for use on bermudagrass greens when temperatures exceed 90°F.

[d] This product is for seed treatment only.

Azoxystrobin, myclobutanil, propiconazole, triadimefon, and trifloxystrobin control rusts when applied in spring or fall when the first signs of rust are visible. Repeat applications every 7 to 14 days are necessary while rust is present. Contact fungicides require applications on a 7 to 10 day interval and are not especially effective.

Bibliography

Anonymous. 1992. Guidelines for water reuse. U.S. Environmental Protection Agency. EPA/ 625/R-92/004. U.S. EPA, Center for Environmental Research Information, Cincinnati, OH.

Anonymous. 1993. USGA recommendations for a method of putting green construction. *USGA Green Section Record* 31(2):1–3.

Brady, N.C. and R.R. Weil. 1999. *The Nature and Properties of Soils.* 12th ed. Prentice Hall, Upper Saddle River, NJ.

Brandenburg, R.L. and M.G. Villani, Eds. 1995. *Handbook of Turfgrass Insect Pests.* Entomological Society of America, Lanham, MD.

Butler, J.D., P.E. Rieke, and D.D. Minner. 1985. Influence of water quality on turfgrass. pp. 71–84. In V.B. Youngner and S.T. Cockerham, Eds., *Turfgrass Water Conversation.* Proc. Symposium ASPA, San Antonio, TX. 15–16 Feb. 1983. Coop. Ext. Univ. of California, Oakland, CA.

Carrow, R.N. 1995. Soil testing for fertilizer recommendations. *Golf Course Management* 63:61–68.

Couch, H.B. 2000. *The Turfgrass Disease Handbook.* Krieger Publishing Company, Malabar, FL.

Davis, W.B., J.L. Paul, and D. Bowman. 1990. The sand putting green—Construction and management. Univ. of California Div. Agric. and Natural Resources Publication 21448.

Dernoeden, P.H. 1995. Turfgrass diseases and their management. pp. 87–170. In T.L. Watschke, P.H. Dernoeden, and D.J. Shetlar, Eds., *Managing Turfgrass Pests.* Lewis Publishers, Boca Raton, FL.

Emmons, R.D. 1995. *Turfgrass Science and Management.* Delmar Publishers, Inc. Albany, NY.

Esnard, J., B. Martin, and L.B. McCarty. 2001. Turfgrass Nematodes. In *Best Golf Course Management Practices,* L.B. McCarty, pp. 505–517. Prentice Hall, Upper Saddle River, NJ.

Foy, J.H. 2000. Going for the gold with bermudagrass greens: Part II. *USGA Green Section Record* 38(6):1–5.

Gorsuch, C., D. Short, and L.B. McCarty. 2001. Turfgrass Insects. In *Best Golf Course Management Practices,* L.B. McCarty, pp. 465–504. Prentice Hall, Upper Saddle River, NJ.

Harivandi, M.A. 1994. Wastewater quality and treatment plants. In *Wastewater Reuse for Golf Course Irrigation.* pp. 106–129. Lewis Publishers, Boca Raton, FL.

Hummel, N.W., Jr. 1998. Which root-zone recipe makes the best green? *Golf Course Management* 66(12):49–51.

Hurley, R.H. 1990. Best turfgrasses for southern winter overseeding. *Grounds Maintenance* 26(1).

Jones, J.B., Jr., B. Wolf, and H.A. Mills. 1991. *Plant Analysis Handbook*. Micro-Macro Publishing, Inc., Athens, GA.

Martin, B. and L.B. McCarty. 2001. Turfgrass Diseases. In *Best Golf Course Management Practices*, L.B. McCarty, pp. 415–464. Prentice Hall, Upper Saddle River, NJ.

McCarty, L.B. 2001. *Best Golf Course Management Practices*. Prentice Hall, Upper Saddle River, NJ.

McCarty, L.B. and M.L. Elliott, Eds. 1994. *Best Management Practices for Florida Golf Courses*. Cooperative Extension Service, SP 141. University of Florida, Gainesville, FL.

Miller, R.W. and D.T. Gardiner. 1998. *Soils in Our Environment*, 8th ed. Prentice Hall, Upper Saddle River, NJ.

Niemczyk, H.D. and D.J. Shetlar. 2000. *Destructive Turf Insects*, 2nd ed. H.D.N. Books, Wooster, OH.

Snow, J.T. 1993. USGA explains its new greens specifications. *Ground Maintenance* 28(1):20–22.

Tisdale, S.L., W.L. Nelson, and J.D. Beaton. 1985. *Soil Fertility and Fertilizers*. Macmillan Publishing Co., New York, NY.

Westcot, D.W. and R.S. Ayers. 1984. Irrigation water quality criteria. In G.S. Pettygrove and T. Asano, Eds. pp. 3:1–3:37. *Irrigation with Reclaimed Municipal Wastewater—A Guidance Manual*. Report No. 84-1 wr. Calif. State Water Resources Control Board, Sacramento, CA.

Index